Religious Giving

D0370365

PHILANTHROPIC AND NONPROFIT STUDIES

DWIGHT F. BURLINGAME AND DAVID C. HAMMACK, EDITORS

Religious Giving

FOR LOVE OF GOD

EDITED BY
DAVID H. SMITH

INDIANA UNIVERSITY PRESS
BLOOMINGTON AND INDIANAPOLIS

This book is a publication of

Indiana University Press
601 North Morton Street
Bloomington, Indiana 47404-3797 USA

www.iupress.indiana.edu

Telephone orders 800-842-6796
Fax orders 812-855-7931
Orders by e-mail iuporder@indiana.edu

© 2010 by Indiana University Press
All rights reserved

No part of this book may be reproduced or utilized in any form or by any means,
electronic or mechanical, including photocopying and recording, or by any
information storage and retrieval system, without permission in writing from
the publisher. The Association of American University Presses' Resolution on
Permissions constitutes the only exception to this prohibition.

⊖ The paper used in this publication meets the minimum requirements of the
American National Standard for Information Sciences—Permanence of Paper for
Printed Library Materials, ANSI Z39.48-1992.

Manufactured in the United States of America

Library of Congress Cataloging-in-Publication Data

Religious giving : for love of God / edited by David H. Smith.
p. cm. — (Philanthropic and nonprofit studies)
Includes bibliographical references and index.
ISBN 978-0-253-35459-4 (cloth : alk. paper)
ISBN 978-0-253-22188-9 (pbk : alk. paper)
1. Generosity. 2. Abrahamic religions. 3. Generosity—Religious aspects. 4. Charity.
I. Smith, David H., [date]
BJ1533.G4R45 2010
204'.46—dc22
2009037258

1 2 3 4 5 15 14 13 12 11 10

CONTENTS

PREFACE

Just before sitting down to write this preface, I dutifully went to church. My pledge—for once in cash—secure in my pocket, I passed a panhandler twenty yards from the church door. I ignored him and hurried into the lovely sanctuary, listened to a fine sermon, and heard a wonderful choir. But I confess to having a troubled conscience. And I am not alone.

Whether to "walk on by" someone begging for money is not an uncommon issue for urban Americans, but something feels peculiar about failure to help while on the way to a religious service. Why is that? Does it make sense? This collection of essays begins with the assumption that there is something inherently right or natural about the connection between religion and giving, but just exactly what is that connection? To whom should we give, how much should we give, and what is the relationship between our giving and our relationship to God? Why is religious commitment associated with giving?

The list of issues that might be discussed under these headings is long. Despite meeting together over a two-year span, we are under no illusions about our book's comprehensiveness, but we had to work within the constraints of finitude. We limit ourselves to the Abrahamic traditions, and we focus most of our attention on the philosophical or theological dimensions of the problematics of giving. The reader will look in vain for a discussion of Buddhist or Hindu issues with giving, or for analysis of fundraising strategies. We write for an introspective donor, congregational leader, or student of various ways of meeting human need. We build on the traditions as we critically read them, but for the most part this is not a report on institutional practices. Rather, it is an argument—better, a series of related arguments—about the connection between religion and giving. We begin with a report on the practices of some religious persons in the United States and conclude by discussing some very specific and timely religious and moral issues.

The relationship between religion and giving is a topic of enormous importance. Even if the data that Paul Schervish cites are way off, which is unlikely, his basic introductory point would remain forceful: the magnitude of wealth transfer from one generation to another that we will see in the next decade or two is enormous. What current wealth holders or their heirs choose to do with this wealth may well determine the human prospect on this planet. Democratic governments in truly pluralistic societies will never be able to do all that needs to be done to cope with aging populations, energy shortfalls, and global climate and environmental issues. Strong government action on all these fronts is necessary, but it will surely be insufficient so long as people resist paying taxes.

The driving concern behind the two years of work that led to these essays is to try to ensure that, insofar as the Abrahamic religious traditions inform and motivate persons, this guidance—and, if you will, inspiration—is thoughtful, constructive, and helpful to giver, recipient, and the larger society.

Our book begins with Patrick Rooney's helpful summary report on the facts about religious giving in the United States today. Some data are clear; many things we'd like to know, for example, about the giving practices of American Buddhists, are not available. We learn that many Christians and Jews give; for the most part they don't give very much. Shariq Siddiqui's essay on giving among American Muslims follows, giving attention to the traditions, rationale, and responses to the American context of the diverse American Muslim community.

These two introductory essays are followed by five that relate to basic religious rationales for giving. We consider the language that Christians and Jews use when they speak to each other, but in a way that is understandable beyond those faith communities. Judith Failer considers the rationale for giving of self and treasure among Hassidic Jews and the Modern Orthodox. Bangert, Wheeler, and Vacek probe scripture, tradition, and moral psychology to make claims about motives for Christian giving, hardness of heart, love and justice, and learning to give. Both the distinctiveness of Jewish tradition and the parallels between Christianity and Judaism are evident.

The three essays that comprise the final section of the book tackle some very specific problems of religious giving: the reformation or education of donors (Schervish), the powerless giver in a culture of debt and consumption (Dempsey), and the changing needs of the peoples of God (Katz). The authors deal with these issues in very specific contexts but in ways that suggest more general applications. The concluding chapter is my attempt to pull together some of the major themes in, and problems raised by, the essays.

The authors and editor of this collection are grateful for the help given us by a group of critics—Scott Alexander, Dwight Burlingame, David Craig, David Daniels, Robert Gianini, Carol Johnston, Don Jones, Fred Kniss, Glenda Murray, Joseph Rautenberg, and Nancy Marie Robertson—who contributed considerable time and thought so that this book might be improved. Our greatest debt, however, is to the Lake Institute on Faith and Giving, particularly Lauren Wright, Natalie Ingle, and William Enright, whose encouragement and support have made our work possible.

Religious Giving

Dispelling Common Beliefs about Giving to Religious Institutions in the United States

PATRICK M. ROONEY

The aim of this chapter is to test the validity of eight assumptions about religious giving in the United States. "Religious giving" refers to giving to religious organizations, by which we mean charities whose primary mission is religious discovery, enhancement, and so forth. It includes giving to religious ministries on TV, radio, and in print. However, it does not include giving to religious organizations whose primary mission is not religious per se, such as Catholic schools or Jewish hospitals.

The first three assumptions address general issues:

1. Is religious giving declining?
2. Do most Americans tithe—especially those affiliated with religious organizations?
3. Do members of some faiths give more than members of other faiths?

The remaining five have to do with potential demographic disparities in giving:

4. Do minorities give more to religious organizations than Whites?
5. Do women give more than men?
6. Do poor persons give more than wealthy persons?
7. Do less-educated people give more than well-educated people?
8. Do Southerners give more than those from other geographic areas?

Some other interesting questions will not be addressed here for lack of adequate tools and data. For example, although we can measure how much households give to religious organizations, we can not isolate how much religious values affect giving to other subsectors. Is giving to a Jewish hospital or a Catholic university *religious* giving or religiously motivated giving? While such gifts might be motivated by religious values or beliefs, they are not technically counted as giving to religion. Another question that we cannot yet answer is why religious giving *as a share of total giving* is declining. Finally, a policy question that is outside the scope of this chapter is whether religious giving is actually philanthropy or is more like membership fees or dues in a club. For example, Robert Payton (2008) has defined philanthropy as "voluntary action for the public good." A question can be raised about whether giving to religious organizations is supporting a public good.

This chapter measures household giving to religious organizations in the aggregate and per household, both overall and to a lesser degree by religious affiliation and frequency of religious attendance. It also looks at a number of socioeconomic demographic factors to determine their effects on giving to religious organizations. It uses the largest datasets ever collected on household religious giving in the United States: the Center on Philanthropy Panel Study (COPPS) for giving by households in the lower 97 percent of income and wealth (see Appendix A for more information on COPPS and its methodology); and the Bank of America Study of High Net-Worth Philanthropy, conducted by the Center on Philanthropy at Indiana University, for households in the top 3 percent of income and wealth (see Appendix B for more information on the BOA study and its methodology). Similarly, Giving USA is the longest running and only data series that looks at all of the sources of giving (i.e., personal giving, corporate giving, foundation giving, and bequest giving) as well as all of the major uses of philanthropy (e.g., religion, education, health, human services, etc.). Comparisons are made to prior research results to the extent available.

Keep in mind that we are not able to address how much of total giving, secular giving, or even religious giving is driven by religious values. We can only measure giving to religious organizations, giving to secular organizations, and total giving. One might reasonably assume that religious values motivate giving to religious charities, but that might not be what drives all of religious giving. For example, a concern for the poor, whether local, national, or international, might be a determinant of some giving to local religious organizations, which is counted as religious giving; the donor may know that a portion of that gift is actually distributed to poor households and may for that reason give more to that particular religious charity. Conversely, many might give to the local United Way campaign or CARE or other "secular" charities because of a desire to help the poor, but that desire to try to ameliorate the conditions of poverty might, in fact, be driven primarily by religious values.

We must acknowledge that we can only measure what is feasible with these datasets. We can reasonably assume that giving to religious organizations is motivated by religious values and thus represents the lower bound of total giving that is motivated by religious beliefs and values. For example, my gifts to the University of Notre Dame count as gifts to education, given that institution's primary mission. However, my decision to attend Notre Dame and to continue to donate might, in fact, be deeply affected by the linkage of Catholic values and traditions with educational achievements. Others enrolling at a religiously affiliated college or university might select that institution based only on its perceived intellectual and/or market value (e.g., my Jewish roommate at Notre Dame).

Likewise, we must acknowledge that we cannot disaggregate the giving to specific organizations or even to specific faith-group-affiliated organizations because the questions are not asked that way. For example, when we look at tithing behaviors, we assume that those who report being Latter-day Saints give to their church, that Jews give to synagogues, and so on, but we cannot isolate that.

Finally, it must be acknowledged that each of the datasets (Giving USA, COPPS, and Bank of America) was designed to measure different things; each has a different methodology; each has numerous sources of potential measurement error; and each has some aspects that appear to contradict the results of other research. That does not invalidate their utility for what they were designed to measure, however, and in each case they are unarguably the best dataset available at this point to measure, explain, and predict the various aspects of philanthropy. These are simply limitations on what we can measure, explain, and predict. They do not repudiate the basic results of the study. Rather, they limit the number and types of analyses we can make and the strength of the conclusions and implications we can assert in some cases.

COMMON BELIEF #1:
RELIGIOUS GIVING IS DECLINING

Every year since Giving USA started tracking it in 1955, religious giving has grown in both nominal and inflation-adjusted dollars, even during recessions. However, it has grown relatively slowly, averaging only 2 percent per year over the last 40 years compared to 5 percent per year for total giving (both adjusted for inflation). Over the last decade, religious giving has grown 2.1 percent per year versus 6.5 percent per year for total giving (again, both adjusted for inflation). The result is that religious giving, as a share of total giving, has fallen dramatically from approximately one-half of total giving for many years to under one-third today (Giving USA 2008).

In virtually all of the major religious affiliations for which there was data in both 1987/89 (Hoge et al. 1996) and 2004 (COPPS 2005), religious giving as a share of income fell by between one-tenth and one-half. Most of the larger Christian-based faiths (e.g., Catholics, Baptists, Methodists, Episcopalians) experienced a decline in religious giving as a share of income of approximately one-third. The smallest percentage of decline was among the "Other Protestants" group, which fell by 11 percent. Jehovah's Witnesses experienced the greatest percentage decline (79%), followed by Presbyterians (54%) (see table 1.1).

This result is despite the fact that more households give to religion than to any other subsector (46% per COPPS) and that a larger share of household philanthropy goes to religion than to any other subsector (60% per COPPS). In 2007, $102.32 billion were given to religion, making up 33.4 percent of total giving (Giving USA 2008). Thirty years earlier, only $14.18 billion (inflation-adjusted) were given to religion, but these donations made up 44.5 percent of total giving (Giving USA 2008). Thus, while religious giving increased substantially, even after adjusting for inflation, it did so at a slower pace than giving as a whole. Iannaccone (1998) noted that religious giving as a percentage of GDP had been fairly constant (1%) since 1955. However, this percentage has not held in recent years. Using data from Giving USA 2008, we can readily calculate that religious giving as a percentage of GDP is now at 0.7 percent. Approximately one-third of total giving is now religious giving, and total giving is now around 2 percent of GDP as compared to 1984, when religious giving was half of total giving and total giving was 1.7% of GDP.

Considering this historic data, we find that the evidence does not support the assumption that giving to religion is declining in terms of total dollars. However, there is ample evidence that religious giving is declining as a share of total giving as well as a share of household giving. This result is affected by a variety of factors, such as lowered rates of religious affiliation and attendance[1] and the growth in the role of foundation giving nationally. Foundations are the fastest growing source of giving over the last forty years, but foundations give very little to religious organizations.

TABLE 1.1. RELIGIOUS GIVING AS A SHARE OF TOTAL INCOME

	1987/1989 (Hoge 1996)	2004 (COPPS 2005)	Difference (1987–2004)	Percentage changes
Latter-day Saints	7.3%	5.6%	1.7%	23.9%
Pentecostal/ASG	4.6%	2.9%	1.6%	35.6%
Other Protestant	2.9%	2.6%	0.3%	11.0 %
Baptist	2.8%	2.0%	0.7%	27.2%
Lutheran	1.7%	1.5%	0.2%	13.1%
Methodist	2.0%	1.2%	0.7%	37.6%
Episcopal	1.7%	1.2%	0.4%	26.3%
Presbyterian	2.6%	1.2%	1.4%	54.3%
Catholic	1.2%	0.7%	0.5%	38.6%
Jehovah's Witness	2.7%	0.5%	2.1%	79.5%

The Foundation Center estimates that only 2.3 percent of foundation grants in 2006 were made to religious charities (Giving USA 2008). Therefore, a partial explanation for the decline in the share of religious giving as a percentage of total giving is a change in the share of the sources (relatively less reliance on households and more emphasis on foundation giving) combined with differences in the allocations of giving to various subsectors by these sources.

COMMON BELIEF #2:
AMERICANS GIVE "THE BIBLICAL TITHE"

In spite of the fact that many talk of the biblical tithe, only 2.6 percent of U.S. households give 10 percent or more to religious organizations, and only 8.3 percent give 5 percent or more of their income to religion (including the 2.6% who give 10% or more). In table 1.2, we see that 54 percent of Americans give none of their income to religious organizations and 21 percent give between zero and 1 percent. Almost 8 percent give between 1 and 2 percent of their incomes to religious charities, and 9 percent give between 2 and 5 percent. Therefore, 75 percent give less than 1 percent of their income to religious charities, and 82 percent give less than 2 percent! Clearly, most Americans do not "tithe," biblically speaking.

Furthermore, while a few individual households may tithe, *none* of the religious affiliations overall come close to tithing the traditional ten

TABLE 1.2. PERCENTAGE OF U.S. HOUSEHOLDS GIVING TO
RELIGION AT VARIOUS SHARES OF INCOME

% of income given to religion	% of households	Cumulative % of households
0%	53.9	53.9
0.001%–1%	20.6	74.5
1%–2%	7.8	82.4
2%–3%	4.2	86.6
3%–4%	3.0	89.5
4%–5%	2.1	91.6
5%–10%	5.7	97.4
10+%	2.6	100.0

Source: COPPS 2005

percent of income—at least not on average. Only Latter-day Saints (5.55%) give more than 3 percent of income to religious organizations, and only Pentecostal/ASG (2.93%), Other Protestants (2.57%), and Baptist (2.01%) give more than 2 percent of income to religious organizations. The other religious affiliations give an average of between 0.5 and 2 percent of income to religion (see table 1.3).

COMMON BELIEF #3: SOME FAITH GROUPS ARE MORE GENEROUS DONORS THAN OTHERS

This assumption will be discussed first with respect to total giving and then to religious giving.

TOTAL GIVING

Religious affiliation makes a big difference in the likelihood of being a donor to charity in general (secular and religious) and in the mean amounts given. Table 1.3 compares total charitable giving by religious affiliation after taking into account differences in household incomes (but not wealth, educational attainment, etc.). If generosity is measured as a share of income, Latter-day Saints hold the top spot for total giving (6.2%), followed by Other Protestant (3.7%), Pentecostal/ASG (3.5%), and Jewish (3.1%). These shares of income are conspicuously greater than those of

TABLE 1.3. TOTAL GIVING AND RELIGIOUS GIVING AS A SHARE OF INCOME BY RELIGIOUS
AFFILIATION SORTED BY RELIGIOUS GIVING AS A SHARE OF INCOME

	%Who Give	Mean Giving	Family Income	Religious Giving	Total Giving as % of Income	Religious Giving as % of Total Giving	Religious Giving as % of Income
Latter-day Saints	93.7%	$4,016	$64,334	$3,574	6.24%	89.0%	5.55%
Pentecostal/ASG	64.4%	$1,405	$40,038	$1,172	3.51%	83.4%	2.93%
Other Protestant	80.2%	$2,495	$67,028	$1,723	3.72%	69.1%	2.57%
Baptist	64.4%	$1,402	$53,534	$1,078	2.62%	76.9%	2.01%
Lutheran	77.4%	$1,615	$67,954	$1,004	2.38%	62.1%	1.48%
Greek/Russian/ Eastern Orthodox	70.7%	$1,091	$50,577	$677	2.16%	62.1%	1.34%
Jewish	88.3%	$3,822	$123,305	$1,552	3.10%	40.6%	1.36%
Methodist	73.3%	$1,257	$64,140	$790	1.96%	62.9%	1.23%
Episcopalian	80.4%	$2,006	$85,833	$1,044	2.34%	52.0%	1.22%
Presbyterian	81.9%	$1,461	$69,147	$827	2.11%	56.6%	1.20%
Catholic	73.7%	$1,122	$75,861	$559	1.48%	49.8%	0.74%
Muslim/Buddhist	69.9%	$1,248	$74,245	$450	1.68%	36.1%	0.61%
Missing	70.2%	$929	$63,034	$368	1.47%	39.6%	0.58%
Jehovah's Witness	64.8%	$472	$35,228	$193	1.34%	40.9%	0.55%
None	56.0%	$792	$71,556	$191	1.11%	24.1%	0.27%

Source: COPPS 2005

other faith groups, which ranged from 1.3% to 2.6%, as well as non-believers (1.1%).

RELIGIOUS GIVING

Among the five most generous religious affiliations—Latter-day Saints (6.2%), Other Protestant (3.7%), Pentecostal/ASG (3.5%), Jewish (3.1%), and Baptist (2.6%)—when measured by *total* giving as a percentage of income, all but Jewish remain in the top five of *religious* giving as a share of income (table 1.3). This suggests that Jewish households are relatively generous with respect to giving to "secular" causes. The middle five of total giving as a share of income (Lutheran, Episcopalian, Greek/Russian/Eastern Orthodox, Presbyterian, and Methodist) are also largely in the middle five of religious giving as a share of income (Greek/Russian/Eastern Orthodox, Jewish, Methodist, Episcopalian, and Presbyterian), with Lutheran being the exception. The bottom five of "total giving as a share of income" (Muslim/Buddhist, Catholic, Missing, Jehovah's Witnesses, and None) are also the least generous for religious giving as a percentage of income. Clearly, there are conspicuous differences in generosity in religious giving by various faith groups.

In multiple regression analyses designed to estimate the *differences in the probability of being a religious donor*, we found, not surprisingly, that those who were religiously affiliated were more likely to be religious donors than those who were not religiously affiliated. Religious attendance was also positively associated with the likelihood of religious giving (table 1.4). Similarly, in multiple regression analyses designed to estimate the differences in the *amounts donated to religious charities*, we found, also not surprisingly, that those religiously affiliated were more generous donors to religion than those who were not religiously affiliated. Religious attendance was significantly associated with increased religious giving (table 1.5). For both the probability of being a religious donor and the amounts donated to religious causes, the marginal effects of more frequent attendance were small but highly significant, and adding religious attendance tended to swamp the significance of other variables (e.g., number of children, being in good health, race, and being from the South).

COMMON BELIEF #4:
THE WEALTHY GIVE LESS TO RELIGION

Religious giving grows fairly dramatically with both income and wealth. Of those with less than $50,000 in income, just over one-third (36%)

were religious donors, and among those donors the average gift to religion was $1,248. Of those with incomes between $50,000 and $100,000, over one-half (54%) gave an average gift to religion of $1,889. High-income households in COPPS (>$100,000) were much more likely to be donors to religion (62.5%) and to give much more ($3,019) (table 1.6). Almost two-thirds (64%) of households with net worth in excess of $200,000 (excluding their homes) were religious donors, giving an average of $2,798. Those with a negative net worth (excluding their homes) were much less likely to be religious donors (32%) and to give relatively small amounts ($1,330).

Among high net-worth households (the top 3% of all households by income), religion is the most important subsector for giving, measured by dollars given (19% of high net-worth households) and is one of the subsectors most frequently donated to (72%). More high net-worth households donate to education (79%) and basic needs (75%), but these subsectors garner smaller shares of the total dollars given (24% and 4%, respectively). High net-worth households that donate to religion give an average of $12,167 (median = $4,000) compared to the rest of the population in which donors to religion give an average of $1,858 (median = $700) (Rooney and Frederick 2007).

Brown and Rooney (2007b) examined data on religious giving from COPPS and the Bank of America study by income as a share of total giving and found that the share of total giving going to religion declined fairly precipitously moving from lower to higher income brackets. For example, households earning less than $100,000 per year donated an average gift to religion of $1,423 and accounted for 59 percent of all household giving to religious charities. Those earning between $100,000 and $200,000 gave an average of $2,316 to religious charities, or 11 percent of the total giving to religion. Those earning from $200,000 to $1 million gave an average of $12,105 to religion and accounted for 21 percent of the total giving to religion. Finally, those earning $1 million or more donated an average of $61,060 to religious organizations, which amounted to 9 percent of the total dollars given to religion.

We used Probits (COPPS 2005) to determine the marginal effects of various socioeconomic factors on the probability of an individual being a donor to religion. Surprisingly, after controlling for wealth and tax itemization status as well as for several other variables, we found no significant effect between income and the probability of being a donor—except in the base model when controlling for religious attendance, in which case

TABLE 1.4. PROBIT MODELS—DEPENDENT VARIABLE: GIVING TO RELIGION

Independent Variables	Model 1 Base model w/o religious attendance	Model 2 Base model with secular giving	Model 3 Base model with religious attendance	Model 4 Base model with all interactions
Log average income	0.015	-0.016	0.046*	0.004
Log positive average wealth	0.026***	0.020***	0.028***	0.021***
Log negative average wealth	-0.028***	-0.021**	0.032***	-0.025***
Tax itemizer	0.207***	0.157***	0.176***	0.115***
Tax itemizer unknown	0.073	0.055	0.060	0.040
Age of head of household	0.006***	0.005***	0.004***	0.004***
Male head of household	-0.034	-0.012	0.018	0.042
Married	0.170***	0.166***	0.125***	0.118***
Marital status unknown				
Number of children	0.028**	0.029**	0.016	0.017
Good health	0.072**	0.061*	0.055	0.052
Health unknown	-0.242	-0.257	-0.303	-0.313*
College attendee	0.087***	0.071**	0.072**	0.051
Bachelors degree	0.101***	0.070**	0.069*	0.023
Postgraduate education	0.037	0.015	0.010	-0.038
Education Unknown	0.118*	0.117*	0.093	0.094
Black	0.073*	0.095**	-0.010	0.009
Latino	0.009	0.051	-0.058	-0.026
Race Others	0.060	0.079	0.032	0.047
Race unknown	-0.060	-0.020	-0.158	-0.116
Catholic	0.330***	0.145*	0.275***	0.168*
Jewish	0.228***	0.192	0.260***	0.142
Protestant	0.316***	0.202***	0.234***	0.162*
Religion others	0.210**	-0.187	0.125	-0.146
Religion unknown	0.151*	0.072	0.143*	0.143
Retired	0.012	0.006	0.022	0.025
Unemployed	-0.187***	-0.191***	-0.152**	-0.164**
Other employment status	-0.134***	-0.136***	-0.158**	-0.157**
Employment unknown	0.326	0.304	0.383	0.383
South	0.052**	0.051**	0.013	0.013
Region unknown	-0.128	-0.194	-0.258	-0.269

TABLE 1.4. (*continued*)

Independent Variables	Model 1 Base model w/o religious attendance	Model 2 Base model with secular giving	Model 3 Base model with religious attendance	Model 4 Base model with all interactions
Metropolitan community	-0.002	-0.017	0.000	-0.016
Community type unknown				
Religious attendance last year			0.009***	0.009***
Religious attendance last year-squared			0.000***	-0.000***
Secular giving		0.110		
Secular giving by Catholic		0.269***		
Secular giving by Jewish		0.079		
Secular giving by Protestant		0.179*		
Secular giving by other religion		0.426***		
Secular giving by religion unknown		0.093		
Log secular giving amount				0.026*
Log secular giving by Catholic				0.030*
Log secular giving by Jewish				0.025
Log secular giving by Protestant				0.020
Log secular giving by religion others			0.058*	
Log secular giving by religion unknown			-0.005	
Sample Size	5725	5725	5663	5663

Statistical Significance Note: * p <0.05 ** p <0.01 *** p <0.001

Source: COPPS 2005. (See appendix C for a brief discussion of Probits.)

TABLE 1.5. TOBIT MODELS—DEPENDENT VARIABLE: GIVING TO RELIGION

Independent Variables	Model 1 Base model w/o religious attendance	Model 2 Base model with secular giving	Model 3 Base model with religious attendance	Model 4 Base model with all interactions
Log average income	0.157*	0.197**	0.322***	-0.020
Log positive average wealth	0.129***	0.087***	0.111***	0.089***
Log negative average wealth	-0.137***	-0.097***	-0.125***	-0.093**
Tax itemizer	1.087***	0.575***	0.771***	0.819***
Tax itemizer unknown	0.454*	0.246	0.351*	0.354
Age of head of household	0.029***	0.017***	0.019***	0.026***
Male head of household	-0.174	0.075	-0.019	-0.073
Married	0.905***	0.609***	0.656***	0.862***
Marital status unknown				
Number of children	0.144***	0.087*	0.091*	0.134***
Good health	0.304**	0.154	0.204	0.282*
Health unknown	-1.000	-0.936	-0.934	-1.004
College attendee	0.435***	0.278**	0.361***	0.334**
Bachelors degree	0.474***	0.188	0.337**	0.247*
Postgraduate education	0.320	0.137	0.253	0.097
Education unknown	0.586*	0.339	0.402	0.528*
Black	0.395*	0.178	0.098	0.447**
Latino	0.079	0.089	-0.060	0.296
Race Others	0.195	0.102	0.070	0.259
Race unknown	0.019	0.012	-0.126	0.193
Catholic	1.893***	0.711	1.345***	0.845*
Jewish	1.401***	1.496	1.705***	0.244
Protestant	1.749***	0.945**	1.253***	1.262***
Religion others	1.336**	-0.449	0.904*	-0.523
Religion unknown	0.858*	0.740	0.740*	0.625
Retired	0.009	0.036	0.062	0.005
Unemployed	-0.970***	-0.745***	-0.749***	-0.989***
Other employment status	-0.694***	-0.579***	-0.602***	-0.672***
Employment unknown	1.310	1.492	1.572	1.195
South	0.283***	0.048	0.056	0.278***
Region unknown	-0.565	-0.298	-0.110	-0.612

TABLE 1.5. (*continued*)

Independent Variables	Model 1 Base model w/o religious attendance	Model 2 Base model with secular giving	Model 3 Base model with religious attendance	Model 4 Base model with all interactions
Metropolitan community	0.004	0.002	0.059	-0.060
Community type unknown	5.499***	1.415***	2.152***	3.653***
Religious attendance		0.029***	0.030***	
Religious attendance-squared		0.000***	0.000***	
Secular giving		0.729*		
Secular giving by Catholic		0.722		
Secular giving by Jewish		0.244		
Secular giving by Protestant		0.452		
Secular giving by other religion		2.014		
Secular giving by religion unknown		-0.063		
Log secular giving amount				0.068
Log secular giving by Catholic				0.197***
Log secular giving by Jewish				0.176
Log secular giving by Protestant				0.125*
Log secular giving by religion others				0.366***
Log secular giving by religion unknown				0.034
Sample Size	5726	5663	5664	5726

Statistical Significance Note: * p <0.05 ** p <0.01 *** p <0.001
Source: COPPS 2005. (See appendix C for a brief discussion of Tobits.)

TABLE 1.6. RELIGIOUS GIVING BY SOCIOECONOMIC FACTORS (2005)

Socioeconomic Factors		All Religious Mean	Donor Households Percent of giving
Head-sex	Female	$1,083	38.9%
	Male	$2,150	49.1%
Head-age	Age <40	$1,278	30.7%
	Age 40–64	$2,086	49.2%
	Age 65+	$1,979	62.9%
Head-race	White	$2,004	48.8%
	Black	$1,674	36.1%
	Native American	$476	46.7%
	Asian, pacific islander	$1,869	49.0%
	Latino origin or descent	$899	37.5%
	Others	$1,854	47.9%
	Race-missing	$2,287	34.3%
Head-education level			
	H.S. or less	$1,488	38.8%
	Some college	$1,946	47.5%
	B.A./B.S.	$1,938	58.3%
	Post-graduate	$3,675	59.4%
Head-marital status			
	Married	$2,316	58.4%
	Never married	$731	23.0%
	Widowed	$1,641	55.9%
	Divorced/annulled	$1,039	36.3%
	Separated	$1,069	25.7%
Income	<$50K	$1,248	36.4%
	$50K-$100K	$1,889	54.0%
	>$100K	$3,019	62.5%
Wealth	w/o Home <$0	$1,330	31.7%
	w/o home </=$50K & >/=0	$1,338	37.3%
	w/o home >$50K, </=$200K	$1,923	59.3%
	w/o home >$200K	$2,798	64.4%

Source: COPPS 2005

income does have a positive and significant effect on the probability of being a religious donor (see table 1.4). Wealth has a highly significant but relatively small effect on the probability of being a religious donor. We split wealth into positive and negative net worth. A 10 percent increase in positive net worth is associated with between a 0.2 and 0.3 percent increase in the likelihood of being a religious donor, and a further decline in negative net worth by 10 percent is associated with between a 0.2 and 0.3 percent decrease in the likelihood of being a religious donor. After controlling for income and wealth, tax itemizers were between 12 and 21 percent more likely to be religious donors.

We used Tobits (COPPS 2005) to determine the marginal effects of various socioeconomic factors on the amounts households donated to religion. We found varying levels of significance and varying levels of the significant effect between income and the amounts donated to religion after controlling for wealth and tax itemization status as well as for several other variables—except in the model with all of the indicators, including secular giving (see table 1.5). A 10 percent increase in income is associated with an increase in the amount given to religion ranging from 1.6 to 3.2 percent. Wealth has a highly significant but relatively small effect on the amounts donated to religion. We split wealth into positive and negative net worth. A 10 percent increase in positive net worth is associated with between a 0.9 and 1.3 percent increase in the amount donated to religion, but further declines in negative net worth of 10 percent is associated with between a 0.9 and 1.4 percent decrease in the amounts donated to religion. After controlling for income and wealth, tax itemizers donated significantly more than non-itemizers, which suggests that even religious donors are tax price sensitive—that is, religious donors give more when they can itemize their donation than when they cannot, even after controlling for differences in income, wealth, and other factors.

Over half (56%) of high net-worth households in the Bank of America Study of High Net-Worth Philanthropy (BOA) reported that their religious beliefs were an important or very important motivator for their giving overall. We also found a fairly linear relationship between religious participation and religious giving among high net-worth households. Those who report not attending religious services gave an average of $591. Those who attend weekly gave several times more (average = $24,020) than those who attend once or twice every six months (average = $4,105). Giving drops a bit for those who attend more often than weekly ($16,574).

The anomaly was that those who attend once or twice a year gave an average of $13,087, which was bigger than expected based on the trend.

Hence, whether one sees the wealthy as being generous to religion is a matter of interpretation. High-income households are more likely than other households to give to religion, and they give a higher amount on average. Giving also increases with increases in wealth, but the increases in religious giving grow more slowly than the increases in income and wealth, which suggests that the overall share of income (or wealth) going to religion falls as income (or wealth) grows. Therefore, very high-income and high net-worth households give a lower share of their income (or wealth) to religious charities than do the rest of the population—even though they give very large amounts on average.

COMMON BELIEF #5: RELIGIOUS GIVING IS INVERSELY RELATED TO EDUCATIONAL ATTAINMENT

Education seems to have a positive effect on religious giving, both with respect to being a donor at all and to the amounts donated. Examining the average levels of religious giving and education, we find that just over one-third (39%) of those with a high school education or less give to religious causes, and they give an average of $1,448 per year. Households headed by those with some college are more likely to be donors (48%) and to give much more ($1,946). Similarly, those graduating from college are much more likely to be donors (58%) and to give more ($1,938) than those with a high school education or less. Those with a postgraduate degree are about as likely as college grads to be donors (59%), but they give substantially more than college grads ($3,675).

Using Probits to look at the pure education effects, holding constant income, wealth, and an array of other variables, the likelihood of being a religious donor increases significantly with educational attainment, especially in the models that do not control for religious attendance. Those who have attended college are between 7 and 9 percent more likely to be religious donors than are those with a high school education or less, holding other factors constant. Those with a BA or BS degree are between 7 and 10 percent more likely to be religious donors than those with a high school diploma or less, holding other factors constant—except in the model with religious participation and all of the religious affiliation interactions. Those with a postgraduate education are no more or less likely to be religious donors than those with high school or less, holding other factors constant.

Using Tobits to estimate the pure educational effects on how much is donated to religion, we find that the amounts donated to religion increase significantly with educational attainment, especially in the models that do not control for religious attendance. In all of the specifications, those who have attended college donate more to religion than those with a high school education or less, holding other factors constant. Those with a BA or BS degree give significantly more to religion than those with high school or less, holding other factors constant—except in the model with religious participation and all of the religious affiliation interactions. Perhaps surprisingly, those with a postgraduate education give no more or no less to religion than those with high school or less, holding other factors constant.

Overall, religious giving grows with educational attainment. These relationships hold both on the simple averages and in more sophisticated multiple regression analyses. The one exception is that those who have a postgraduate degree give more on average (unconditional means) but are no more likely to be donors or to donate more money than those with a high school diploma or less—once we have statistically controlled for differences in income, wealth, and other factors.

COMMON BELIEF #6: MINORITIES GIVE MORE TO RELIGION THAN WHITES DO

There are fairly wide variations in the mean levels of giving by race/ethnicity and percentage of donors, but much smaller ranges in the differences when examining median gifts. The two most generous groups (not controlling for income or wealth, etc.) are Whites (48% give, with a mean gift of $2,004) and Asian/Pacific Islanders (49% give, with a mean gift of $1,869). Blacks are less likely than Native Americans to give (36% vs. 47%), but Blacks give substantially more than Native Americans ($1,674 vs. $476). "Other" races/ethnicities are more likely than Latinos to be donors (48% vs. 38%), and donate more ($1,854 vs. $899) (table 1.6).

We used Probits to isolate the pure differences in the probability of being a religious donor that are due to differences in race/ethnicity after controlling for differences in income, wealth, education, and an array of other variables. There were no significant differences in the likelihood of being a religious donor by race or ethnicity in the models that control for religious attendance. However, Blacks were between 7 and 10 percent more likely to be religious donors than Whites if we do not control for differences in religious attendance (table 1.4).

We used Tobits to isolate the pure differences in the amounts of money donated to religion that are due to differences in race/ethnicity after controlling for differences in income, wealth, education, and an array of other variables. Blacks donated more than Whites if we do not control for differences in religious attendance, but that difference goes away once we control for religious attendance. Not surprisingly, those religiously affiliated donated significantly more to religion than those who were not religiously affiliated. Religious attendance had a small but significant effect that was independent of religious affiliation.

These results suggest that there are differences in religious giving by race and ethnicity at the mean levels. However, these differences are actually due to differences in income, wealth, and/or educational attainment since the differences in religious giving become statistically insignificant after these controls are implemented to make more direct comparisons of households in similar circumstances. Finally, after controlling for differences in income, wealth, education, and so forth, Blacks appear more likely to give to religious charities and to give more than Whites. However, these differences also become statistically insignificant once we control for differences in religious attendance. This suggests that Blacks attend religious services more than do Whites but that, when comparing Black households and White households with similar socioeconomic status and with similar frequency of religious attendance, there are no significant differences in the propensity to give to religion or in the amounts donated to religion by race and/or ethnicity.

COMMON BELIEF #7: WOMEN GIVE MORE TO RELIGION THAN MEN DO

In table 1.6, we see that male-headed households are both more likely to be donors to religion than female-headed households (49% vs. 39%) and to donate more ($1,940 vs. $962) (COPPS 2005). When we used Probits to isolate the pure differences in the probability of being a religious donor that are due to differences in gender, after controlling for differences in income, wealth, education, and an array of other variables, we found no difference between male-headed and female-headed households. Married couples were between 12 and 17 percent more likely to be religious donors than singles. Similarly with Tobits, after controlling for socioeconomic differences we found no difference between male-headed and female-headed households in the amounts donated to religious charities. However, married couples donated significantly more than singles to religion.

COMMON BELIEF #8: SOUTHERNERS AND THOSE LIVING IN RURAL AREAS GIVE MORE TO RELIGION THAN PERSONS IN OTHER PARTS OF THE COUNTRY DO

Those living in some rural areas and those living in some parts of the South give more to religion on average. The East South Central region has the highest average gift to religion ($753) and the highest percentage of people giving to religious organizations (65.1%). The next most generous region is the West North Central where the average gift to religion is $554 and 58.4 percent of the people give to religion (see table 1.7). The South Atlantic was closer to the average giving levels, while the South West Central was much lower. Clearly, the data show mixed results about this common belief in relation to Southern regions.

The data relating to rural areas are a little more difficult to interpret. The populations most likely to give to religious charities are those from completely rural areas (64.8%), not adjacent to a metropolitan area (table 1.7), while people from completely rural areas adjacent to a metropolitan area were the least likely to give to religion (23.7%). The average gifts also ranged drastically from $629 to $100 respectively. More research on the differences of these apparently distinct demographics is needed to determine the causes of such a discrepancy. Perhaps the disparity of wealth in rural areas adjacent to metropolitan areas is much greater than that of other rural areas.

We used Probits (table 1.4) to isolate the pure differences in the probability of being a religious donor that are due to differences in region, after controlling for differences in income, wealth, education, and an array of other variables. Those living in the South are 5 percent more likely to be religious donors in the base model, but once we controlled for religious attendance the South is not significantly different from the rest of the country. We used Tobits to isolate the pure differences in the amounts donated to religious charities that are due to differences in region after controlling for differences in income, wealth, education, and other variables. Those living in the South donate significantly more to religion in the base models, but once we controlled for religious attendance the South is not significantly different from the rest of the country.

CONCLUSIONS

We used several different datasets and empirical techniques to test eight assumptions about giving to religious charities. In this conclusion, we

TABLE 1.7. RELIGIOUS GIVING BY REGION AND RESIDENTIAL AREA

Region-census	Mean	Percent of giving
East South Central	$753	65.1%
West North Central	$554	58.4%
Pacific	$531	32.8%
South Atlantic	$509	53.0%
New England	$432	57.2%
Mid-Atlantic	$427	57.0%
East North Central	$380	47.7%
West South Central	$307	47.0%
Mountain	$284	41.0%
Residence		
Completely rural, not adjacent to a metropolitan area	$629	64.8%
Urban population of less than 20,000; not adjacent to a metropolitan area	$616	60.6%
Fringe counties of metropolitan areas population of 1 million or more	$842	56.6%
Urban population of 20,000 or more; not adjacent to a metropolitan area	$764	56.0%
Counties in metropolitan areas of 250 thousand to 1 million population	$683	49.4%
Foreign	$489	49.0%
Urban population of less than 20,000; adjacent to a metropolitan area	$1,079	47.0%
Central counties of metropolitan areas of 1 million population or more	$1,186	46.9%
Counties in metropolitan areas of less than 250 thousand population	$1,263	43.5%
Urban population of 20,000 or more; adjacent to metropolitan area	$848	30.6%
Completely rural; adjacent to a metropolitan area	$100	23.7%

Source: COPPS 2005

briefly review those assumptions and whether or not the data are consistent with them.

- COMMON BELIEF: RELIGIOUS GIVING IS DECLINING
  The data do not support this. While religious giving as a share of total giving is declining, religious giving has grown substantially over time—even after adjusting for inflation.

- COMMON BELIEF: AMERICANS GIVE THE "BIBLICAL TITHE"
  The data do not support this. Only 2.6 percent of Americans give 10 percent or more of their income to religious charities. In fact, 75 percent of U.S. households give 1 percent of their income or less to religious charities.

- COMMON BELIEF: SOME FAITH GROUPS ARE MORE GENEROUS RELIGIOUS DONORS THAN OTHERS
  The data do support this. There are dramatic differences in giving to religion by religious affiliation at the unconditional means (averages), and we found that the differences in religious giving, even after controls for differences in income, remain significant differences. For the most part, religious attendance is much more important to understanding these differences in behavior than are differences in religious affiliation. However, Latter-day Saints are the only denomination to give more than 5 percent of their income to religious charities.

- COMMON BELIEF: THE WEALTHY GIVE LESS TO RELIGION
  The data do not support this. Religious giving grows fairly dramatically with both income and wealth. While income and wealth have little or no effect on the probability of being a donor to religious organizations, they do positively and significantly affect how much donors give. While religious giving increases with increases in income and wealth, after controlling for other variables, the increases in religious giving grow at less than a proportionate rate with respect to both income and wealth, which suggests that the overall share of income (or wealth) going to religion falls as income (or wealth) grows. Perhaps high-income or high net-worth donors view the needs of their religious organizations as fixed and thus do not increase their religious giving as rapidly as their income/ wealth grows.

- COMMON BELIEF: RELIGIOUS GIVING IS INVERSELY RELATED TO EDUCATIONAL ATTAINMENT

  The data do not support this. Education seems to have a positive effect on religious giving, both with respect to being a donor at all and to the amounts donated. This result holds in mean-level analyses as well as in multiple regressions.

- COMMON BELIEF: MINORITIES GIVE MORE TO RELIGION THAN WHITES DO

  The data do not support this. When comparing the simple means for giving to religion by race/ethnicity, one might decide that there are differences in religious giving by race/ethnicity. However, after controlling for income, wealth, education, and religious attendance, we find that the race/ethnicity differences go away. This suggests that differences observed at the racial levels are attributable to differences in income, wealth, and/or religious attendance.

- COMMON BELIEF: WOMEN GIVE MORE TO RELIGION THAN MEN DO

  The data do not support this. Male-headed households are both more likely than female-headed households to be donors to religion and to donate more, but these differences become statistically insignificant when we control for differences in income, wealth, educational attainment, and so forth. Therefore, these are income and wealth effects—not gender effects.

- COMMON BELIEF: SOUTHERNERS AND THOSE LIVING IN RURAL AREAS GIVE MORE TO RELIGION THAN PERSONS IN OTHER PARTS OF THE COUNTRY DO

  The data for this are mixed. When we look at the cross tabulations, some Southern regions are more generous than average, and some are actually less generous than average. Furthermore, while those living in the South were 5 percent more likely to be religious donors in the base Probit model, once we controlled for religious attendance, the South was not significantly different from the rest of the country. The same phenomenon occurred when we used Tobits to look at differences in amounts donated to religion. This suggests that Southerners are somewhat more generous to religious organizations. However, the key difference seems to be driven by the fact that they attend religious services more frequently.

APPENDIX A:
CENTER ON PHILANTHROPY PANEL STUDY (COPPS)

This chapter uses The Center on Philanthropy Panel Study (COPPS) at Indiana University-Purdue University Indianapolis to ascertain religious giving behavior and its determinants for the majority of American households (i.e., those in the lower 97th percentile of income and/or wealth). The data allow us to track a sample family's economic and demographic characteristics over time and relate this history to the family's current philanthropic behavior.

COPPS is ideally suited for this because it appended philanthropy questions to the Panel Study of Income Dynamics (PSID) conducted by the University of Michigan's Institute for Social Research, the largest and longest running panel study in the world. In each module since 2001, the PSID has added questions about household giving and volunteering. Given that the PSID is a large representative sample (and has an over-sample of low-income and minority households), and given that for many years the PSID interviewees have been asked a series of detailed questions about their income and wealth, we feel that adding questions about their specific giving patterns is likely to produce more accurate data than most surveys (whether by mail or Random Digit Dialing [RDD]). These households are accustomed to answering financial questions and doing so with expected levels of specificity that might annoy many households. Furthermore, because these questions about household giving are embedded in a 90-minute survey, it is highly unlikely that there should be concerns about selecting into or out of the sample, concerns that might confront a traditional RDD survey about any given topic. Wilhelm (2006) documents why COPPS is the "gold standard" compared to other household surveys of philanthropy.

Given that COPPS has scores of other variables in the dataset, we are able to utilize many variables in estimating the determinants of giving. We can look at these differences both at the simple mean level and also after controlling for income, wealth, educational attainment, race/ethnicity, and so forth in a regression model to estimate the marginal effects of these other variables on religious giving. We use Probits and Tobits (see Appendix C) to take into account the fact that donations are truncated at zero (i.e., one cannot make a negative gift—no matter how badly one might want to do so!).

APPENDIX B:
BANK OF AMERICA STUDY OF HIGH NET-WORTH PHILANTHROPY

In addition to using COPPS results, we incorporate some general results from the Bank of America Study of High Net-Worth Philanthropy (BOA), which was conducted by the Center on Philanthropy to ascertain giving at the high end (i.e., the top 3% of income earners). While not going into as much detail from the BOA study as we do with the COPPS data, we can use it as a backdrop to see how much high net-worth households give to religion and how this differs not only in absolute dollar amounts but also in share of giving. The BOA study is the first national, proportionally random sample of high net-worth households and their philanthropy. It is also the first large-scale (n = 1,398) study addressing these issues. Finally, it is the most comprehensive study of high net-worth households and their philanthropy as well as of the factors that motivate them to give more or less and the vehicles through which they give (Rooney and Frederick, 2007).

APPENDIX C:
PROBITS AND TOBITS

We use two statistical procedures to analyze these data. The first, which evaluates the probability that a respondent gives one answer rather than the opposite, is called a *Probit*. It is most often used for "yes/no" types of questions. Using this method, there is a dependent variable (the thing we are trying to predict or estimate) and independent variables (factors that are potentially associated with the dependent variable). To evaluate whether or not someone gives, for example, the dependent variable is the answer the person provides to the question: Did you give to charity last year? Independent variables are measures of things known already—or hypothesized—to be associated with the giving decision. These include income level, education level, marital status, whether or not the person lives in a certain size of community or certain region of the country, and so on.

When we report the results of a Probit, each finding is always compared with a reference group or "omitted" value and takes into account all of the independent variables at once. Taking into account all variables at once is called "with controls," or "controlling for other variables." So we could say in an example that people who are single are less likely than people who are married to make a charitable gift, after controls. We would also say that, after controls, people with a college degree are more likely than people with a high school diploma to give. When we say "after controls," that means we have included in the analysis all of the other factors such as income, education level, frequency of religious attendance, region of residence, age of children, and so on that might be linked with their giving behavior.

The idea is to compare differences in the probabilities of two individuals being donors when the two are identical in all other ways except the aspect being compared. For example, we might compare two people who have actually (or statistically adjusted) the same age, education, income, and so on, but differ in race (or gender). This enables us to determine the effect of race (or gender) on the propensity to give, holding all other factors constant. The tables included in this chapter show the "omitted" variables against which the others are compared.

The other technique, called a *Tobit*, is similar to a Probit, but rather than estimating or predicting a yes/no answer, it estimates a specific measure of something continuous (e.g., dollars). Tobits are used when the thing measured cannot fall below zero (one cannot make a negative contribution). Tobits tell us how much each factor, or variable, influences or is linked to the dependent variable. In this work, Tobits are used for dollar amount donated, holding all the other factors constant. Results are also reported in comparison to a reference group and with controls for all other variables. For example, we might compare two people who have actually (or statistically adjusted) the same age, race, gender, and so on, but differ in income (or educational attainment). Holding all other factors constant enables us to determine the pure impact of income (or education) on the amounts donated.

APPENDIX D:
METHODOLOGICAL CONCERNS

There are some important methodological concerns in examining the decline in religious giving as a share of income. First, not all faith groups were examined in the first wave as reported by Hoge et al. (1996), based on data from the General Social Survey (GSS) (1987–89), so we lack a comprehensive picture of what has happened. Second, the GSS sample replies are based on those who attend religious services at least annually, whereas the replies for the second wave of data (COPPS, 2001) are based on self-reported religious affiliation but are not restricted by religious attendance parameters. Third, the GSS and COPPS are two different surveys with two different survey methods and two different samples.

Rooney, Steinberg, and Schervish (2001 and 2004) and Wilhelm (2007) clearly document how important methodological differences in giving surveys can be in yielding differences in reported levels of giving. The differences in methods and/or sampling could account for much of the reported differences in giving as a share of income. In spite of all of these methodological concerns, the very large differences in religious giving as a share of personal income between 1987/89 and 2001 strongly suggest that religious giving has fallen as a share of income in that period of time.

NOTES

The author thanks Mark Wilhelm for sharing several relevant calculations. I also want to thank Ke (Samuel) Wu, Brian Getz, Dan Heist, and Xing Wei for research assistance. In addition, I thank Fred Kniss for suggesting organizing the material in this chapter along the line of common beliefs about religious giving, Paul Schervish for pointing out the pros and cons of each of the datasets used, the other participants of the Lake Institute's authors' conferences, and Patricia Dean for other editorial comments and suggestions. Of course, any remaining errors or omissions remain the sole responsibility of the author.

1. While the number of churchgoers has increased, the percentage of the population attending religious services nearly every week or more declined from 34.9% to 32.8% over a 30-year period (ARDA 2007). Also, the percentage of household income given to religion declined over this period (Wilhelm, Rooney, and Tempel, 2007).

REFERENCES

Azzi, Corry, and Ronald Ehrenberg. 1975. "Household Allocation of Time and Church Attendance." *Journal of Political Economy* 83 (1): 27–56.

Brown, Melissa S., Joseph C. Harris, and Patrick M. Rooney. 2005. "Reconciling Estimates of Religious Giving." Working Paper available at www.philanthropy.iupui.edu.

Brown, Melissa, and Patrick M. Rooney. 2007a. "Is There a Hierarchy of Giving?" Working Paper available at www.philanthropy.iupui.edu.

———. 2007b. "Giving to the Poor." Working Paper available at www.philanthropy .iupui.edu.

Center on Philanthropy Panel Study (COPPS). 2005, 2008. The Center on Philanthropy at Indiana University.

General Social Survey (GSS). 1987. National Opinion Research Center, University of Chicago. www.norc.org/GSS.

Giving USA 2008. 2008. Researched and written by the Center on Philanthropy at Indiana University. Published by the Giving USA Foundation, Chicago.

Hodgkinson, Virginia A., Murray S. Weitzman, and Arthur D. Kirsch. 1990. "From Commitment to Action: How Religious Involvement Affects Giving and Volunteering." In *Faith and Philanthropy in America*, ed. Robert Wuthnow and Virginia A. Hodgkinson. San Francisco: Jossey-Bass.

Hoge, Dean R., Charles Zech, Patrick McNamara, and Michael J. Donahue. 1996. *Money Matters*. Louisville, Ky.: Westminster John Knox Press.

Hoge, R. 1994. "Introduction: The Problem of Understanding Church Giving." *Review of Religious Research* 36 (2): 101–10.

Iannaccone, Laurence. 1998. "Introduction to the Economics of Religion." *Journal of Economic Literature* 36 (3): 1465–95.

Long, Stephen H., and Russell F. Settle. 1977. "Household Allocation of Time and Church Attendance: Some Additional Evidence." *Journal of Political Economy* 85 (2): 409–13.

Meslin, Eric, Patrick Rooney, and James Wolf. 2008. "Health-Related Philanthropy and Traditional Philanthropy: Is There a Universal Donor?" *Nonprofit and Voluntary Sector Quarterly* 37 (1): 44–62.

Payton, Robert. 2008. *Understanding Philanthropy: Its Meaning and Mission*. Bloomington: Indiana University Press.

Religious Service Attendance. The ARDA. www.thearda.com/quickstats/qs_55.asp.

Rooney, Patrick, and Heidi Frederick. 2007. "Bank of America Study of High Net-Worth Philanthropy." Working Paper available at www.philanthropy.iupui.edu.

Rooney, Patrick, Kathy Steinberg, and Paul Schervish. 2001. "A Methodological Comparison of Giving Surveys: Indiana as a Test Case." *Nonprofit and Voluntary Sector Quarterly* 30 (3): 551–68.

———. 2004. "Methodology Is Destiny: The Effect of Survey Prompts on Reported Levels of Giving and Volunteering." *Nonprofit and Voluntary Sector Quarterly* 33 (4): 628–54.

Smith, Adam. 1991. *The Wealth of Nations*. Buffalo, N.Y.: Prometheus Books.

Wilhelm, Mark O. 2006. "New Data on Charitable Giving in the PSID." *Economic Letters* 92:26–31.

Wilhelm, Mark O., Patrick M. Rooney, and Eugene R. Tempel. 2007. "Changes in Religious Giving Reflect Changes in Involvement: Age and Cohort Effects in Religious Giving, Secular Giving, and Attendance." *Journal for the Scientific Study of Religion* 46 (2): 217–32.

2 Giving in the Way of God: Muslim Philanthropy in the United States

SHARIQ SIDDIQUI

CHARITY BEGINS AT HOME

During Ramadan, the Muslim month of fasting and increased dedication to prayer and charitable activity, I regularly receive calls from my mother commending me on the civic work I do in and on behalf of the community in which I live—Greater Indianapolis, Indiana. This commendation, however, is usually the preface to an important admonition: "Just don't forget that charity begins at home." Lest anyone think my mother uses Ramadan as an opportunity to solicit me for funds to support herself, I had better explain. Even though she has lived in England for many years, for my mother, as for most immigrants, "home" is the land of the ancestors. In my family's case, this would be that part of the world known to most as India and Pakistan. When my mother reminds me that "charity begins at home," she is reminding me that successful South-Asian Muslims now living in the West have a responsibility to those family members and others whom they've left behind. I say that my mother is "reminding" me of this responsibility because, in many ways, it's a responsibility of which I've been aware from a very young age. Even though my immediate family lived all over the world as I was growing up, the bulk of our annual charitable contributions would be forwarded to my maternal grandmother in Lahore, who, as matriarch of our extended family, would distribute the funds as needed to our less-fortunate relatives and friends in South Asia.

That the adage "charity begins at home" may well have first been coined by Charles Dickens[1] and that my mother lives in England are strictly coincidental. This principle is deeply embedded in the ways Muslims think about charitable giving, as it is in the thought of a wide variety of religious traditions and cultures.[2] In his grand classical synthesis of

Islamic law and spirituality, the great Sunni scholar Abu Hamid al-Ghazali (d. 1111 CE) emphasizes how important it is for the Muslim giver first to come to the aid of those closest to him or her. In his discussion of the importance of giving to appropriate recipients (*man tazku bi-hi al-sadaqatu*),[3] Ghazali lists kinship as the sixth of six key attributes of the appropriate recipient.[4] In fact, he quotes a hadith (report) attributed to cousin and son-in-law of the Prophet Muhammad Ali b. Abi Talib in which Ali is depicted as having once said that he prefers giving one dirham[5] to one of his brothers in need (*akha min ikhwani*) than twenty dirhams as alms for needy strangers. He also quotes Ali as saying that he would prefer giving a hundred dirhams as a gift to needy kin even over the manumission of a slave.[6] The point here is not at all to diminish the importance in Islam of charitable giving to strangers, or of the manumission of a slave. In fact, although slaveholding is functionally no longer sanctioned by Islamic law, in the classical Muslim jurisprudence of the medieval period the manumission of a slave was considered to be one of the greatest acts of charity and mercy in which a human being could engage. Rather, what Ghazali is attempting to do is to underscore the primacy of being charitable to those closest to the giver. "Both friends [*al-asdiqâ'*] and the brethren of the good [*ikhwân al-khayr*]," Ghazali concludes, "should be given preference over acquaintances [*al-mâ'arif*], just as relatives [*al-aqârib*] are given precedence over non-relatives [*al-ajânib*]."

As a contemporary Muslim American with roots and extended family in South Asia and with immediate family living in Europe, my understanding of "home" has very little by way of geographic, cultural, or national boundaries. Like so many of my fellow Muslims in this era of globalization and unprecedented mobility, I have many "homes" where my solemn duty of charitable giving must "begin." It must begin with those members of my immediate and extended family who may be in need, wherever they might be. It must, however, also "begin" with those around me to whom I have no blood relation but whose needs I must address if I dare claim to be a Muslim. If I make no effort to give to charitable causes in Indianapolis and in the wider American society which I have made my home, then I cannot claim to be following the *sunna* or "lived example" of the Prophet Muhammad (s.),[7] who never turned a blind eye or a deaf ear to a soul in need and who made untold sacrifices for the benefit of the community in which he lived. To put it simply, regarding "appropriate recipients," there are many places where my charitable giving as a Muslim American with an immigrant background must begin. But what about the role charitable giving plays in the lives of Muslims in general? What, for Muslims, is the source of the imperative to give, and what are some of its basic principles, besides the fact that it must "begin at home"?

CHARITABLE GIVING IN ISLAMIC TEACHING

In the simplest terms, a Muslim's commitment to charitable giving can be found inscribed on his or her religious genes. "Almsgiving," or *zakât*, is one of the five "pillars" of Islam—one of the five crucial elements of what it means to live one's life in "submission" to God (the literal meaning of the Arabic word *islâm*). After testimony to the existence of the one God and the recognition that Muhammad (s.) is God's messenger, and after a commitment to prayer at least five times daily, comes the solemn duty to give "alms" (*zakât*).

The semantic field surrounding the word *zakât* renders some important insights regarding what the Qur'an teaches about the duty to give to those in need. *Zakât* comes from a tri-consonantal Arabic root (*z-k-y*) having to do with "purity" and "purification" as well as with "growth" and "increase."

The sense in which almsgiving is an act of purification[8] operates on a few different levels. One level has to do with the quranic teaching that everything a human being possesses belongs to God. In order, therefore, for the human being legitimately to use one's material wealth—over and above what one requires to meet one's basic needs and the basic needs of those for whom one might be financially responsible—one must first give God God's due. One does this by rendering to the poor a certain percentage of one's net worth, providing it has been in one's possession for at least a full lunar year and providing it exceeds a certain minimum amount (*nisâb*).[9] In the case of people whose net worth largely takes the form of monetary wealth, the alms one would pay on a yearly basis would be the equivalent of 2.5 percent of one's monetary assets[10] minus liabilities.[11] Through the solemn obligation to give God God's due in the form of *zakât*, one not only purifies one's net worth for legitimate use but also takes an important step toward the purification of one's soul by warding off the sins of greed and miserliness.

The sense in which almsgiving is an act of "growth" and "increase" has to do with the many blessings—in both this life and in the hereafter— that are connected with this practice. According to the Qur'an, "You will never attain true godliness until you expend what you love" (Q 3:92). "A simile for those who spend their wealth in the path of God is a [single] grain which yields seven ears in each of which are a hundred [more] grains; and God multiplies [God's bounty] for whomever God wills— God's knowledge is all-encompassing" (Q 2:261);[12] and "Whatever you lend at interest in order that [your wealth] might increase through the wealth of [other] people, [your wealth] will not increase in God's sight, [but] whatever you give as alms (*zakât*), longing for the face of God— these are those [whose wealth] will be multiplied" (Q 30:39).

As significant as are the rewards for fulfilling one's obligation to give *zakât*, however, this particular form of mandated charitable giving is understood as only a minimum designed to prime the spiritual pump of the human heart for a lifetime of what is known in Arabic as *sadaqa*. This is a cognate of the Hebrew word *tzedakah*, a word that means "righteousness" in both Hebrew and Arabic. Although the two words are sometimes used interchangeably in classical Muslim sources, obligatory almsgiving (*zakât*) is actually just one genus of the much broader category of *sadaqa*, which entails any act done in obedience to God and for the sake of another. *Sadaqa* thus entails everything from the establishment of a pious endowment for the welfare of others, known as a *waqf* (e.g., an endowment for a mosque, school, or hospital), to the simplest acts of kindness. The Prophet Muhammad (s.) once famously taught that even the act of smiling at someone in need of encouragement can be *sadaqa*.

Islam teaches that the best forms of *sadaqa* are those that are given at the right time for the right reason for the right cause. But how can one be sure, when one gives a gift, that all these principles are operative? There is a story from the life of the Prophet Muhammad (s.) about a man who unwittingly gave alms to a thief. When he found out that he had done so, he feared that God would not accept his *sadaqa*, so he decided to try again. This time he accidentally gave charity to a prostitute. When he eventually discovered what he had done, he was once again anxious that God would not accept this act of righteousness because it was once again done for the wrong recipient. So the man decided to make at least one more attempt. This time he wound up unknowingly giving alms to a wealthy, and thus entirely undeserving, man. Feeling overwhelmed by his three-fold error (and perhaps running out of expendable wealth), the man went to the Prophet in despair. To his surprise, the Prophet comforted him, telling him that his *sadaqa* was valid in all three instances. Just as the donor had no knowledge of the true identity of the three recipients, he cannot discount the possibility that, in the infinite wisdom of God's plan, the alms he gave may well have helped prevent the thief from stealing, the prostitute from selling her body, and the rich man from withholding his wealth from the needy. Although this story does not absolve the donor from the obligation of diligence in attempting to discern the appropriateness of the recipient, it does emphasize the central Islamic teaching regarding all acts of worship (charitable giving included) that the ultimate criterion for determining its acceptability to God is that the doer's intent be as pure as possible. It also emphasizes that, even if something about the act of giving is less than ideal, the result of the act may well be salutary.

Another central principle to Islamic teaching on charitable giving is that it is for the benefit of both the giver and the recipient. The Qur'an says: "If you openly demonstrate acts of charity (sadaqât), it is all well and good, but if you conceal them and perform them on behalf of the poor, that is better for you and [God] will forgive your evil deeds—God is well aware of what you are doing" (Q 2:271). In the first case, the act of giving clearly has practical benefit for the recipient in that he or she is relieved of some distress. It also may have practical benefit for the rest of the needy and the society at large if, through someone's public act of giving, awareness of need increases and encourages more people to give. It is clear from this verse, however, that the giver receives his or her crucial spiritual benefit if the giving is done in secret.[13]

Ghazali speaks of this benefit in terms of three different types of obligatory acts in the context of Islamic law. The first type are those acts of worship that are acts of pure religious devotion that have the important spiritual effect of rooting the practitioner in a deeper humility before God but that have no apparent "rationally perceivable" or "practical benefit."[14] The example he gives is the stoning of the three stone pillars (jamarât)—which represent the three appearances of Satan to Abraham as the latter was preparing to sacrifice his son—as one of the rites of the Hajj. The second type is acts of worship that have "rationally perceivable benefits,"[15] like repaying a debt or restoring stolen property to its rightful owner. The third type combines both the spiritual and practical benefit, and it is as this third type that Ghazali classifies as charitable giving that has—if done properly—the dual effect of making for a more just society and deepening the giver's sense of devotion and indebtedness to God. In simpler terms, God knows our intent and gives us credit for good intent. If, however, the motivation behind our giving is personal glory or material gain, it defeats the *spiritual* purpose of giving, and thus we end up cheating ourselves out of an opportunity for spiritual growth. Moreover, if one boasts of one's giving, the act can actually bring about practical harm to the recipient in the form of embarrassment, and to the giver in the form of increased pride. "O you who are faithful," enjoins the Qur'an, "Do not invalidate your acts of charitable giving (*sadaqâtikum*) by making [the recipient feel] beholden [to you or by otherwise] doing [the recipient] harm like the one who gives his wealth in order to show off before the people, and who neither believes in God nor the Last Day. The simile here is [that such a person is] like a rock upon which there is [some measure of soil] and then which is pelted by a downpour, leaving it barren. They have no control over what they have acquired and God does not guide the un-faithful people" (Q 2:264).

CHARITABLE GIVING AND THE STRUGGLE FOR JUSTICE

With *zakât* as one of its core expressions, *sadaqa* encompasses all forms of giving to others beyond one's minimum obligation; as such, it is an indis-pensable element of the struggle (*jihâd*) to live a righteous Muslim life. From the quranic perspective, performing acts of *sadaqa* is one of the pri-mary ways in which every Muslim—no matter how wealthy or how poor—can participate in the single most important imperative for the human creation of the quintessentially compassionate God: to work assiduously for justice (*'adl*) against each and every force of oppression (*zulm*) in the world.

The quranic term for "oppression"—*zulm*—comes from a tri-consonantal root (*z-l-m*), which also connotes "darkness" and "obscurity." According to classical lexicographers, *zulm* has a literal sense of disor-der—of things not being in their proper places and therefore not in proper relationship with one another.[16] In two places, the Qur'an explicitly speaks of *zulm* as "transgressing the limits set by God"[17] (Q 2:229 and 65:1), and in one very well-known verse (Q 31:13), it identifies *shirk*—the sin of associating anything with God (i.e., ascribing "partners" to God)—as a paradigmatic instance of the human self's being out of right relationship with God and thus in the mode of oppressing or wronging itself. Accord-ing to the logic of quranic teaching, the source of all oppression and in-justice is the human being's failure to recognize the rightful sovereignty of the one true God and thus his or her failure to adhere to God's com-mandments. If, therefore, some human beings are deprived of their mate-rial needs and the opportunity to support themselves and their families, while others have an abundance of both, then those who are hoarding for themselves the bounty that can come only from God are transgressing the boundaries of right relationships set by God. They are oppressing others by depriving them of what is rightfully theirs, and they are oppressing themselves by bringing upon themselves God's punishment for transgressing the divinely appointed limits.[18]

It is in this context that *sadaqa* takes on its central role in quranic morality. To give to others in ways that meaningfully address the inequities in the world, one is acting in accordance with the limits God has established for the individual human being and is thus committing oneself to living in right relationship with both God and the rest of humanity. To the extent that *zulm* implies the "oppression" that results from transgressing God's limits, it also implies living out of right relationship with the natural environment (i.e., with other living creatures and the entire ecosystem). This is why certain Muslim scholars are increasingly arguing for acts of *sadaqa* that benefit the natural environment as well as one's fellow human beings.[19]

According to Islamic tradition, the Prophet Muhammad (s.) once told the story of a very thirsty man walking on a deserted road. On his way, he found a well and climbed down to quench his thirst. When he climbed back up, he found a dog that was breathing hard due to thirst. The man climbed down and brought the dog some water for its thirst. The Prophet conveyed the message that this was a great act of *sadaqa*, indicating that, just as is the case with the Jewish notion of *tikkun ha-olam*, or "repair of the world" (see Judy Failer's essay in chapter 3 of this book), from the Islamic perspective, charitable giving is a key element of living a life of right relationship with God and all of God's creation. To practice *sadaqa* is to live a life of justice in the sense of striving to maintain the balance that God has decreed should exist between and among all God's creatures. In other words, philanthropy in Islam is indeed about making the world a better place.

THE DEMOGRAPHICS OF MUSLIM GIVING IN THE UNITED STATES

A quick overview of the history of the Muslim communities in the United States is necessary background for any attempt to say something about the demographics of Muslim giving in this country. As I indicated earlier, Muslims in America are a very diverse group and have come from different places at different times. Contrary to what some might think, Islam may not be entirely alien to premodern North America; there are reports that Muslims may have come to the shores of the New World as early as 1492 from Spain, as part of the mass exodus that resulted from the infamous

Spanish Inquisition. There is no hard evidence, however, to support this claim. As far as the historical record seems to indicate, the first known Muslims in what is now the United States came as chattel slaves via the horrendous Middle Passage.[20] According to Sylvianne Diouf, we have at least five so-called "slave narratives" written by Muslim African Americans who thus document their lives as slaves from West Africa.[21] Some historians estimate that fully 10 percent of African American slaves were Muslim. But most were unable to maintain an Islamic way of life, so this group never crossed the threshold of historical visibility in any significant way and thus has been largely neglected.[22]

Instead of acquiring their religious identity directly through their ancestry, today's African American or "indigenous" Muslim Americans came to Islam largely through various African American Muslim movements that were established well after Reconstruction. One of the first of these movements was the Moorish Science Temple of America, established by the Noble Drew Ali in the early 1900s. This group maintained that African Americans were Asiatic and not African. Although it had some teachings that diverged in major ways from that of the brands of Islam found in the traditional Muslim world (e.g., it had its own Qur'an, which was written by Noble Drew Ali), the movement did seek to connect itself, through its narratives and theology, to mainstream Islam.[23]

Another important African American Muslim movement is Elijah Muhammad's Nation of Islam. The Nation was initially formed by Fard Muhammad, who, according to Nation tradition, first came to the United States in 1930 as an incarnation of God from Mecca. According to this tradition, it was in Detroit, Michigan, that Fard met the young Elijah Poole, whom he eventually anointed as his latter-day prophet and messenger to the oppressed people of God in North America, and who thus took the name "Elijah Muhammad." Not long after they met, Fard mysteriously disappeared and Elijah Muhammad took over the direction of the movement. He taught a radically new liberationist mythology, which saw Whites as a race of bleached "demons" designed by an evil scientist/ Satan figure for the express purpose of oppressing God's original people of color. Because of its deification of Fard and its racial separatism, among other things, most mainstream Sunni or Shi'i Muslims denounced the Nation as heretical. As Edward Curtis has shown, however, despite these condemnations, the Nation continued to build connections with mainstream Muslim communities.[24] After the death of Elijah Muhammad, his son Warith Deen—or simply W. D. Muhammad—took over a large part of the movement, which he fairly soon led to accept a mainstream Sunni Muslim identity. What remains of the Nation today are those who continue to adhere to the original teachings of Elijah Muhammad by following Minister Louis Farrakhan, and those who identify themselves as members of Nation splinter groups, such as the Nation of Gods and Earths (also known as the Five Percenters), founded in 1964 by Clarence 13X.

Not all African American Muslims have roots in the Nation. The Darul Islam Movement, for example, was established in Brooklyn in the 1960s as a group dedicated to a strict interpretation of Sunni Islam as a basis for attaining independence from the unjust and immoral structures of American society. For a time, a significant part of this movement came under the leadership of a South Asian Sufi shaykh. Those who did not accept the shaykh's authority followed the leadership of Imam Jamil al-Amin (formerly H. Rapp Brown). Today they comprise a federation of some thirty primarily African American Muslim communities in North America.

The first wave of Muslim immigrants to the United States were Arab, and from 1875 until the outbreak of World War I, they came largely from the Middle East.[25] The next wave took place between the two great wars. These initial waves of Arab Muslim immigrants were generally uneducated, unskilled, and of peasant background. They came to the United States seeking the economic prosperity that had been achieved by their Arab Christian brothers and sisters who had come before them. The next wave of Muslims came between 1947 and the mid-1960s to escape political oppression in Egypt, Iraq, Syria, Yugoslavia, Albania, and the Soviet Union. The largest number consisted of displaced Palestinians. This group was different from previous groups, consisting primarily of educated and influential families. The current wave of immigration started in 1967, when the Johnson administration introduced favorable changes to immigration laws. That led to educated, English-speaking, Westernized Muslims immigrating to the United States from all over the Muslim world.[26] Although mosques and Islamic centers had been established in the 1900s, the number of mosques and Islamic organizations rose rapidly after 1967.

For a number of reasons, it is difficult to say just how large the U.S. Muslim population is: the U.S. Census Bureau does not collect information about religious affiliation; the Muslim community in the United States includes considerable ethnic diversity; and the vast majority of U.S. Muslims probably are not *officially* affiliated with a Muslim institution like a mosque, school, or Islamic center. The various demographic studies that have been conducted place the U.S. Muslim population anywhere between two and seven million. It is estimated that more than 60 percent are immigrants and that the largest ethnic group is African American.[27]

To get a clearer understanding of the Muslim American community and its philanthropic activities, it is important to know something about the demographics of this population. It is estimated that 54 percent of Muslims in America are male and 46 percent are women. Fifty-six percent are between the ages of 18 and 39, while only 13 percent are 55 or older. Forty-two percent report that their financial situation is excellent, and 41 percent report that they are homeowners. Sixteen percent report having incomes over $100,000; 10 percent, from $75,000 to $99,999; 15 percent, from $50,000 to $74,999; and 24 percent from $30,000 to $49,999. Twenty-four percent report that they are self-employed or small business owners. Eighty-four percent of Muslim households have multiple people living in them; 59 percent have children living in them.[28] Fifty-eight percent are college graduates, while an additional 24 percent report that they have some college. Seventy-eight percent report that their faith is very important; 17 percent that it is somewhat important. Thirty-one percent report that they attend mosque more than once a week; an additional 24 percent report attending the weekly congregational Friday (*jumaah*) prayers. Ten percent attend mosque once or twice a month, while 14 percent attend a few times a year, especially for Eid prayers.[29]

Although the number of Muslim Americans is in dispute, most studies agree that there are over 1,200 mosques and 200 full-time Islamic schools in the United States.[30] (It should be noted that in 1998 the *Tablighi Jamaat* went from city to city and released a directory of over 3,000 mosques that they had visited.)[31] The number of full-time Islamic schools is generally considered to be larger than 200: *Philanthropy in America* puts the number at 300,[32] and a survey by The Islamic School's League of America found 235 full-time Islamic schools in America.[33]

In addition to mosques and schools, every Muslim community is also home to multiple small nonprofits dedicated to causes dear to the founder. Nonprofits dealing with issues such as domestic violence, scholarships for Muslims, feeding the poor, assisting the homeless, interfaith outreach, and media relations can be found in U.S. Muslim communities. Although there are at least twelve major Muslim relief organizations in the United States that raise money to be spent on relief projects primarily in the Muslim world, there are countless smaller organizations that also do meaningful work. For example, in Plainfield, Indiana, alone there are two relief organizations that raise over $100,000 a year. One of them, ObatHelpers, reports having raised more than $250,000 for stranded Pakistanis in Bangladesh. That organization was established by a Muslim family in 2005 with the intention of sponsoring one Pakistani family. The project grew so large that they are now establishing an endowment to support long-term service in the refugee camps.[34]

Nearly every U.S. college with a Muslim population has established a Muslim Student Association, as have many high schools. Youth groups that encourage high school and middle school youth to be more involved with civic activities as well as with activities related to their faith are popping up all over the country. Muslim Boy Scout and Girl Scout organizations are being established across the country. Their members take part in the Scout programs, but the troops are all Muslim, they are run by Muslim parents, and they incorporate Islamic events and programs into their activities.

Professional associations like National Association of Muslim Lawyers, Islamic Medical Association of North America, American Muslim Social Scientists, Islamic Social Services Association, Association of Muslim Mental Health Professionals, and American Muslim Scientists and Engineers are just a few of the organizations that have been established in the United States and that hold annual conventions to bring their members together.

A number of public advocacy organizations have also been established. The Council of American-Islamic Relations, with more than 32 chapters, is probably the largest. Other major advocacy organizations are Muslim Public Affairs Council, MAS Freedom Foundation, and American Muslim Alliance. There are also many smaller regional or local public advocacy organizations that have been established by Muslims.

Muslim nonprofits are not limited to the causes cited above and are as diverse as the Muslim population: thepenandinkpot foundation sells Islamic art and pushes for environmentally friendly and sustainable development; Muslims for a Safe America focus on issues of national security; Muslim Re-entry Network of Indiana offers re-entry assistance to ex-offenders; Islamic Broadcasting Network has an internet radio station and is trying to establish a Muslim TV channel. The list goes on.[35]

Although it is clear that Muslim Americans are active in charitable endeavors, there have been no studies measuring giving and volunteering specifically by Muslim Americans. The Center on Philanthropy Panel Study (COPPS) measures Muslims and Buddhists together, due to the small size of those groups within the sample.[36] Furthermore, most studies of Muslim Americans are focused on politics, beliefs, and demographics and thus do not provide much information about philanthropy.

Despite their limitations, these studies do provide a window into Muslim American philanthropy. The American Muslim Poll by the Zogby organization asked the Muslims polled if they were involved in various kinds of civic engagement. "Involved" was defined as having donated time or money or serving as an officer of an organization. Of those polled, 77 percent reported involvement with an organization to help the poor, sick, elderly or homeless; 71 percent with a mosque or religious organization; 69 percent with a school or youth program; 46 percent with a professional organization; 45 percent with a neighborhood, civic or community group; 42 percent with an arts or cultural group; 36 percent with an ethnic group; 33 percent with a Muslim political or public affairs committee; 24 percent with a veteran or military service organization; and 17 percent with a trade or labor union.[37]

Most intriguing is that, at a time when Muslim Americans are reporting a high number of hate crimes, discriminatory acts, and concern about civil liberties, their highest philanthropic priorities are helping the poor, sick, elderly, and homeless and participating in mosques and religious organizations, while public affairs and political organizations are third from last. The same survey showed that 96 percent believed they should donate to non-Muslim social service organizations; 96 percent that they should be involved with American civic and community development organizations; 93 percent that they should be involved in the American political process; and 88 percent that they should support interfaith activities.[38]

In the Pew Study, 76 percent of Muslim Americans said that giving to charity (*zakât*) was very important, while an additional 14 percent thought it was somewhat important. Only 8 percent stated that it was not too important or not at all important.[39] When ranking the five major religious practices, respondents placed *zakât* second only to fasting and ahead of a pilgrimage to Mecca, reading the Koran daily, and daily prayer. If those who ranked it "very important" and "somewhat important" were combined, it would be first.[40]

Mosques are also important sources of philanthropy for Muslim Americans, since 84 percent are reported to give cash assistance to families or individuals; 74 percent provide counseling services; 60 percent have prison or jail programs; 55 percent have a food pantry or soup kitchen or collect food for the poor; and 53 percent have a thrift store or collect clothes for the poor. In addition, 28% have a tutoring or literacy program, 18 percent have an anti-drug or anti-crime program, 16 percent have a daycare or preschool program, and 12 percent have a substance abuse program.[41]

These studies provide only a partial picture of philanthropy among Muslim Americans. I looked at the 990 tax forms of 12 large Muslim American relief organizations. These organizations reported that they raised over $43 million in 2006 from individual donors. I did not find a current 990 for Islamic Relief, the largest Muslim American charity; I spoke with their development director, who reported that they had raised over $50 million last year. Since the organizations I looked at were large organizations that raised over $500,000 and that were known to me through my years of work, they do not include the countless smaller relief organizations like ObatHelpers (discussed above), which are also able to raise significant amounts of relief money, or the money raised by individuals and sent as relief funds through money transfers to family and friends overseas.

Not even Muslim Americans realize the scope of their philanthropy. A recent article in *Islamic Horizons* (the flagship magazine for the largest Muslim American organization, Islamic Society of North America) estimated that Muslim Americans' annual *zakât* was $37.5 million. The article lamented, "If the entire amount of zakat among North Americans were collected, the progress made by the community would be staggering."[42] In reality, it seems that Muslim American relief charities alone raised over $93 million from individual donors. This amount does not include the amounts raised to sustain the major national organization, the more than 1,200 mosques, the more than 200 Islamic schools, and the innumerable other philanthropic activities. The problem for many Muslim American organizations that serve Muslim Americans is not that Muslim Americans do not give large sums of money to charity but that much of it is focused on relief efforts across the world.

It is also important to look at how Muslim American philanthropy reacts to emergency situations. Three major events have mobilized philanthropic resources in the past few years: the tsunami, Katrina, and the 2005 Pakistani earthquake. At least one major sustainable Muslim American relief organization, Asia Relief, was established specifically to work on the aftermath of the tsunami. In the cases of Katrina and the Pakistani earthquake, the major Muslim American organizations came together and created special task forces. These task forces coordinated the efforts of the major organizations' charitable work in these crises. For Katrina they pledged and raised $10 million; for the Pakistani earthquake they pledged and raised over $20 million.[43] These numbers do not include the incredible amount of work that was done at the mosque, community, and individual levels. Anecdotal reports include stories of individuals personally taking $500,000 to Pakistan for earthquake relief—money that was raised individually without institutional or organizational support.[44]

These figures suggest an incredible amount of philanthropic activity by Muslim Americans. Muslim Americans are motivated not only by their religious calling to engage in charity but also by the opportunities that America provides for civic engagement. In most Muslim countries giving is individual in nature rather than organizational. Mosques and religious institutions (including schools) are organized and funded by the state. In fact, one of the pioneers in Islamic philanthropy, the ISNA Development Foundation, suggests that this is a major difference between Muslim American and Muslim world philanthropy.[45] Muslim American philanthropy has its own unique American flavor, albeit rooted in faith.

PORTRAITS OF MUSLIM AMERICAN PHILANTHROPY

The nature of Muslim American philanthropy cannot be understood through numbers alone. The following are a few illustrations of how philanthropy among Muslim Americans is affected by the situation in which they live as well as by their unique Muslim American identity.

While there is no evidence that the ten percent of slaves who were Muslim were able to carry on their Islamic traditions, there is evidence that Islam affected African American traditions. As was discussed earlier, Muslims are required to give *zakât*, or charity, from their wealth. While one would not expect slaves to give *zakât*, there is evidence that *zakât* was practiced within the slave population. Slaves in Georgia are reported to have saved small quantities of the rice they harvested every day and small quantities of sugar from their rations. The female slaves would then make a saraka cake for the children to eat. Sylvianne Diouf believes that the word *saraka* comes from the Arabic word *sadaqa*, which as we have seen is a form of Islamic charity. The granddaughter of a slave described it this way: "She wash rice, an po off all duh watuh. She let wet rice sit all night, an in mawnin rice is all swell. She tak dat rice an put it in wooden mawtuh, an beat it tuh paste wid wooden pestle. She add honey, sometime shuguh, an make it in flat cake wid uh hans. . . . Duh cake made, sha call us all in a deah she hab great big fannuh full an she gib us each cake. . . . Den we all stands roun table, and she says 'Ameen, Ameen, Ameen' an we all eats the cake."[46] Muslims use the word 'Ameen' on various occasions, including when they ask God to accept a prayer. One can imagine how special these cakes would be to the children of slaves. Having no money, they did the only thing they could to continue to practice the charity that their faith asked of them. Their faith and circumstance influenced the nature of their philanthropy.

Carolyn Rouse provides some beautiful narratives of contemporary African American Muslim women who practice various forms of philanthropy while they live their lives as Muslims. She tells about Alia and Karim, a middle-class couple doing religious charitable work.[47] Karim counsels inmates and lectures about Islam and incarceration; Alia is a housewife who does *dawah* (shares the Islamic faith). They live in a cheap apartment in a poor neighborhood in order to continue their religious work. For Alia and Karim, charity is not in the form of money but consists of making sacrifices and contributing time to make the lives of other better. In the United States, Alia and Karim's *dawah* and work with inmates is necessary for the propagation of Islam. Unlike an Islamic country, where the government takes on this burden, in the United States it is the hard work and sacrifice of philanthropists like Alia and Karim that allows Islam to be the fastest growing religion in the country. Again, the situation they were placed in resulted in a unique Muslim American form of philanthropy.

Rouse also shows us the importance of "African American Muslim soul food." After major Muslim celebrations, or during Ramadan, families get together and share food. This allows poorer families to share in the success of well-to-do families. For example, Rouse describes Safa as "clearly one of the best and most generous cooks . . . who for Eid brought enough . . . to feed five families."[48] Safa used food as a way to share her wealth. It wasn't enough for her just to buy soul food. Just as important was deciding on the menu, purchasing the ingredients, making the food, and then sharing it with other Muslim families. Safa's sharing of food was a way for her to practice her faith and show her commitment to her community. African American Muslim soul food includes traditional items like macaroni and cheese, collard greens, fried chicken, potatoes, okra, cornbread, black-eyed peas, and barbecued beef ribs. It also has adopted Middle Eastern items like curried lamb and beef kabobs. The influence also goes the other way: at a recent Ramadan gathering of Muslim immigrants, fried chicken and spaghetti were served. This should not be surprising because there has been interaction between the African American and immigrant Muslim communities, an interaction that has helped shape a new Muslim American identity.

Using food as philanthropy is not unique to African American Muslims. Immigrant Muslims also hold large family-sponsored events to feed the community. These events are open to all members of the community, regardless of whether they are known by the hosts. Every Ramadan in my local mosque in Plainfield, Indiana, families get together and have Friday night potlucks and Saturday night community *iftars* (evening meals for breaking the fast during the month of Ramadan). During the 2007 Ramadan, families sponsored three Saturday night *iftars*, at which my small mosque hosted more than 400 community members each Saturday and raised more than $40,000 for philanthropic projects during 15-minute fundraising sessions after breaking the fast. The families that host these *iftars* could simply give money to a food kitchen, but it is important to them that they get together and plan the event, set up the mosque, have announcements made, prepare the food, pray for a large crowd and then, despite fasting all day and laboring to prepare the food, they do not eat until everyone else has been fed. Once the event is done, they clean up before and after the late-night prayers. The time and money devoted to feeding fellow community members are given as an act of philanthropy.

Philanthropy has also highlighted the role of women in Muslim American communities. The women at the All-Dulles Area Muslim Society (ADAMS) Center sell food after every Friday prayer. They get together to prepare the food, buy the paper products and serve and sell the food after prayer. Their time is volunteered so that all of the money raised can be used for an endowment for the center.[49] This is not unique; women in many Islamic centers have taken on this role, which brings in vital funds for the community.

The most dramatic effect of Muslim American women's philanthropic activity can be seen in the American Moslem Bekaa Center in Michigan. The founders of the Bekaa Center used to be members of the Dix mosque in Michigan. In 1978, these members were ousted from the Dix mosque because of disagreement about the way that Islam should be practiced in the mosque. When the Dix mosque was taken over by a new group, the old guard found itself without a mosque or resources to build a new one. However, the Dix mosque had a Women's Society that had raised money that they kept separate from the mosque treasury to further the programs of the Women's Society. When the families of the old guard were ousted from the Dix mosque, the Women's Society was able to provide the necessary funding for a down payment to purchase a building to host the American Moslem Bekaa Center.[50]

Dr. Farooque Khan's book, *Story of a Mosque in America*, shows how his community was able to come together and establish a highly successful Islamic center.[51] The methods of fundraising used by his community are very similar to ones practiced by other Muslim communities across the United States. The fundraising methods include weekly collections before and after Friday prayers, an annual fundraiser that usually brings in a famous Muslim fundraiser/scholar, lunches sold after Friday prayer, and individual solicitations made by mosque leaders.

Not all Muslim communities limit *zakât* to 2.5 percent. Lila and Mohsen describe how the imam of their mosque was able to sustain himself without being paid a salary, while remaining a full-time employee. Lila and Mohsen gave 20 percent of their annual savings to their imam to be given to the poor. It was understood in their community that the imam would use a certain portion of that money toward his own salary. This would be perfectly permissible according to the rules of *zakât*. The imam would probably fall under three categories: first, gifts to those who collect and administer *zakât*; second, gifts for the sake of Allah; and finally, gifts to the poor, because he is an income-less imam.[52]

As an immigrant Muslim American, my own philanthropic story is not very different from many others. There are causes, Muslim and non-Muslim, that I am passionate about, and these are where I focus much of my time and treasure. As a Muslim, I know that I am required to be charitable, but I also know that my faith expects me to make this world a better place. Therefore, it is not surprising that I donate the majority of my charity to organizations that I work with the most. Most of these causes are centered in my community in Indiana and in the United States. However, it is difficult to forget where my parents came from. Like many immigrant Muslims, I donate to my region of origin through family and also through relief organizations. If I had a great deal of money, this would be less of a struggle. However, as a student and public servant, I am forced to make choices. While those choices, in my case, favor the causes I am involved with here, it is difficult to face family and friends in the Muslim world who have great expectations of me. Regardless of where I stand economically in comparison to others in the United States, I am clearly better off than those who live in poorer regions of the Muslim world. Having talked with many friends in the United States, I know they face similar struggles. Some favor giving more to the Muslim world because of its poverty and the greater impact their money will have due to exchange rates; others have patterns similar to mine.

Government raids on Muslim American organizations, based on allegations of support for terrorism, have made the choice to give to the Muslim world more difficult. Although Muslim American relief organizations show a growth in donations, they report that Muslim American donors express concern about the government's actions in raiding and closing Muslim American charities. In fact, scholars in the Muslim community have even been asked whether a Muslim fulfills his duty if a relief organization to which he donates *zakât* is subsequently closed. Most scholars would argue that a Muslim's duty is fulfilled at the time of donation and is dependent upon the intent of the donor. Nevertheless, when I bring up this question to those who raise concerns about charities that have been closed, I receive an interesting response. One friend told me, "Even though I have fulfilled my duty of *zakât*, I still want that money to make the world better. When the government seizes that money, and it is not used for the defense of the charity, it doesn't help the poor and needy that I wanted to help." Therefore, his need to give *zakât* was both selfish and selfless. It was selfish, because he wanted to fulfill his Islamic obligation, but it was also selfless, because he was concerned that the recipient benefit. This concern among Muslim Americans is growing because many charities that have been raided have never been indicted, and many more have been listed as "un-indicted co-conspirators." Furthermore, the list has been accidentally leaked to the media. Recent cases against one charity have resulted in acquittals and a hung jury, embarrassing the government and creating further unease among Muslim Americans.

There is no evidence to suggest that donations to Muslim Americans are diminishing. In fact, since 2001, charities are reporting increased levels of funding. However, with no serious examination of this issue, it is difficult to determine how government action against Muslim American charities is affecting them.

To conclude: Muslim American philanthropy is not very different from the philanthropy of Americans at large. Regardless of whether they were born here or not, Muslim Americans have taken to the voluntary sector like fish to water. Their philanthropy, while motivated by their Islamic faith, is shaped by their unique Muslim American identity. The need to further causes, religious as well as secular, has resulted in a vibrant Muslim American philanthropic sector. The importance of religion among Muslim Americans is similar to the importance of religion among the American population in general. Considering the importance of religion and the special emphasis Islam places on philanthropy, it is not surprising that religious giving is a significant part of Muslim American life.

NOTES

The title, Giving "in the way of God" (i.e., *fî sabîl Allâh*)—a direct reference to Q 2:261—is the quranic expression for authentic giving, which benefits both the giver and receiver and pleases God by helping to build a more just social order.

1. In the midst of a conversation about how usury laws make things "hard" on potential usurers, the conniving Tigg Montague justifies bilking insurance purchasers by famously quipping: "But charity begins at home and justice begins next door" in Charles Dickens' *Martin Chuzzlewit*.

2. One well-known Christian scriptural locus classicus for an articulation of this principle of charitable giving can be found in the strong words of 1 Timothy 5:8: "And whoever does not provide for relatives, and especially for family members, has denied the faith and is worse than an unbeliever" (NRSV).

3. Abu Hamid al-Ghazali, *Kitâb ihyâ' 'ulûm al-dîn*, ed. Dr. Badawi Tabanna (Indonesia: Maktaba wa Matba'a Kariyata Futra, n.d.), 1:221 (hereafter cited as Tabanna with page number).

4. "The sixth [attribute] is that [the recipient] should be a relative close of kin so that the gift would be both charity [*sadaqa*] and a favour to the close of kin. A favour to the close of kin has countless rewards." This translation of Ghazali is from Nabih Amin Faris in *The Mysteries of Almsgiving: A Translation from the Arabic with Notes of* Kitâb asrâr al-zakâh *of al-Ghazali's* Ihyâ' 'ulûm al-dîn (Lahore: SH. Muhammad (s.) Ashraf, 1966), 54. The original Arabic reads: *al-sifatu l-sâdisatu: an yakûna min al-aqârib wa dhûwî l-arhâmi fa-takûna sadaqatan wa silata rihmin wa fi silati l-rihmi min al-thawâb mâ lâ yuhsâ* (*Ihyâ'*, B. Tabanna, ed.), 221.

5. A dirham is a coin—usually silver and weighing anywhere between two and four grams—that was a staple of the currencies of many medieval Muslim societies. Dirham is also the basic currency unit in certain contemporary Arab nations such as Morocco and the United Arab Emirates.

6. Ghazali, *Mysteries of Almsgiving*, trans. N. A. Faris, 54 (hereafter cited as Faris with page number).

7. The (s.) stands for the Arabic expression, *sallâ llâhu 'alayhi wa sallam*, roughly translated as "May God bless him and grant him peace."

8. See Q 9:103. This is the standard notation used for quranic citation (in this case indicating chapter 9, verse 103).

9. The percentage and set minimum are established for each of the six major "types" of *zakât* required by divine law (e.g., 2.5% of cash in excess of 200 Meccan dirhams of sterling silver, or two goats for every ten camels one possesses above the minimum of five). According to the classical formulation of medieval books of Muslim jurisprudence on the subject, such as Ghazali's *Kitâb asrâr al-zakât*, these six major types include *zakât* on: livestock (*na'am*), cash (*naqdân*, i.e., silver and gold coinage), merchandise (*tijâra*), precious minerals and the contents of mines (*rikâz* and *ma'âdin*), a tenth of fungible crops (*mu'ashsharât*), and the per capita per household cost of a fast-breaking (*fitr*) meal at the end of Ramadan. See Faris, 5–16; Tabanna, 209–12.

10. This includes all personal and business bank accounts, all holdings in gold and silver bullion and jewelry, stocks and mutual funds, business merchandise and

accounts receivable, retirement plans, real estate in addition to one's primary residence, etc.

11. Muslims who live in societies in which the government does not collect and distribute the obligatory alms (such as the U.S. and most other countries with a majority non-Muslim population) can visit a Web site like that of the Hidaya Foundation (www.hidaya.org/zakat-calculator.html), enter their annual data, and be told what they owe for that year. It will then be their responsibility to distribute their *zakât* appropriately.

12. Cf. Q 2:265; here givers are compared to "a hilltop garden" (*jannatin bi-rubwatin*).

13. Cf. Matthew 6:2–4; note that there is also a saying ascribed to the Prophet Muhammad (s.) in which one of the seven types of people who will "stand in God's shade on that Day when there will be no shade but God's" (i.e., on judgment day) is identified as "a man who gives charity (*sadaqa*) and hides it such that his right [hand] does not know what his left is giving" (*rajulun tasaddaqa bi-sadaqatin fa-akhfâhâ hattâ lâ ta'lama yamînuhu mâ yunfiqu shimâluhu*).

14. *ta'abbudun mahdun lâ madkhil li-l-huzûz wa l-aghrâd*, Tabanna, 213; Faris, 19–22.

15. *hazzun ma'qûlun*, ibid.

16. Lane's *Arabic-English Lexicon*, in Muhammad (s.) Kamil Hussain, "The Meaning of *Zulm* in the Qur'an," translated with notes by Kenneth Cragg, *The Moslem World* 49, no. 3 (July 1959): 196–212, at 197 n. 1.

17. *yata'adda hudûd Allâh*.

18. Hussain points out that, especially when used in the intransitive mode, the verbal form of *zulm* in the Qur'an almost invariably means to "wrong oneself." He argues that the transitive mode preserves this sense of wronging oneself to the degree that wronging others by transgressing God's commandments ultimately means bringing God's punishment upon—and thus wronging—the self. See "Meaning of *Zulm*," 200.

19. E.g., Muhammad (s.) Haytham al-Khayat, *Environmental Health: An Islamic Perspective* (Alexandria, Egypt: World Health Organization, 1997).

20. Leonard, Karen Isaksen, *Muslims in the United States: The State of Research* (New York: Russell Sage, 2003), 5.

21. Sylvianne A. Diouf, *Servants of Allah: African Muslims Enslaved in the Americas* (New York: New York University Press, 1998), 140.

22. Sulayman Nyang, *Islam in the United States of America* (Chicago: Kazi Publications, 1999), 13.

23. Jane I. Smith, *Islam in America* (New York: Columbia University Press, 1999), 78.

24. Edward E. Curtis IV, *Black Muslim Religion in the Nation of Islam, 1960–1975* (Chapel Hill: University of North Carolina Press, 2006), see generally.

25. Yvonne Haddad, *A Century of Islam in America* (Washington, D.C.: Middle East Institute, 1986), 1.

26. Ibid., 2.

27. There are varying numbers in different studies, which include *Muslims in the American Public Square*, a survey conducted by Zogby International for Georgetown University's Project MAPS, October 2004; *Muslim Americans: Middle Class and Mostly Mainstream* (Washington, D.C.: Pew Research Center, 2007); and Ihsan Bagby, Paul M. Perl, and Bryan T. Froehle, *The Mosque in America: A National Portrait (A Report from the Mosque Study Project)* (Washington, D.C.: Council on American-Islamic Relations, 2001).

28. *Muslim Americans* (Pew Research Center).

29. *Muslims in the American Public Square* (Zogby 2001 and 2004).

30. Bagby, Perl, and Froehle, *Mosque in America*.

31. Interview with Dr. Sayyid M. Syeed, director of ISNA National Office, Washington, D.C., October 2, 2007. It is very possible that, since the project took a few years, mosque addresses changed and that prayer areas rather than full-fledged mosques or Islamic centers were being identified.

32. Dwight Burlingame, ed., *Philanthropy in America: A Comprehensive Historical Encyclopedia* (Santa Barbara, Calif.: ABc-CLIO, 2004).

33. http://www.4islamicschools.org/

34. Interview with ObatHelpers president, Anwar Khan.

35. These are just a few examples of Muslim activities in America. This list is simply provided to give an idea of the diversity of activities and is in no way meant to be exclusive.

36. Center on Philanthropy Panel Study (COPPS), The Center on Philanthropy at Indiana University.

37. *Muslims in the American Public Square* (Zogby 2001 and 2004).

38. Ibid.

39. *Muslim Americans*, Pew Research Center, 2007.

40. Ibid.

41. Bagby, Perl, and Froehle, *Mosque in America*.

42. "The Rewards of Giving," *Islamic Horizons* (September/October 2007): 28.

43. Interview with Mohamed El-sanousi, director of Community Outreach and Communications, ISNA National Office, Washington, D.C., and a member of both task forces, October 2, 2007.

44. Ibid.

45. Interview with Ahmed ElHattab, executive director of ISNA Development Foundation, October 19, 2007.

46. Diouf, *Servants of Allah*, 63.

47. Carolyn Rouse, *Engaged Surrender: African American Women and Islam* (Berkeley: University of California Press, 2004), 26.

48. Ibid., 108–9.

49. Interview with Dr. Iqbal Unus, International Institute of Islamic Thought, Herdon, Virginia, September 19, 2008.

50. Nabeel Abraham and Andrew Shryock, *Arab Detroit: From Margin to Mainstream* (Detroit, Mich.: Wayne State University Press, 2000).

51. Farooque Khan, *Story of a Mosque in America* (New York: Islamic Center of Long Island, 2001).

52. Abraham and Shryock, *Arab Detroit*, 268–69.

Jewish Giving by Doing:
Tikkun Ha-Olam

JUDITH LYNN FAILER

Under Jewish law, all Jews are required to participate in giving to others. This mandate distinguishes Jewish giving at the outset from many other forms of religious giving, which treat charity as praiseworthy but not morally required. Still, there are many Jewish approaches to giving. Among the more prominent are those motivated by *tzedek, chesed,* and *tikkun ha-olam.*

Giving motivated by *tzedek* (justice) itself aims to make the world more just. God commands the Jews to give to others and to their community as part of the pursuit of justice,[1] which, in its ideal sense, helps others become self-sufficient.[2] *Tzedakah* can also take the form of contributions (monetary and otherwise) to communal organizations or individuals. Giving motivated by *chesed* may well take some of the same forms as acts of *tzedakah* (such as helping the needy)—and those are certainly required—but it is done as an act of compassion.

When Jews act out of *tikkun ha-olam,* however, both their motivations and actions may look different. *Tikkun ha-olam* is premised on the notion that the world (*ha-olam*) is fractured and that humans can participate in its repair (*tikkun*). Jews engaging in acts of *tikkun* may well be motivated by justice and compassion, but their motivation also includes an element of spirituality that envisions humans engaging with God in the mending and continuing creation of the universe.

In this chapter, I will explore some contemporary expressions of *tikkun ha-olam* in order to illustrate one small part of the wide variety of motivations for, and modes of, Jewish acts to "repair the world." After explaining the kabbalistic roots of the concept in the work of Isaac Luria, I will draw on both theological explanations and real-life examples of how two kinds of Orthodox Jews (Hasidic and Modern Orthodox) talk about and participate in *tikkun ha-olam.*

I have chosen to focus on Orthodox Jews because most people associate the pursuit of *tikkun ha-olam* with non-Orthodox and even non-religious Jews. Reform, Conservative, Reconstructionist, and unaffiliated Jews often cite their commitment to *tikkun ha-olam* to describe their motivation to engage in social action. Sometimes this involves feeding the hungry in their local community, helping to house the homeless, aiding efforts to recycle and tend to the environment, or getting involved in political lobbying to promote policies that are more just toward the poor, immigrants, or others who are disenfranchised. This kind of commitment to *tikkun ha-olam* is already so well known and documented that even non-Jewish public figures as diverse as Madonna and Vice President Al Gore have invoked the concept to describe part of their motivation for community service. Indeed, some people within the Orthodox Jewish community are almost scornful of such evocations of the concept, since they see it used to justify involvement in liberal and left-leaning social action for which they have little sympathy.

I do not aim to engage the debate here about who gets *tikkun ha-olam* right—the Orthodox or the non-Orthodox. Rather, I hope to point to some lesser-noted examples of *tikkun ha-olam* to enlarge our notion of what the concept is and what it looks like in practice. In short, I aim to identify some of the core values that drive some of those engaged in *tikkun* to think they can actually change and fix the world. I also hope that, by identifying these lesser-known examples of *tikkun*, I can enlarge our commonly held assumptions about what counts as religious "giving."

THE KABBALISTIC ROOTS OF *TIKKUN HA-OLAM*

Although the concept of *tikkun ha-olam* has roots in both written and oral Jewish law, it did not start out as a radical interpretation of theurgy, or divine intervention in human affairs. Indeed, its original meaning had little to do with its eventual connection to the project of repairing the world. The verb itself invokes a variety of meanings, from fixing or repairing items and improving physical appearance to preparing oneself for important activities and passing laws to improve society.[3] In the earliest references to *tikkun*, the verb t-k-n appears three times in the Bible, thirty times in the Babylonian Talmud, eight times in the Jerusalem Talmud, and very few times in other Jewish texts (including the Midrash and Tosefta).[4] It also appears once in the daily prayer book. Oddly enough, few of these invocations of t-k-n connote anything like the project of repairing the universe. There are midrashic appeals to *tikkun* in this sense,[5] but most of the talmudic references are in a section focusing on divorce laws.[6] The biblical references place the verb in the context of economic legislation and torts, and the reference in the daily "Alenu" prayer occurs in a context that Rabbi Arnold Wolf has noted is "anything but universalistic in its original formulation."[7]

The concept now known as *tikkun ha-olam* (or sometimes *tikkun shel-olam*) took on a whole new meaning when interpreted by the kabbalist Isaac Luria and his followers. It moved from connoting simple repairs and restorations to a more complex notion. To Luria, the notion of *tikkun* is part of the complicated three-part process by which God creates and exists in the universe. At the most basic level, Luria's multilayered theory begins with the assumption that God is everywhere and in everything. But this creates a puzzle: how can it be true that (1) God is everywhere and (2) the world contains things that are not God? Luria answers, first, that God makes space for the universe by contracting a little of His infinite self—into himself—to make room for creation.[8] Second, God then creates the universe by emitting divine light back into the newly created space. The divine light was supposed to be kept in special vessels, but as the light filled the vessels too much light emanated all at once, and some of the vessels broke. The holy light scattered, becoming mixed up with the rest of creation.[9] Third, humans participate with God in undoing the damage from mixing divine light with the unholy shards. Once the light fragments are recovered, God can then recreate the world as He intended. When people help undo the damage, they are repairing and helping to complete the creation of God's intended version of the universe—and all by gathering up the scattered light so it may be reunified. This process of gathering the divine light is called *tikkun*. As Gershom Scholem presents Luria's theory,

> [T]he religious act of the Jew, prepare[s] the way for the final restitution of all the scattered and exiled lights and sparks. The Jew who is in close contact with the divine life through the Torah, the fulfillment of the commandments, and through prayer, has it in his power to accelerate or to hinder this process. Every act of man is related to this final task which God has set for His creatures.[10]

In other words, when Jews follow the Torah, obey the commandments, and pray, they help gather the sparks to unify the divine light that was scattered when the vessels containing the light broke, upon creation of the universe. In this way, "it is man who adds the final touch to the divine countenance."[11]

Successful *tikkun* requires its practitioners to engage in the right activities, of course, but also to do so with the right intent (in Hebrew, this is referred to as *kavannah,* or "mindfulness"). As Lawrence Fine describes it, classical Lurianic approaches to *tikkun* entail engaging in the right acts with "contemplative concentration on the various dimensions of divinity and the various combinations of the divine name in order to 'raise up the fallen sparks.'"[12] When the right mystical intent is present, the project of *tikkun* enables humans to help gather up the fallen divine lights as well as to gather up the holy souls caught in the broken vessels. For Fine, this implies the remarkable idea that *people* are responsible for *tikkun ha-olam,* not God. Indeed, God is effectively a "passive beneficiary" of human's *tikkun* actions.[13]

By emphasizing the power of human beings in creation, the Lurianic approach to *tikkun* strikes some contemporary Jews as outlandish. Rabbi Arnold Jacob Wolf, for example, describes the idea that God contracted into himself to make room for the universe as "rank superstition" and complains that it takes "ineffable *hutzpah*" (roughly, "nerviness") for mere humans to presume to "plumb the very essence of the divine."[14] Similarly, Emmanuel Levinas thinks it "dangerous nonsense."[15] Its skeptics notwithstanding, the idea of *tikkun ha-olam* has become so widely appealing that even President Bill Clinton used the phrase to promote Al Gore to Florida voters in 2004.[16]

In the remainder of this chapter, I explore several Jewish examples of *tikkun ha-olam.* Although the examples will get progressively more remote from anything Isaac Luria might have anticipated, I will illustrate how they nevertheless maintain important continuities with the original concept, that is, they emphasize the centrality of human action in making the world a better place. To this end, these examples illuminate contemporary ways of Jewish giving, all of which extend beyond the familiar notion of giving as contributing money.

HASIDIC *TIKKUN*: JEWISH OUTREACH

One of the more visible examples of contemporary *tikkun* that still looks Lurianic is performed by a dedicated group of Lubavitcher Jews. Lubavitchers are "ultra-Orthodox" (*haredi*) Jews centered in Brooklyn, New York, who scrupulously adhere to all of Jewish law. As *haredim* (literally, "those who tremble at His word"), they worry about both following the laws correctly and maintaining Jewish survival.[17] As Hasidic Jews—a subsection of *haredim*—they organize their lives around a rebbe (a holy man and teacher who directs a rabbinic "court") and his leadership.[18] (There are more than two dozen different Hasidic "courts," each led by its own rebbe.) Hasidic Judaism typically brings insights from Jewish mysticism into daily life. The founder of the Lubavitch court, Schneur Zalman, was the third rebbe after the founder of Hasidism, Israel ben Eliezer (known as the "Ba'al Shem Tov"). Both the Ba'al Shem Tov and Zalman were deeply influenced by the mystical teachings of Isaac Luria, and both believed these messages should shape Jewish life. The most recent Lubavitcher Rebbe, Menachem Mendel Schneerson, was particularly inspired by kabbalistic worldviews and used those ideas to help him find a new way to practice *tikkun:* creating an army of Jewish outreach workers called *shlichim* (literally, "those who go out"), who could help other Jews practice *tikkun* as well.

According to Lubavitch philosophy, human beings are temporal but also contain elements of the divine. Like the Lurianic view that God's light scattered into the mundane creation, the central text of Lubavitcher Judaism explains, "The Jew is a creature of heaven and earth, of a heavenly Divine soul which is truly a part of Godliness clothed in an earthly vessel . . . whose purpose is to realize the transcendence and unity of his nature and of the world in which he lives within the absolute unity of God."[19] The problem is that in today's world many Jews do not realize that their souls contain the divine spark, nor do they know how to retrieve that spark for the purposes of *tikkun.*

Luria identified three methods for *tikkun*—living a life of Torah, fulfilling all of the commandments, and praying—all of which need to be done, and with the right intention. None of these are regularly practiced by today's non-Orthodox Jews as Luria intended. But unless all Jews participate in *tikkun*, the world will never be repaired completely.[20] Hence, Lubavitchers teach that it is holy work to help all Jews to engage in the activities that will effect *tikkun.* As Rabbi Schneerson taught,

> A hassid [pious person] is he who puts his personal affairs aside and goes around lighting up the souls of Jews with the light of Torah and *mitzvot* [literally, commandments]. Jewish souls are in readiness to be lit. Sometimes they are around the corner. Sometimes they are in a wilderness or at sea. But there must be someone who disregards personal comforts and conveniences and goes out to put a light to these lamps. That is the function of a true hassid.[21]

Hence, a large group of Lubavitcher Jews, heeding the Rebbe's call, have committed to finding all the Jews whose sparks are lost inside them. As

Sue Fishkoff has observed in her seminal book on Lubavitcher outreach workers, this project is "crucial because only when *all* God's divine sparks are released [from the shards of earthly vessels that entrap them] and reunited with the Divine Oneness will God's purpose be achieved."[22]

One way that Lubavitcher approaches to *tikkun* differ from their Lurianic roots is on the formulation of the ultimate goal. Whereas Luria emphasized the ingathering of divine sparks in order to unify God's light so that He may (re-)create the universe, Lubavitchers focus on the project's messianic implications. According to Lubavitchers, the discovery and elevating of divine sparks—whether in people or things—contributes to the hastening of the coming of the Messiah. Hence, most Lubavitchers do not speak of *tikkun* directly but focus instead on the uncovering and uplifting of sparks as a way to "bring *Mashiach* [the Messiah]." For them, *tikkun* is a means to the end of laying the groundwork for the messianic era.

The *shlichim* in search of Jewish sparks are everywhere. For the past forty years, they have been on the streets of Manhattan in mitzvah tanks (RVs or other large vehicles), helping any willing Jewish man to don tefillin (phylacteries used for morning prayers), or asking Jewish women if they have lit candles for the Sabbath. But they reach far beyond urban locations with large Jewish populations. Going out as young married couples, these *shlichim* settle into communities all over the United States and the world in order to facilitate the development of Jewish living. They are in my hometown of Indianapolis, organizing day camps for children, study groups for men and for women, tutorials for any Jew who is interested, community-wide parties celebrating Jewish holidays, and road trips to visit Jews in more remote locations, including our state's prisons. They are on virtually all American college campuses where there are Jewish students, providing religious services and classes as well as kosher food and social events tied to observances of Jewish holidays. Indeed, they are all over America: in the Northeast, of course, but also in the South, Midwest, West, and even Alaska. Their reach extends beyond the U.S. borders too, to China, Brazil, Germany, Latvia, Lithuania, Russia, Ukraine, Moldova, the Baltics, Central Asia, and beyond. Velvel Green of Ben-Gurion University once quipped, "Sooner or later we'll land an astronaut on Mars, and he'll be met there by a Lubavitcher shliach."[23] Wherever they go, these *shlichim* find the Jews and aim to help them do two things: participate in the activities they believe will help effect *tikkun*, and eventually develop the "right intentions" so that their participation in these activities will be even more effective in repairing the world.

For the Lubavitchers, these forays into the non-Hasidic world come at considerable cost. Financially, they receive little (if any) money to support their first year, wherever they are placed, and no money afterward. Indeed, once the *shlichim* are situated in a new community, they live there for the rest of their lives, finding their own way financially so that they may proceed with their life's work of contributing to the repair and re-creation of the universe.

The practical and spiritual costs are even higher. They often go to communities where there may be few other Orthodox Jews (let alone Lubavitcher Hasids). Of course this means they are living apart—maybe even oceans away—from family, friends, and others who share their values and lifestyle. In addition to the customary challenges of moving to a new community where they likely know no one and may not even speak the language, these moves can create many practical difficulties for religious and personal lives as well. If the new community contains few observant Jews, they will probably need to begin by building a *mikvah* (ritual bath). These are expensive to build, but they are essential for maintaining laws of family purity and kashering (making kosher) certain cooking and eating instruments. The *mikvah* is also used by some Hasidic men in preparing themselves for the Sabbath. Similarly, it may be difficult for the male *shaliach* to find enough other Jewish men to constitute the prayer quorum they need for thrice daily services. Communities where *shlichim* are most needed probably have poor (or nonexistent) access to kosher food, and opportunities to buy kosher meat and dairy products are likely even more challenging.

As young couples who take seriously the commandment to be "fruitful and multiply," the *shlichim* will soon have a houseful of children, all of whom will need a proper Jewish education. Without access to an appropriate Jewish day school, the *shlichim* have to figure out how to educate their children to their exacting standards. When the children are young, the family may be able to make do by some combination of existing Jewish schools and home schooling. But as the children get older and the local Jewish schools are not appropriate for growing Lubavitcher children, the families may feel the need to send their children to boarding schools or back to Brooklyn to live with relatives so they may attend appropriate Lubavitcher schools there. This exacts an enormous cost on many *shlichim* families, who want what is best for their children but also become lonely for them, should the children need to move to a more Lubavitcher-friendly location.

Shlichim live strictly orthodox lives in communities where they and their children are constantly exposed to ideas and values that are inconsistent with their own. This imposes unusual difficulties on them, since they must maintain their own values while becoming familiar with and understanding the values of those they are trying to reach. While other *haredi* Jews would consider this exposure contaminating, the *shlichim* carefully navigate their way through it in order to understand their new community and how best to move it toward *tikkun*. This creates an additional burden for their efforts to raise their children to be good Lubavitchers, since their children will doubtless be exposed to non-Lubavitcher values that may seem tempting.

As the only Lubavitchers—and sometimes the only practicing Jews—in town, the *shlichim* and their families also become prominent representatives of Judaism for their new Jewish neighbors. While their example can encourage others to emulate their religious lifestyles and values, being in the spotlight puts an added burden on both the parents and the children to live up to their highest standards at all times.[24]

For the *shlichim*, these costs pale when compared to the benefits. When they help Jews perform even one more mitzvah, then the world is that much closer to *tikkun* and the coming of *Mashiach*. This can happen when they help a child make a blessing before eating, provide the community with the opportunity to hear the *megilla* (scroll) of Esther on Purim and then celebrate, or hear words of Torah at an otherwise social gathering.

The prayer campaigns for which the Lubavitchers are famous also help effect *tikkun* by encouraging Jewish men to pray for even one daily service in the right way, by wearing the phylacteries required by Jewish law. They also make efforts to help Jews pray by offering learners' services, by organizing day camps for children where they lovingly teach the children to pray in a way that is kid-friendly and fun, and by organizing fun activities for the whole Jewish community at which they lead prayers in an inclusive, nonintrusive way.

Of course, the *shlichim* believe they really hit the jackpot when they successfully encourage and then support a less-observant Jew in becoming Orthodox. Not only do these newly Orthodox Jews follow all the commandments and pray "properly"—two of the central methods for effecting *tikkun*—but they also facilitate the practice of more Jews living a "Torah life," which is the third way into *tikkun*. According to the most recent Lubavitcher Rebbe, Menachem Schneerson, the contribution to *tikkun* of these *ba'al teshuvahs* (newly Orthodox Jews) rivals that of a truly holy man, a *tzaddik*. This is because the "light" generated by their participation is more like the original light that God emitted (*tohu*) than like the broken pieces of light that need to be gathered up to put it all back together (*tikkun*). As the Rebbe puts it,

> There is more enthusiasm in the service of a ba'al teshuvah than in that of a tzaddik. He takes the excitement that was previously directed towards worldly things and redirects it towards Torah, serving G-d with "all your heart" or, as the Talmud interprets, with "both your desires." The Kabbalah explains this concept as taking the great lights of Tohu which are much greater than the lights of Tikun and drawing them into the vessels of Tikun.[25]

To reach these Jews, the *shlichim* set up classes on topics they believe will draw in an audience and then slip in a little Lubavitcher philosophy designed to whet their appetite for more. As Sue Fishkoff described what one *shaliach* told her, "The core of what he teaches remains the same: Hasidus, or Chabad [Lubavitcher] philosophy." Ideally, it will grab them and begin the long process of transforming them into the kind of *ba'al teshuvah* the Rebbe celebrates. But even if it only changes them a little, this is significant, because these newly observant Jews are setting a good example in their families, and "these are the ones whose children will be Jewish"—children who will then go on to lead their own lifetime of commandments and prayer, and maybe even lead a Torah lifestyle.[26] Of equal importance, of course, is that when it comes to *tikkun* every little bit counts.

MODERN ORTHODOX *TIKKUN*

Orthodox Jews have an ambivalent approach to *tikkun ha-olam*. On one hand, they resist the call to practice *tikkun ha-olam* as most contemporary Jews do it because they reject the way most of its practitioners pay short shrift to appropriate grounds for the activity. On the other hand, they recognize that there are some (although few) commands in more mainstream Jewish sources that impel even the most Orthodox Jews to engage in *tikkun ha-olam*. As a result, *tikkun ha-olam is* practiced in the Modern Orthodox community, although not for the same reasons that other Jews engage in it and not with the same sense of urgency found in other branches of Judaism. In short, Modern Orthodox forms of *tikkun ha-olam* take a very low profile.

What distinguishes Modern Orthodox Jews from other Orthodox Jews is their commitment to live their lives immersed in *both* Judaism and the larger communities where they live and work. Like all Orthodox Jews, the Modern Orthodox are committed to following all of Jewish law. This includes scrupulous attention to following the rules of Torah, primarily as explained by the great rabbis in the codification of Jewish law known as the *Shulchan Aruch*, in Responsa literature (which applies Jewish law to particular problems) or in the Talmud. Most "ultra-Orthodox" Jews accept this responsibility and believe that it is best to fulfill it by living in primarily Jewish communities where they can minimize the contaminating influences of the non-Orthodox (and non-Jewish) cultures in their pursuit of Torah-true lives. In contrast, the Modern Orthodox are more open to selected aspects of contemporary life.[27] For example, Yeshiva University, the leading educational institution for Modern Orthodoxy, has the motto of "Torah and Secular Knowledge." Its influential former president, Rabbi Norman Lamm, identified *synthesis* as the "most characteristic aspiration of modern Orthodox Judaism"[28]—a synthesis, that is, of holy and secular lives. Hence, it is common to see Modern Orthodox Jews working as doctors, lawyers, college professors, social workers, bankers, and even politicians. They live and work in the larger community even as they lead scrupulously Orthodox lives.

One might think that the twin commitments to Jewish values and integrated communal living might make *tikkun ha-olam* a popular practice among the Modern Orthodox. After all, *tikkun ha-olam* is all about Jews reaching out in their actions to repair the world. But this has not been the case for at least two reasons. First, the Modern Orthodox are primarily Orthodox Jews, and there is very little rabbinic discussion of *tikkun ha-olam* in the central Jewish texts. As Rabbi Jonathan Sacks, the Chief Rabbi of the British Commonwealth has noted, "If you look at the Shulkhan Arukh and the Responsa, you see that *tikkun ha-olam* occupies a surprisingly limited space."[29] There is discussion of *tikkun ha-olam* in the mystical literature, but the dictates of kabbalistic texts play a very minor role in the daily lives of most Orthodox Jews. What discussion there is in more traditional texts is not widely developed. There is the reference to *tikkun* in the "Alenu" prayer, but the focus there is on repair for the benefit of the Jewish people. There are also references in the Bible and the Talmud, but those focus on tort claims and divorce law, not on participation with God in the creation and repair of the universe.[30] Without a substantial mandate from the central texts of Orthodox Judaism to go out and practice *tikkun*, it is not particularly surprising that there is at least visceral resistance to the idea that Modern Orthodox Jews should make *tikkun ha-olam* a core practice in their lives.

A second reason why *tikkun ha-olam* plays such a minor role in Modern Orthodox practice is that the kinds of activities typically associated with it are similar to activities the Modern Orthodox already practice—although within (and not without) the Jewish community. Insofar as *tikkun ha-olam* requires Jews to feed the hungry, house the homeless, and free the captive, Orthodox Jews are already very busy with these activities—within the Jewish community. Without much fanfare, Modern Orthodox Jews regularly and quietly take care of the needy Jewish families and individuals within their communities. All of these activities are explicitly required by and extensively discussed within traditional Orthodox texts, albeit as matters of justice and mercy, not as opportunities to participate in the (re-)creation of the universe. Were the Modern Orthodox to replace these activities with similar activities aimed at non-Jews, many fear that the time they spend helping non-Jews (something that is not extensively discussed and not clearly required) would take away from time spent fulfilling their obligations to take care of the needs of fellow Jews (which is extensively discussed and very clearly required). This is certainly the perception of many Orthodox Jews of the *tikkun* activities conducted by Conservative and Reform Jews. They worry that those movements' emphasis on *tikkun ha-olam* and social action takes the place of appropriate emphasis on following the Torah (including the obligation of all Jews to take care of each other).

Those concerns notwithstanding, there has been a small but growing trend among some Modern Orthodox rabbis to promote the practice of *tikkun ha-olam* within a Modern Orthodox framework. These rabbis have taken steps to sanction *tikkun ha-olam* because it is required by Jewish law, even though it receives less attention in the rabbinic literature than other forms of Jewish social action. They also believe that it is possible to engage in *tikkun ha-olam* in a way that will not lead Jews too far away from their responsibilities to other Jews. Modern Orthodox *tikkun* takes at least two forms.

First, many Modern Orthodox Jews choose to pursue helping professions so that they might fulfill their obligations to *tikkun ha-olam* even as they provide for their families. For example, many Jews, following the example of Maimonides, pursue careers in medicine. As doctors, these Jews can help heal any sick person—Jewish or not—and thereby help heal the world. Others pursue social work or choose other forms of public service, including politics. As one prominent Modern Orthodox Jew, Senator Joseph Lieberman, describes his decision to enter into a life of public service,

> My parents and my rabbi . . . taught me that our lives were a gift from God, the Creator, and with it came a covenantal obligation to serve God with gladness by living life as best as we could, according to the law and values that God gave Moses on Mount Sinai. The summary of our aspirations was in the Hebrew phrase *tikkun olam*, which is translated "to improve the world" or "to repair the world" or, more boldly, "to complete the Creation which God began." In any translation, this concept of *tikkun olam* [involves] the inherent but unfulfilled goodness of people and requires action for the benefit of the community. . . . These beliefs were a powerful force in my upbringing and seem even more profound and true to me today.[31]

Note that Lieberman, like other Orthodox Jews, premises his interpretation of his religious obligations on his covenantal obligations, the terms of which are specified in the oral and written Jewish law that "God gave Moses on Mount Sinai." His interpretation of *tikkun ha-olam* makes no mention of its kabbalistic or mystical roots, although his recognition that the idea involves the completion of creation clearly evokes Luria's development of the concept. Note too that he understands the concept as one that applies to all people for the benefit of all people. Hence, he pursues *tikkun ha-olam* by serving all of the people of Connecticut (and the United States), not only the Jewish citizens therein.

A second way that contemporary Modern Orthodox thinkers have advocated participating in *tikkun ha-olam* is acting as a "light unto the nations." As Jonathan Sacks has noted, God made three promises to Abraham, the first two of which are well known. He promised him land, which turns out to be a difficult promise to fulfill. After all, Abraham struggles to buy even a burial plot for Sarah; Isaac fights with the Philistines over the wells he dug; Jacob is forced to buy a small plot of land for his tent at an inflated price; and Moses is not even able to enter the promised land before his death. God also promised him children, which proved just as difficult. As we know, Sarah, Rebecca, and Rachel all struggled with infertility, and the Torah concludes with Moses' recognition that God couldn't have chosen the Jewish people for their number since they turned out to be so small in number. The third promise, however, often receives short shrift. In Genesis 12:3, God promises Abraham that through him all the families of the earth shall be blessed. This is the promise that Sacks associates with *tikkun ha-olam*.[32]

Sacks finds this third promise paradoxical, since it is only by transforming themselves into the Jewish people that the Jewish people can then transform the world. It begins with the Jewish people being true to themselves—by being good Jews. Historically, when Jews have lived their lives as a Jewish people, others have taken note and have learned from them. It became the Jewish vocation, Sacks writes, "to be a particular, specific living example of how to live. Somehow the Jewish people would be the people in whose daily lives the will of G-d, and in whose collective history the presence of G-d would be particularly evident. You could look at Jews and see G-d." The examples Jews set, however, were not about universal truths but about the truths born of a distinct history and experience. As Sacks describes it,

> We were the people who were born in slavery to teach the world the meaning of freedom. We were the people who suffered homelessness to teach humanity the importance of every people having a home. We were the people who were the quintessential strangers to teach humanity that "Thou shall not oppress the stranger." . . . We were the people who walked through the valley of the shadow of death to teach humanity the sanctity of life. We were the people who were always small but yet survived to teach the world a people does not survive by might nor by strength but by My spirit, says G-d. Above all, we were the people that was always different to teach humanity the dignity of difference. Against all expectations it happened, and no other people before or since has had the impact that we have had on the civilization of the world.[33]

What emerges from this is that, when Jews focus on following all of the Jewish laws for themselves, when they persist in their commitment to Jewish laws and life no matter what life throws at them, then they can not only survive as Jews but also inspire others to survive. In short, he concludes, "the essence of *Tikkun Olam* is that by being particularist, by being who we are, we have universal consequences, we help change the world."[34]

From this perspective, Modern Orthodox Jews have a unique opportunity to engage in *tikkun ha-olam* in today's world. Importantly, the existence of the state of Israel provides a unique chance to create a "macro-society run on Jewish principles." If the Jewish state of Israel can govern with justice and compassion, it can be a light unto the nations like no other.

But *tikkun* also works if all Jews strive to be the best Orthodox Jews they can be. Exhorting more Modern Orthodox Jews to participate in *tikkun ha-olam*, Sacks writes that the message that Judaism works for the Jews can only be conveyed,

if we as Orthodox Jews . . . are willing to play our part in the public domain
of our shared life as citizens of the nation and of the world. . . . Our task
is to become a particular living example of a set of universal truths . . .
because it is only by being Orthodox Jews that we are able to [do Tikkun
Olam]—it is only by being true to ourselves that we can be true to other
people. Only if we preserve the sanctity of [the] Jewish family can we talk
with authority about the sanctity of the family to the world. Only by
studying Torah can we speak compellingly about the value of education
and human dignity. Only by having the courage to be different can we be
role models to the dignity of difference. That is why Tikkun Olam is in
my view the special responsibility of we [Orthodox] who are the guardians
of Torah.[35]

In other words, Orthodox Jews can be role models to others in those things
that matter most to Jews: strong families, education, treating others with
dignity. This need not require preaching or even implying that Orthodox
Jews know best. Rather, Orthodox Jews can make an important gift to the
world by simply being their own best Jewish selves.

CONCLUSION

Whether in the form of Jewish outreach or efforts to stay within, and focus
on developing, Jewish identity, many Orthodox Jews are involved in *tikkun ha-olam*, even though the non-Orthodox streams of Judaism have
monopolized the term of late. Whether grounded in the mystical thought
of Isaac Luria or in the sketchier references found in more mainstream
Jewish texts, Orthodox Jews have developed new ways of giving that
extend beyond the traditional forms of giving to achieve justice or, out of
compassion, to assist those in need.

The Lubavitch *shlichim* give of themselves to help find and foster God's
lost lights, thereby hastening the repair of the universe and the arrival of
the Messiah. And at least some Modern Orthodox Jews work to live holy
lives not only for themselves but also to be a light unto the nations, thereby
making the whole world a better place. Although none of these examples
necessarily involve the financial donations commonly associated with philanthropy, they are nevertheless important examples of how some Jews
understand part of their moral obligation to give.

NOTES

I gratefully acknowledge the helpful comments I received on this chapter from David
Smith and the other participants in the Lake Institute on Faith and Giving's Working
Group on Religion and Giving. I also extend profound thanks to Rabbi Aaron Spiegel

for his careful and generous advice on how to improve this text as well as to David Orentlicher and Fraidel Schusterman for their conversations and consultations. Needless to say, any remaining errors remain my own and do not reflect on the advice I received from anyone else.

1. "Justice, justice shall thou pursue" (Deut. 16:20).

2. Maimonides, Mishneh Torah, Laws of Gifts to the Poor 10:7–14.

3. Gilbert S. Rosenthal, "*Tikkun ha-Olam:* The Metamorphosis of a Concept," *Journal of Religion* 85, no. 2 (2005): 214, 215–16.

4. Ibid., 217.

5. Rosenthal cites three examples where the connotation is "propagating the species and saving God's creations" (ibid., 216 and n. 8).

6. Ibid., 217.

7. Arnold Jacob Wolf, "Repairing Tikkun Olam," *Judaism*, September 22, 2001, 479.

8. Gershom Scholem, *Major Trends in Jewish Mysticism* (1946, rpt. New York: Schocken Books, 1995), 260. Scholem's Seventh Lecture is widely seen as an authoritative restatement of Luria's writings.

9. Scholem, *Major Trends*, 265–66.

10. Ibid., 274.

11. Ibid., 273.

12. Lawrence Fine, "*Tikkun:* A Lurianic Motif in Contemporary Jewish Thought," in *From Ancient Israel to Modern Judaism: Intellect in Quest of Understanding, Essays in Honor of Marvin Fox,* ed. Ernest S. Frerichs (Tampa: University of South Florida, 1989), 38.

13. Ibid., 39.

14. Wolf, "Repairing Tikkun Olam," 479.

15. Discussed by Wolf in "Repairing Tikkun Olam," 479.

16. Manuel Roig-Franzia, "Campaign Trail Takes Clinton to South Florida; He Touts Kerry to Jewish, Hispanic Voters," *Washington Post*, October 27, 2004, A14.

17. Samuel Heilman, *Defenders of the Faith: Inside Ultra-Orthodox Jewry* (New York: Schocken Books, 1992), 13–14.

18. Jerome R. Mintz, *Hasidic People: A Place in the New World* (Cambridge, Mass.: Harvard University Press, 1992), 2.

19. Schneur Zalman of Liadi, *Tanya*, English translation (Brooklyn, N.Y.: Kehot Publication Society, 1962), vii, quoted in Sue Fishkoff, *The Rebbe's Army: Inside the World of Chabad-Lubavitch* (New York: Schocken Books, 2003), 19.

20. In recent years, Rabbi Schneerson also introduced the Noahide Project (also known as the Hasidic Gentile Campaign) to reach out to non-Jews to help do their part in *tikkun* through following the basic Noahide laws. See www.noahide.com/rebbe .htm. For the purposes of this chapter, however, I focus on the Lubavitch efforts to reach out to other Jews.

21. Jacob Immanuel Schochet, *Chassidic Dimensions*, vol. 3 of *The Mystical Dimension* (Brooklyn, N.Y.: Kehot Publication Society, 1990), 198, quoted in Fishkoff, *Rebbe's Army*, 21.

22. Fishkoff, *Rebbe's Army*, 22.

23. Quoted in ibid., front matter.

24. Of course not all Jews welcome or admire the presence of the *shlichim.* Indeed, their presence may be off-putting to some and stand as a reason not to become more

observant. Still, the focus here is on how the Lubavitchers believe their outreach can help effect *tikkun*, not on how successful they are at that endeavor.

25. Excerpts of Sichos [public lectures] delivered by The Lubavitcher Rebbe, Rabbi Menachem M. Schneerson, vol. 8—Kislev-Adar 5741, "Shabbos Parshas Vay-ishlach" (14th Day Of Kislev, 5741), www.chabad.org/search/keyword.asp?kid=2354.

26. Fishkoff, *Rebbe's Army*, 236, 238.

27. David Singer, "The New Orthodox Theology," *Modern Judaism* 9, no. 1 (1989): 35, 36.

28. Norman Lamm, quoted in Singer, "New Orthodox Theology," 36–37.

29. Jonathan Sacks, "Tikkun Olam: Orthodoxy's Responsibility to Perfect G-d's World," published on the Orthodox Union's Institute for Public Affairs' official Web site at www.ou.org/public/Publib/tikkun.htm.

30. Wolf, "Repairing Tikkun Olam," 479.

31. Joseph I. Lieberman and Michael D'Orso, *In Praise of Public Life: The Honor and Purpose of Political Science* (New York: Simon & Schuster, 2001), 25.

32. Sacks, "Tikkun Olam."

33. Ibid.

34. Ibid.

35. Ibid.

4 What Does God Require of Us?

BYRON C. BANGERT ——————————————————

Not long ago my local daily newspaper carried an article with the following banner headline: "Food bank accepts donation of 2,500 pounds of chicken thighs." The gift, as the article explained, was part of a twenty-ton donation of chicken by Tyson Foods to the Indiana Poultry Association, which passed it along to a statewide network of food banks, which in turn would dole it out to the network's nine member food banks. The gift was being touted as a wonderful thing, celebrated by local politicians, citizens, and food bank workers and volunteers. Presumably, it would help to alleviate the hunger experienced by the more than 600,000 Hoosiers who, according to the article, go to bed hungry every night.[1]

Whatever the merits of this gift, I confess to being genuinely provoked by the amount of media exposure that it received. Twenty tons may sound like an enormous amount of food, but only if one does not do the math. We are talking about some 40,000 pounds of chicken thighs that surely cost Tyson Foods less than a dollar per pound.[2] What is there to celebrate about a gift worth less than $40,000 in the face of 600,000 hungry Hoosiers? This works out to only about one ounce of chicken per hungry Hoosier, at a value of less than seven cents apiece. One may be glad that Tyson officials saw fit to make this gift. We can only guess with what motives the gift was given, however, and we can be assured—quite contrary to the impression one might gather from the politicians and others who heralded this gift—that it did little to alleviate the problem of hunger in my state of Indiana. Consequently, it is hard to see it as a very meaningful or significant expression of giving.[3]

In this chapter I want to explore the question, what makes a gift meaningful and significant? More basically, since this chapter is part of a book on religious giving, I want to address the question, what is the place of giving in the religious life? Is giving a kind of spiritual grace? Is it a virtue? Is it a moral obligation? How central is it to the vocation, or call-ing, or the religious person—in my case, the Christian? In other words, what is the relationship of giving to life lived in faithfulness before God? In what follows I hope also to make a case that warrants my judgment that the gift described above hardly calls for celebration. The most mean-ingful gifts are those that spring from the depths of gratitude and love, that are responsive to the giver's sense of obligation as foremost a recip-ient, that are appropriate to the giver's resources and circumstance, and that promote justice as determined by the needs of individuals within their communities and society.

The giving of gifts, as any experienced person knows, is often prob-lematic. This is so for many reasons, one of which is that people give gifts for all kinds of reasons, not all of them benevolent or meritorious. This is no less true for religious people than for people in general. Sometimes people give in order to exercise influence, power, or control. Sometimes they give out of guilt or shame. Sometimes they seek recognition or re-ward, or wish to curry favor. Gifts bear social as well as individual mean-ing. Gift-giving can be a highly complex form of human transaction and interaction.

Back in 1968, the National Council of Churches published a little book by Martin E. Carlson, titled *Why People Give*, that reflected very helpfully on a number of the various factors that motivate people to give.[4] Carl-son's work is informed especially by psychology and psychiatry, and thus focuses in particular on individual psychological motivations such as the human needs for safety, love, identity, commitment, and self-actualization. He notes in passing another classification of motives in terms of the human desires for new experience, security, response, and recognition.[5] But then he turns to the subject of Christian faith and motivation, and seeks to identify some normative grounds for giving. He describes five motivations for giving that are characteristically (though not necessarily distinctively) Christian: gratitude, love, personal identification with God's purposes, obedience, and reward.[6] The important point here for my purposes is not whether Carlson's list is satisfactory, but rather that he found it necessary to identify several diverse motivations as basic even to a normative Chris-tian view of giving. The fact is that people give for all kinds of reasons, and among all these reasons there are at least several that seem to be valid from within a Christian faith perspective.

Notwithstanding all the complexities of giving, it has been my expe-rience that many religious people, and perhaps others as well, have a fairly particular notion of what constitutes the ideal or exemplary gift. The exemplary gift, in their view, is one given freely, joyously, almost spontaneously, and without any sense of obligation. It is a gift of charity, or love. It is given without calculation, without reserve, without ulterior motive or instrumental aim. It is the sort of gift that seems to be portrayed in the Gospels of Matthew and Mark by the woman who anoints Jesus with the jar of very costly ointment.[7]

As Mark tells the story, Jesus is with friends in Bethany when a woman enters the house and breaks open an alabaster jar of precious ointment, which she proceeds to pour over Jesus' head. Some of Jesus' companions view this as a profligate act, complaining that the ointment could have been sold for a substantial sum and the proceeds given to the poor. Jesus, however, defends the woman, stating that "she has performed a good service for me."[8] In some earlier English translations (e.g., KJV and RSV), Jesus is reported to have called her act "a beautiful thing." Jesus further explains, "She has done what she could; she has anointed my body beforehand for its burial . . . [W]herever the good news is proclaimed in the whole world, what she has done will be told in remembrance of her."[9]

It is hard to imagine higher praise for a gift. That it comes from Jesus tends to lend it the greatest possible authority for Christian teaching. But, someone may say, this is a gift given under the most extraordinary of circumstances, bestowed on the most extraordinary of individuals. Consequently, it can hardly serve as an example for our giving. Such a view is possible, but then we have to wonder why this story was told.

The more compelling view is that the story is told to counter certain conventional ideas about giving. In particular, the story challenges a merely utilitarian calculus for giving. Are we not inclined to question the extravagant gift? Do we not agree that selling the ointment and giving the proceeds to the poor would accomplish a greater good? Yet Jesus commends this gift. Moreover, he reminds those who have voiced objections, "you always have the poor with you, and you can show kindness to them whenever you wish."[10] In effect, Jesus is chiding them: "You want to help the poor? Go ahead. What's keeping you? You hardly need to wait till someone comes along with a valuable commodity before you begin. Meantime, don't condemn this woman for her extravagant devotion."

It is important to see here that Jesus does not in any way denigrate giving to the poor. This text is commonly misappropriated in the service of an attitude of nonchalance toward the lot of the needy. Nothing could be further from the mark. If anything, the text contains a rebuke to those who think that poor relief is somebody else's responsibility, to be paid for by somebody else's largesse. The text is not celebrating one form of giving at the expense of another. The extravagant gift does not preclude the gift that is practically useful or morally and socially responsible. Nonetheless, there does seem to be something special if not exceptional about this particular extravagant gift. In the history of the Christian church, this text surely has served to sanction acts of full-hearted religious devotion.

Should this text be central to our understanding of religious giving? Yes and no. The truth and power of the text, it seems to me, lie in the fact that it presents us with an act of giving that arouses our aspirations. Here is a gift that is costly, generous, personal, and uncalculating, given in a transparent act of love and devotion. At least it is possible to read these qualities into the woman's gift. Thus we are presented with a vision of true beauty, an act of graciousness like unto which we might aspire. The story evokes from us some sense of that purity of heart that is the wellspring of all true giving. The true gift, we see in this light, is an expression of unselfish love. No matter their magnitude, our gifts are meager and impoverished if they lack this quality of love. As the apostle Paul wrote to the Corinthians, "If I give away all my possessions, and if I hand over my body so that I may boast, but do not have love, I gain nothing."[11]

In terms of its presumed motivation, then, and what it suggests about the character or virtue of the giver, the woman's gift of precious ointment is exemplary. It is suggestive of a dimension of grace and spirit in human existence that transcends the economic materialism governing our daily existence. It reminds us that human beings cannot live "by bread alone." Or, as a former president of Costa Rica famously put it, "Why have tractors without violins?"[12] (It may be taken as a given that human beings must have bread, and that we would not want violins without tractors.) Indeed, the woman's gift requires us to recognize that the good cannot be reduced to any calculus, not even a moral calculus. This gift transcends any moral measure.

On the other hand, it is all too easy to exploit the story of the woman's gift in ignoble ways. If the story is employed to suggest that the proper devotion of religious adherents may require them to give up their most precious possessions without regard for their future needs or those of their families, then we have a problem. In many third world countries and communities one can find magnificent houses of worship, funded by the labor and resources of the general population, surrounded by grinding poverty. One must question whether the gifts of religious devotion that built and continue to maintain such edifices are truly commendable. To be sure, such houses of worship often provide a focal center of hope for people whose daily lives seem hopelessly grim. But surely, also, one can imagine that, by shifting significant resources away from dominant religious institutions to people on the margins, a different distribution of economic and social power would result that could elevate the lives of the general population at little if any spiritual cost.[13]

The story of the woman with the precious ointment evokes an awareness of those qualities of the human spirit that are most gracious and ennobling. It tells us something about those motivational qualities of our giving that are most to be cherished. It invites us to behold and celebrate a dimension of goodness beyond the moral measure. But insofar as we seek moral guidance regarding what sorts of gifts we should give, under what circumstances, and to whom, it has little to say. The highest form of giving may be the loving, generous, joyous, uncalculating offering of ourselves and our substance in relation to another, but when, where, how, and to whom should such offering be made? Or does it matter?

Does it appear that I am attributing too much influence to this idealized view of giving as a kind of unconditional virtue? What concerns me is the widespread tendency to celebrate a highly romanticized, and thus distorted, version of the exemplary act of giving. Let us recall that only a few years ago we could readily find bumper stickers on cars throughout our nation inviting us to "Commit random acts of kindness and senseless acts of beauty." This saying was discussed in books, newspapers, and magazines, and a foundation was even established called "The Random Acts of Kindness Foundation." The idea had clearly captured the public imagination. And the idea that came across was that one could do something especially felicitous and virtuous for another quite apart from any obligation, calculation, or planning. One did not even need any personal knowledge of the recipient, nor did one need to envision a continuing relationship with the recipient. In fact, the absence of any particular personal connection to the recipient was judged to make the presumably helpful and/or favorable action all the more virtuous. Presumably committing a random or senseless act of a kindly or beautiful sort could only spring from the goodness of one's heart.

It is not my intent to disparage the random act of kindness. I share the sense that there is something virtuous about the realized capacity to engage in actions that may enrich the lives of others, irrespective of any claims those persons may have upon oneself and irrespective of any relational benefits that may accrue to oneself because of such actions. In terms of its virtuous character, the random act of kindness is surely to be celebrated over the guilt-ridden overture, the strategically calculated effort to gain personal advantage, the gratuitous show of power, or the gift with strings attached. But it must be observed that we do not have in the random or spontaneous act of generosity an adequate set of criteria for all the sorts of giving that may be commended as contributions to the lives of others. We must also think about the giving of gifts in the context of our ongoing relationships with other persons and groups, and in view of the circumstances in which giving may occur and the consequences that may result.

To this point I have suggested that one reason we find the random act of kindness, and the "beautiful thing" done by the woman with the costly ointment, especially appealing lies in the character of the motivation behind such actions. As a matter of fact, however, we have at best a rather thin account of motivation in such actions. It appears that the woman with the precious jar of ointment acted out of love and devotion, but that is our surmise only because we behold Jesus' commendation of her. As for the random expression of generosity or kindness, who knows what may prompt such a spontaneous act? Virtually by definition such actions are viewed as "senseless" or "random," therefore not subject to any account based on antecedent events.

For a normative account of motivation in giving, we need something like the ethics of gratitude that William F. May has proposed.[14] May notes that, for Christians as well as Jews, the treatment of God's people at God's hands becomes the basis for their subsequent treatment of others who find themselves in similar straits. For example, the story of God's solicitude for the Hebrew slaves while they were "strangers" in Egypt is invoked in the scriptures of Israel to warrant special treatment for the "strangers" in their midst. In the New Testament the exhortation to love is predicated upon God's prior love: "In this is love, not that we loved God but that he loved us. . . . Beloved, since God loved us so much, we also ought to love one another."[15] Throughout the Bible God is portrayed as taking the initiative, extending solicitude, offering aid to comfort and strengthen, deliver and bless, the people of God. From this religious perspective, says May, human giving needs to be put "in the context of a primordial receiving."[16]

As recipients of God's gifts, our first calling is to enjoyment and appreciation of God's gifts of love, manifest in our relationships to all that exists and by the very fact of our existence. We are to recognize ourselves as those who have "freely received" the gift of life and all that sustains and enriches it. The true enjoyment and appreciation of what we have been given issues in gratitude and thanksgiving, expressed not only to God but also to others, in acts that imitate the divine graciousness. Religious giving, at least within the Christian perspective, is fundamentally a form of thanks-giving.[17]

In an important respect, therefore, religious giving is rooted in the sense of obligation.[18] This sense of obligation impels us, less as a matter of duty than as a matter of opportunity, to extend to others the graciousness that has been extended to us. The feeling of being blessed is not peculiar to religious people. It is, however, a basically religious sensibility, an awareness of a gift unwittingly received. In Reformed theology it might be regarded as an evidence of prevenient grace. Many people who experience themselves as blessed feel a deep need to "make good" on the gifts they have received. To some extent this need may be understood as the need to discharge a great debt. The debt, though not intentionally incurred, is no less significant as an experienced reality that helps to motivate the desire to contribute to the lives of others. The sense of indebtedness is part and parcel of a desire to honor what one has been given, and not to let it dissolve into meaninglessness or insignificance. For many, it prompts the desire to make a contribution, to make a difference.

An insight of the philosopher, Charles Hartshorne, is relevant here. "Far from our valuing others only for their usefulness to ourselves," Hartshorne observed, "it is in no small part for our usefulness to others that we value ourselves."[19] To a very considerable extent, we find the meaning and purpose of our lives, their overall significance, precisely in the positive differences we are able to make in the lives of others. Often it is our contributions to others that confirm, honor, and shape the meaning of the gifts of which our senses of gratitude and indebtedness make us initially aware. This realization helps us to fathom the truth that we love because we have first been loved. What we have been given enables us to give. What we have been given empowers us to give. What we have been given motivates us to give. What we have been given also impels us to give. In a profoundly important sense, we need to give to others in order fully to realize the gifts given to ourselves.

I have stated that the sense of obligation is more a matter of opportunity than of duty. Nonetheless, a sense of the imperative attaches to the sense of obligation. The imperative has to do, at the very least, with enacting the meaningfulness of the gift that has been received. One would not want what one has received to come to nought. Thus, the gifts we have received do impose a certain burden or demand upon us. With them, or with the awareness of them, comes a sense of responsibility. Although we may be able to do what we please with what has been given us, the economy of giving is such that our gifts will ultimately be diminished if we fail to employ them in ways that truly contribute to the lives of others. The greatness of these gifts is to be found in the sharing of them as fully as possible.[20]

My argument thus far is that a gift is meaningful when it is an expression of love that springs from the heart of gratitude for all that one has been given. To be meaningful, a gift hardly needs to be employed in such a way that it accomplishes some measurable goal. There are gifts that lie beyond any moral measure. A meaningful gift, however, is never given in a vacuum, or simply as a spontaneous, random act, but always in a context of multiple relationships with various levels of felt obligation and envisioned possibility.

As I now turn from questions of motivation and character to questions of context, purpose, means, and effects, I wish to focus primarily on the *moral* dimension of giving.[21] The crux of the following argument can be expressed in these words attributed to Jesus: "From everyone to whom much has been given, much will be required."[22] There are two major points to be made regarding this maxim. The first is that gifts are not unencumbered. That is to say, contrary to much popular thinking, once having received a gift one is not *morally* free to do with that gift whatever one chooses. This does not mean that the giver retains the right to reclaim the gift, or to dictate how the gift is to be used. Rather, it means that in receiving a gift one is placed under a certain obligation, if not to the giver directly, then to some other or others who may benefit from one's appropriation of the gift. In a Christian context, this obligation is understood to arise in relation to God. However, it requires expression, first of all, in relation to the neighbor who is present and visible to us. As stated in 1 John, "We love because [God] first loved us. . . . [T]hose who do not love a brother or sister whom they have seen, cannot love God whom they have not seen."[23]

The second point is that a principle of justice inheres in the maxim. The more that one has received, the more that will be required. The degree of one's obligation with respect to the gifts one has received is a measure of the magnitude of the gifts themselves. Those who have been given little are hardly obliged to give as much as those who have been given more. The principle of justice here seems to be one of elementary fairness and equitable distribution. The burdens or encumbrances that accompany gifts are distributed in proportion to the magnitude of what has been received.

There is nothing novel or radical about either of these points, but they are extraordinarily important to the claim I now wish to make. In brief, that claim is that, in a biblical perspective, we should understand ourselves as stewards of the gifts we receive. Moreover, the receipt of these gifts requires us to seek ways in which to deploy these gifts, in some proportionate measure to what we have received, on behalf of others. If we do so in a spirit of gratitude and generosity, so much the better. But we should do so nonetheless.[24]

There are several further implications to be drawn from this way of framing the matter of our giving. First, giving as seen in this perspective is a matter of justice, not charity. It is only right that we do this. We are not talking here about acts of supererogation, but about a general obligation and requirement regarding the disposition of our resources. Second, because it is not transparently obvious that the language of "gift" and "giving" yields this understanding, we need to add to our conventional notions of "gift" and "giving" the notions of "trust" and "entrustment." Whatever we are given is a trust. As a gift entrusted to us, it is never permanent and absolute. It is always temporary and in some ways contingent. For one thing, none of us is immortal. All of us must eventually relinquish whatever we have been given, including life itself. But more basically, and in keeping with earlier comments about the nature of the gift itself, the full realization of whatever is given to us requires that it be shared. All that we have and all that we are is given to us in trust, not for safekeeping, and not only for our own enjoyment and well-being, but also for investment (to continue the fiduciary language) in the lives and fortunes of others.[25]

One further elaboration is needed here to complete the basic argument. Giving as a matter of justice must be measured not only in proportion to the resources of the giver but also in significant measure in accord with the needs of the recipients. It is difficult to state this point more precisely. I am not suggesting that we must place the needs of others above our own. Nor do I think we should aim at simple equality in the distribution of resources. No scheme of distributive justice can approach the meeting and fulfillment of all human needs. More is required than a simple redistribution of wealth. Our social, political, and economic arrangements are instrumental to the capacity of individual human beings (as well as groups of human beings) to flourish and to engage fully in the tasks of living in a democratic society, including active and meaningful participation in the political processes of civic governance. My claim is that those who lack this capacity stand in need. Meeting that need may require supplementation in the provision of food, clothing, shelter, education, health care, transportation, child care, or other resources, as well as alteration in other material conditions and social circumstances of existence, in order for individuals and groups to attain that capacity.

It cannot be too strongly emphasized that the need to be addressed here is never simply a matter of providing physical resources to individuals of limited financial means. It is much more important that systemic changes be made to alter the political, social, and economic structures that create and maintain disadvantages in power, opportunity, and prospect for some persons due primarily to their life circumstances and largely irrespective of their innate abilities.[26] It is a requirement of justice that such changes be made for those in need. Moreover, the provision of justice for individuals in need must be based on the simple fact of need, not on any calculus of desert. Every human being has an intrinsic claim to the provisions necessary for human flourishing and—in a democratic society—to the resources requisite for full engagement in civic life.[27]

As already noted, the biblical notion of stewardship, widely popularized these days in association with the environmental movement, serves as a primary category for interpreting the nature and meaning of religious giving in the Christian tradition. Unfortunately, in most Christian congregations stewardship continues to be associated primarily with the raising or pledging of funds for the support of the facilities, program, staff, and mission of the congregation. However, most churches these days are also increasingly familiar with the notion of the stewardship of the earth and earth's resources. And most Christians, I believe, understand in at least a rudimentary way that stewardship is not exactly tantamount to ownership. Stewardship involves the care and use of resources that have been given to them as a trust, not as a permanent and enduring possession. The words to a nineteenth-century hymn by William H. How, found in many church hymnals, capture this dimension of stewardship quite well:

> We give Thee but Thine own,
> Whate'er the gift may be;
> All that we have is Thine alone,
> A trust, O Lord, from Thee.

The main challenge posed by the perspective presented here is not to enliven the notion of stewardship itself, then, but to conjoin this notion with that of justice and its demands. And with respect to the notion of justice, it is not the idea that more is demanded of those who have been given more that poses the real challenge. Rather, it is the idea that this is a matter of justice, not charity, and that justice further requires the meeting of human need irrespective of human desert.[28] Voluntaristic notions of charity continue to have wide currency among religious adherents when it comes to responding to those in our society who have unmet needs. Moreover, past social research surveys and other research suggest that actively religious people are more likely to come to the aid of those in need than are those who are not actively religious.[29] But there is often a parting of the ways among religious people regarding the requirements of love in the form of social justice.[30]

In a 1959 essay subtitled "The Ethics of Stewardship," Joseph Fletcher wrote, "There is a rock-bottom difference between being stewards of wealth because it is God's and we are acting on [God's] behalf, on the one hand, and being stewards of wealth because it is *ours* and we are acting on behalf of our own charity." Fletcher's statement implicitly accents the confusion that exists in the minds of some people regarding the meaning of stewardship as a non-ownership relationship. The central thrust of Fletcher's statement, however, is the recognition that a biblical understanding of stewardship is incompatible with a purely voluntaristic notion of charity. As Fletcher went on to point out, the biblical doctrine of creation means that God is the only owner, and that God's creation "is provided for [God's] children on earth on a familial basis, intended for all and not just for some." That is to say, "We all have an inalienable equity in God's patrimony, so that contributing to a community fund or paying taxes for social security is not *largesse* or *noblesse oblige* but simple, obligatory stewardship."[31]

In agreement with Fletcher, I maintain that Christian stewardship is another way of speaking about Christian vocation.[32] Stewardship simply accents the fact that our calling to a life of faithfulness before God involves not only a life of fidelity and moral virtue, nor even a life of labor in accord with one's particular sense of vocation, but more basically a life that is invested in the promotion of the commonwealth that is the gift of Divine Providence. We are called to exercise stewardship with respect to all of our resources, all of our gifts, not just our labors and their rewards. Our time and our talents, as well as our treasures, are in some measure to be invested, shared, committed, for the sake of the greater and common good. This may be understood as a work of love, but it is not something to be done merely out of the goodness of our hearts. It is also a work of justice, and it is no less than what is required to honor all that we have been given.

Fletcher criticized the "petty moralism" of the small-scale, private, individualistic, voluntaristic ethics of charity. He argued for a macro-ethics appropriate for a large-scale, highly organized society. He recognized that the needs of today's society exist on such a massive scale that they can hardly be met even by the combined efforts of individual givers. The politically controversial "faith-based initiatives" approach to solving social problems, touted by the Bush II administration, would have been seen by Fletcher as hopelessly inadequate. Government spending and taxation policies will have to become primary means through which Christians exercise their stewardship if anything significant is to be accomplished. Stewardship, he wrote,

> cannot remain a private, small-scale, individualistic affair—in the form of purely voluntary and private "tithing" or anything of the kind. Post-modern man [sic] is going to have to exercise his stewardship, his social use of wealth, in forms that fit the way he gets it—i.e., in social planning and public welfare, in corporate or community giving. In a way this will be returning from modern individualistic attitudes and mores to the essentially social or corporate character of stewardship at its biblical sources in the Old Testament—when it was a "role" assigned to and accepted by the whole covenant-community of Israel, and not a private or individual election.[33]

I discovered Fletcher's essay on stewardship, delivered as an address to a National Council of Churches conference on stewardship in 1959, while I was engaged in research for this chapter. In more than twenty-five years as a parish minister, I cannot recall ever having encountered it among all the materials and resources customarily provided to parish ministers to inform and enhance their stewardship endeavors. His ideas apparently have yet to take the Church by storm. Yet I believe he was fundamentally correct. I will not attempt a critique of what I take to be some minor failings in his essay, but I do want to highlight two claims he makes that remain especially challenging if not problematic for our thinking about stewardship today. These are claims beyond what I have already identified as the notion that stewardship is a matter of justice, not charity. In so doing, I want to be clear that the claims I am discussing are challenging chiefly because they meet with so much resistance in our individualistic culture, not because they are somehow at odds with an authentic appropriation of Christian scripture and tradition.

The first claim is that stewardship has to do with what is simply oblig-atory. I have also made this claim, but it needs further attention. Custom-arily, stewardship has been associated with giving—for example, the giving of time, talents, and treasure. Giving has been seen as a basically voluntary activity. Many people resist the notion that anyone else, even God, has a rightful claim on their resources. They may feel a general sense of obli-gation to give out of their abundance, but that sense of obligation is sel-dom tied to particular claims upon them. Must we abandon the notion of giving if we are to move to a notion of stewardship as the obligatory deployment of one's resources? I do not think so.[34]

With reference to any particular situation one may speak both of what God requires and of what individual human beings choose or will to do. The language of requirement is the language of divine purpose and possi-bility, not the language of coercion. God does not, and in my view cannot, force us to be good stewards. Our failures to do what God requires are truly failures to realize the highest possibilities presented to us and to all of God's creation in a particular context or situation. We consistently choose less than what is possible, which is to say, less than is required to realize the fullest potential of the commonwealth of God. In this sense we really do fail on our obligations—obligations that often can be rather clearly identified—but that hardly means that we are thereby cast outside the realm of divine providence or grace. We simply fall short in our actions, including our giving. We do not measure up to our divine calling.

The second claim made by Fletcher is tied to his claims about taxa-tion and the corporate distribution of resources. Taxation is typically under-stood to be quite involuntary, and enforced by coercive measures. Many of us doubtless view some uses of our taxes as anything but good steward-ship. In my view, the largest single portion of my federal income taxes, which goes for something called "national defense," is badly misspent. I would not want to make the mistake of asserting that all taxes are good, or that the payment of all taxes is an act of faithful stewardship. But Fletcher does not make that mistake, either.

Rather, Fletcher's point is that, as a matter of stewardship, Christians should be engaged in the creation of tax policy, and should regard the pay-ment of taxes as a means for addressing the social welfare and social justice needs of the greater commonwealth. Fletcher was insufficiently cautious in noting the pitfalls of democratic decision making and the inevitable failings and unseemly compromises of actual tax policies. Nonetheless, he was right to claim that in a democratic society it is possible and desirable to have a much more positive view of taxation than we do, and that it is crucial for Christians to recognize that in the setting and implementation of tax policies and practices they have a means of exercising stewardship over the resources with which they have been individually and corporately entrusted. One might at least realistically hope that if most Christians had this more favorable view of taxation, their influence would result in actual reformation and improvement of governmental taxation and spending policies and practices. Moreover, insofar as democracy affords us the possibility of determining how and for what purposes we are to be taxed, there is clearly a voluntary dimension to taxation. Taxes in a democracy are not primarily forms of wealth expropriation. They are an imperfectly but nonetheless corporately agreed-upon means of pooling and sharing of material resources for the benefit of all. When appropriately structured and conjoined with strategic social policies, including but hardly limited to both fiscal and monetary policies, taxes can aid significantly in the long-term redistribution of power and wealth. For Christians, taxes should be seen as a price we agree to pay for the sake of the common good.[35]

In my state of Indiana, as I noted earlier, some 600,000 residents are said to go to bed hungry every night. That is an integral feature of the context in which I and my fellow Christians in this state must begin our thinking about Christian giving and Christian stewardship.[36] If twenty tons of chicken thighs will hardly make a difference in this situation, then my limited material resources will prove next to insignificant. Yet I am not prepared to say that only the Bill Gateses and Warren Buffetts of this world have what it takes to exercise meaningful stewardship in the face of such large-scale need. Indeed, even the Gates Foundation recognizes that it lacks the resources to be more than "a drop in the bucket compared to what's needed" in a world where huge disparities exist in our worldly estates. As recently noted by the Gates Foundation's chief executive officer, "It's essential that other people and organizations, *especially governments*, get involved in addressing inequity. . . . [W]e recognize that we have a shared responsibility to create a world where every person—no matter where they were born—has the opportunity to live a healthy, productive life, and that's what we're going to keep driving toward."[37]

Let us not stifle the springs of gratitude and generosity. But let us be serious about what is required, long-term, if our well-intentioned efforts to share ourselves and our substance with others are really going to make much difference to those in greatest need. On the one hand, our thinking about the fundamental character of religious giving must be informed by an ethics of gratitude for all that we have been given. But on the other hand, our thinking about the moral pragmatics of giving—how much, when and where, to whom, and under what conditions—must be shaped by an ethics of stewardship that takes into consideration all the resources, energies, skills, time, talents, and opportunities available to us for structuring our political, economic, and social relationships in new ways that afford to everyone whatever is needed to grow, develop, and flourish as individual human beings within our respective communities.

In short, we are called not simply to love one another and thereby share ourselves with one another. Recognizing that love must be mediated by the various structures and relationships of our daily existence, we are also called to do justice. There is no real love that is without justice, and no true justice that is without love. Justice gives form to love in all our relationships. Social justice is the goal toward which we must aim if our love is to become effective and enduring in our larger social world. Social justice entails just social relationships, some measure of equality in opportunity, sufficient material resources for health and welfare, and effective mechanisms—including taxation—for the distribution of wealth and other resources consistent with the meeting of basic individual and social needs. Christian stewardship, therefore, is not primarily a matter of ecclesiastical economics.

We must give ourselves to the tasks of democratic citizenship, guided by Christian principles and social values, in concert with all who share a concern for individual human dignity and the common good.[38] We must regard all of our resources as gifts, entrusted to us as means to help us attain the commonwealth of all God's creatures, not least but not exclusively our fellow human beings. Our stewardship must encompass the earth and all earth's inhabitants. But it must first encompass our social, economic, and political systems—all that we human beings have constructed to organize, manage, regularize, and control our engagements and exchanges with one another. We must endeavor to make these humanly created habitats conducive to the realization of the highest possibilities for human existence. And we must insist that the price for doing so, and for conserving our natural world, be paid, *in accordance with our means*, by us and our contemporaries, not by future generations.[39]

What does our God require of us? The answer has not changed all that much in over 2,500 years: "To do justice, to love kindness, and to walk humbly with our God."[40] We do justice when we accept and practice an ethics of stewardship with respect to all that we have and all that we

are, for the sake of the common good. We love kindness when we celebrate and practice an ethics of gratitude and generosity, seeking in love
to enact the meaningfulness of the gifts we have been given. We walk
humbly with God when we acknowledge our ultimate indebtedness to
God for all things and recognize how blessed we are to be able to contribute to the realization of the commonwealth of all creation.

NOTES

1. Bloomington (Indiana) *Herald-Times*, May 4, 2006, A5.

2. In my grocery shopping experience, one can frequently purchase a pound of
Tyson chicken thighs on sale at retail cost at the local Kroger store for less than $1.00
per pound.

3. Most likely the gift was a business decision made by Tyson officials as a matter of public relations. Businesses that sell consumer products typically have economic
motivations for enhancing their corporate image by making contributions that presumably make them more attractive to the consumers they want to buy their products.
Moreover, the free publicity that often attends such gifts serves as a form of advertising and may be less costly than the outright purchase of advertising space. However,
my claim about Tyson's gift has to do with its inadequacy in meeting the need, i.e.,
alleviating hunger, irrespective of the motives for the gift.

4. Martin E. Carlson, *Why People Give* (New York: Council Press for Stewardship and Benevolence, National Council of the Churches of Christ in the U.S.A.,
1968). In 1998 Robert F. Hartsook came up with "77 Reasons Why People Give" in
Fund Raising Management 29, no. 10 (1998): 18–19. His list was geared toward successful fund raising, however, and was little more than a list of tips for soliciting. He
did not reflect substantively on the basic motives for giving and failed to contemplate
seriously any of the less-admirable reasons why people make gifts of money. Nonetheless, his list helps to illustrate the fact that it is impossible to summarize neatly and
succinctly the various reasons people have for giving.

5. Carlson, *Why People Give*, 46.

6. Ibid., 130–47.

7. Matthew 26:6–13; Mark 14:3–9 (NRSV). Note, however, as Paula Dempsey
points out in chapter 8 of this volume, this ostensibly spontaneous act of giving is not
the sort of giving most strongly encouraged by U.S. religious organizations and denominations in their official statements on giving.

8. Mark 14:6; also Matthew 26:10.

9. Mark 14:8, 9; cf. Matthew 26:12–13.

10. Mark 14:7.

11. 1 Corinthians 13:3. The idea of love as central to a Christian understanding
of giving is more richly and fully developed by Ed Vacek in chapter 6 of this volume.

12. Attributed to José Figueres Ferrer, in his inaugural speech in 1970. Though it
lies beyond the scope of this essay to elaborate on the ethical perspective that informs
my thinking, it may be helpful to note that implicit in my remarks here is an aesthetic
ethics that is also theocentric, in that the ethical (i.e., the good, the right, the true, the
beautiful, or that which is of intrinsic value) is understood not only to transcend the
moral but also to lie beyond *human* measure.

13. It is worth noting in this connection an essay by Addison G. Wright on the so-called widow's mites, in which he argues, convincingly in my view, that this Gospel story (Mark 12:41–44 and Luke 21:1–4) presents the widow's gift to the maintenance of the Jerusalem temple as lamentable rather than praiseworthy. See "The Widow's Mites: Praise or Lament?—A Matter of Context," *Catholic Biblical Quarterly* 44 (April 1982): 256–65. The article may also be found at www.visionsofgiving.org/studywidowsmite .htm. Further corroboration of this interpretation is provided by Sakari Häkkinen's essay, "Two Coins Too Many: Reflections on the Widow's Offering," in *The Fourth R* 20 (July–August 2007): 9–12. I must therefore disagree with the conventional interpretation Ed Vacek gives to this passage when he writes, "The implication is that the widow is the one who made the truly deep gift of herself."

14. William F. May, *Beleaguered Rulers: The Public Obligation of the Professional* (Louisville, Ky.: Westminster John Knox Press, 2001), 224–25. See also May, "Images That Shape the Public Obligations of the Minister," in *Clergy Ethics in a Changing Society: Mapping the Terrain*, ed. James P. Wind, Russell Burck, Paul F. Camenisch, and Dennis P. McCann (Louisville, Ky.: Westminster John Knox Press, 1991), 54–83. For a most helpful, thorough, and succinct review of social science research on gratitude as a moral category, see Michael E. McCullough, Robert A. Emmons, Shelley D. Kirkpatrick, and David B. Larson, "Is Gratitude a Moral Affect?" *Psychological Bulletin* 127, no. 2 (2001): 249–66.

15. 1 John 4:10–11.

16. May, "Images That Shape the Public Obligations of the Minister," 66.

17. Catholic theologian Ed Vacek has more to say about giving as response to God and to God's love in his essay in this volume, "A Theology of Philanthropy." Since I largely agree with him, I consider his theology to be congruent with the best of Protestant theology. The most important point of theological agreement is that we both regard giving, in its ultimate context, as response to God, who is love and who is the ultimate giver of all good things.

18. My argument here bears strong affinity with that of Sondra Wheeler in her essay in this volume, "'Freely Give': The Paradox of Obligatory Generosity." However, I would prefer to speak of the tension, or dialectical relationship, between generous giving and obligation rather than the paradox. The characterization of the relationship as one of paradox suggests a degree of incoherence than I do not find experientially true. But the larger point is that we agree that the idea of giving cannot be adequately elaborated within a Christian theology without recourse to the idea of obligation. Ed Vacek also rightly notes that "acts of philanthropy are obligatory yet voluntary" (in the sense of uncoerced), and that "frequently, our obligation to give will feel like an opportunity rather than an obligation."

19. Charles Hartshorne, "Beyond Enlightened Self-Interest: A Metaphysics of Ethics," *Ethics* 84, no. 3 (1974): 205.

20. Jesus' parable of the talents may be interpreted as a commentary on the need to venture ourselves and our gifts in the world. Nothing could be worse than to hoard what we have been given, for then no one benefits. Ultimately, the self-preoccupied attempt to preserve what we have been given will leave us with nothing to show for ourselves at all. See Matthew 25:14–30; Luke 19:12–27.

21. I have previously noted that our giving often transcends any human calculus. Here I am focusing on giving only insofar as it is regarded and intended as a moral activity, subject to assessment in terms of moral categories such that one can make comparative judgments regarding the moral superiority or inferiority of one form of

giving with respect to another. In other words, I remain committed to the view that not all forms of giving are commensurable. I am seeking in the latter half of this essay to offer a critical and prescriptive perspective on giving within my own twenty-first-century American context precisely insofar as it can be—and actually is—regarded as a moral undertaking.

22. Luke 12:48. Interestingly enough, Andrew Carnegie, America's greatest past philanthropist in terms of sheer dollars given, and America's greatest current philanthropists by the same measure, Bill Gates and Warren Buffett, have all articulated their understanding of the obligations of their philanthropy in terms of this maxim. It is one of the two stated principles invoked by the Gates Foundation as a core value.

23. 1 John 4:19, 20.

24. My point here is not that we can discount motivation and set aside the ethics of gratitude. Rather, I am simply and implicitly acknowledging the fact that no one spends 100 percent of his or her time infused with the spirit of gratitude and generosity, not even when engaged in acts of giving. Indeed, according to one study, only approximately 10 percent of American adults indicated that they experience the emotion of gratitude "regularly and often" (McCullough et al., "Is Gratitude a Moral Affect?" 250). The lack of an immediate sense of gratitude hardly invalidates the meaningful gift, nor does it excuse the potential giver from engaging in acts of giving until the mood strikes.

25. In Jesus' parable of the talents, the steward who is given but one talent is chastised and divested of that talent, not because he failed to garner a return on his master's money, but because in self-preoccupation (expressed in terms of his unfounded fear of the consequences of possible failure) he made no attempt even to invest what he was given. He simply buried it in the ground for safekeeping, thereby insuring that it would yield no return. It would have been better to have ventured and lost than never to have ventured at all. See note 20 above.

The perspective and argument I am presenting here seem to be significantly at odds with the view of religious giving developed by Paul Schervish in chapter 7 of this volume. While I heartily agree with Schervish that religious giving is not limited to "giving that goes to congregations or religiously run organizations" and that such giving should be understood as emerging from "discerned reflection on ultimate origins and ultimate goals," my conviction is that such a discernment process should lead to the awareness that all that one possesses has been given and must in some way be ventured or shared. Schervish's focus on philanthropy, viewed primarily as the giving of wealth, constricts his vision and tends to limit the discernment process to a financial accounting process in which distinctions are made to distinguish "a conservatively defined stream of present and future financial resources," "a liberally defined stream of present and future expenditures to support" a desired standard of living, and "a stream of excess resources potentially available for philanthropy," only the latter of which is understood to be available for "charitable purposes." Thus, despite his claim that the process of discernment can apply to all our choices, he really attends to the special circumstances of the wealthy and lacks an adequate phenomenology and ethics of giving applicable to the common lot of humanity.

26. Paula Dempsey's observations in this volume on the structural or systemic causes of debt are relevant here. Debt is not simply a manifestation of poor personal financial management, but is often the result of structural inequities and societal failures, e.g., inadequate educational services, lack of employment opportunities, deceptive lending and credit practices, and especially the absence of universally affordable health care services.

27. In his landmark book, *A Theory of Justice*, John Rawls developed the notion of primary goods as those goods to which all persons in democratic society have a justice claim. See *A Theory of Justice*, rev. ed. (Cambridge, Mass.: Harvard University Press, 1999), 54–55, 78–81. The capabilities approach of economist Amartya Sen and social philosopher Martha Nussbaum represents a further development and modification of Rawlsian thought that explicitly recognizes that provision of the primary goods, or requisite capabilities for full human flourishing, is a matter of entitlement or justice, not charity. See, e.g., Nussbaum, *Frontiers of Justice: Disability, Nationality, Species Membership*, (Cambridge, Mass.: Belknap Press, 2006). For an explicitly religious statement of what social justice requires primarily in economic terms, see United States Catholic Conference of Bishops, *Economic Justice for All*, 10th anniversary ed. (UCCSB, 1997). My intent here is not to elaborate a specific set of primary goods or requisite capabilities, the provision of which I regard as morally obligatory, but merely to indicate the scope and magnitude of the sphere of social justice.

28. In Jesus' parable of the laborers in the vineyard, the laborers work varying amounts of time. At the end of the day, however, each receives the same amount—a living wage. The parable is typically given a spiritualized interpretation, but surely it is also a commentary on God's intentions for all of God's children to be adequately provided for whether or not, in the circumstances at hand, they have earned what is needed for their daily sustenance. See Matthew 20:1–15.

29. See, for example, the summary of recent research presented by Vassilis Saroglou, "Religion's Role in Prosocial Behavior: Myth or Reality?" in *Psychology of Religion Newsletter*, American Psychological Association Division 36, vol. 31, no. 2 (Spring 2006): 1–8. See also Peer Scheepers and Manfred Te Grotenhuis, "Who Cares for the Poor in Europe?" *European Sociological Review* 21, no. 5 (2005): 453–65, and V. Hodgkinson and M. Weitzman, *Giving and Volunteering in the United States* (Washington, D.C.: Independent Sector, 1992).

30. My final revisions to this chapter were already completed when I discovered Donald E. Messer's congenial essay, "More Than Random Acts of Kindness," in which he endorses charity but also argues for social justice, claiming that these are not matters of "either/or" but of "both/and." "We need to rethink certain religious practices and reappropriate biblical and theological imperatives related to social justice," he claims, corroborating the observation he cites from journalist and social commentator Bill Moyers: "Charity is commendable; everyone should be charitable. But justice aims to create a social order in which, if individuals choose not to be charitable, people still don't go hungry, unschooled, or sick without care. Charity depends on the vicissitudes of whim and personal wealth; justice depends on commitment instead of circumstance. Faith-based charity provides crumbs from the table; faith-based justice provides a place at the table." Messer's essay is in George McGovern, Bob Dole, and Donald E. Messer, *Ending Hunger Now: A Challenge to Persons of Faith* (Minneapolis: Fortress Press, 2005), 87–107. The specific citations are on pages 88–89.

31. Joseph Fletcher, "Wealth and Taxation: The Ethics of Stewardship," in *Stewardship in Contemporary Theology*, ed. T. K. Thompson (New York: Association Press, 1960); I am quoting from an online version at www.visionsofgiving.org/document.php?loc=3&cat=4&sub=19.

32. I take Sondra Wheeler to be making a similar point when she writes in chapter 5 of this volume, "Formation for stewardship will be identical with spiritual formation generally."

33. Fletcher, "Wealth and Taxation."

34. On this point, as previously noted, I am in close accord with Sondra Wheeler in her essay in this volume.

35. Most public discussion and ethical debate about the justice of government economic policy focuses on fiscal policies. It is important to note that government monetary policies also exercise enormous influence over economic activity, both for good and for ill. For a helpful treatment of monetary policy in theological and ethical perspective, see John B. Cobb Jr. and Herman E. Daly, "Afterword: Money, Debt, and Wealth," in *For the Common Good*, 2nd ed. (Boston: Beacon Press, 1994), 407–42.

36. Other integral features could be summarized in terms of the general statistics regarding *state* and *national* poverty statistics, educational attainments, health care coverage, and other dimensions of material well-being. More poignantly, the statistics about *world* hunger, disease, poverty, and death would accent the fact that there is hardly anything ordinary about the experience of most Americans in the context of the prevailing global conditions for human existence. The disparities of wealth, power, and quality of life on the planet are so well known, and yet remain so overwhelming, that it may seem pointless to call attention to them. Nonetheless, if any other human being is potentially one's neighbor, then the fact is that most of our potential neighbors lack the basic necessities fully to realize their God-given capacities as human beings. We can hardly ignore this reality in our thinking about Christian giving as an expression of our calling to love God and neighbor.

37. Patty Stonesifer, in an interview titled "Evaluating the Gates Foundation: A Response from the CEO," *Chronicle of Philanthropy*, 22 March 2007, 52 (emphasis added). Stonesifer's view, which I share, runs counter to the claim made by Paul Schervish in this volume to the effect that current levels of wealth in the world are sufficient "to accomplish what the world has never been able to do before—to solve so many of its pressing needs for so many of its people." It may be that current levels of wealth, if put at the disposal of the appropriate agencies, would be *financially* sufficient to meet the most pressing *material* needs of most people in the world today, but clearly other sorts of resources, as well as various sorts of systemic social, political, economic, and other structural changes are also necessary.

38. The latest available statistics continue to show a huge and growing income gap in the United States, with the incomes of the wealthiest growing the fastest. The latest tax data, based on 2005 figures, show that the top 1 percent of Americans, with average annual incomes well over $1 million, now have the largest share of national income since 1928. Meanwhile, cuts in government services in recent years have had the most negative impact on those with low incomes. (See David Clay Johnston, "Income Gap is Widening, Data Shows," *New York Times*, March 29, 2007.) The inequities that accompany this widening gap in incomes and the corresponding and even more dramatic gap in wealth are hardly to be remedied by traditional philanthropy. Only changes in taxation and social policy are likely to make much difference.

39. I am thus in basic agreement with Franklin Gamwell, who argues that all Christians who inhabit a liberal democratic society are under a general obligation to engage in political activity as part of their calling "to pursue the community of love and to act for justice as general emancipation"; see Gamwell, *Politics as a Christian Vocation: Faith and Democracy Today* (Cambridge: Cambridge University Press, 2005), 5.

40. Micah 6:8.

"Freely Give": The Paradox of Obligatory Generosity in Christian Thought

SONDRA WHEELER

The question of how to live faithfully with possessions—how to sustain our material lives in the world and yet keep from being corrupted or held captive by what we own, how to decide what we may keep and what we are to give away—these are just particular, and particularly difficult, forms of a more general question: How are we to live? That question is more ancient than Christianity—one posed to Moses on Sinai, to John at the Jordan, to Jesus on the road, and to the apostles outside the upper room. It is, in fact, the origin of all religion, rooted in the human sense of dependency and awe, and it has driven every human culture we know anything about to ask, what do the gods demand of us? The trouble is, if the Christian gospel is true, the question posed in that way can never be answered truthfully. Or to put it a little more exactly, the answer is always both "everything" and "nothing at all."

On the one hand, Christians share with Muslims and Jews a doctrine of God as transcendent—manifested in creation but not contained within it, the absolute Author and Source of all that exists. Moreover, God's claim on us and on all life is not merely the claim of the Maker upon what is made. God has also blessed and nourished and sustained all things, "giving each creature its food in due season" (Ps. 145:15), as the psalmist sings, ordering all according to the divine will. Regarding humankind, God has further condescended to enter into covenant: first with Noah and then with Abraham, and through him with all of Abraham's children and with the church, which is incorporated into the people of God by adoption. That relationship makes comprehensive claims on how we live—from how we sustain our bodies, to how we order our communities, to how we relate to those outside them.

For Christians, over all these claims stands the ultimate obligation: the response to God's grace in Jesus Christ, which is the life of discipleship. This is modeled on the one who offered all without reservation and was "obedient unto death, even death on a cross" (Phil. 2:8). Thus, it is proper to say that we are obliged to and by God at every point, without limit or reserve, so that Jesus himself can say, "Anyone who does not hate father and mother and even his own life cannot be my disciple" (Luke 14:26). This is the "everything" piece of what God requires. John Wesley, eighteenth-century Anglican priest and founder of my own tradition of Methodism, captures it in a characteristically vigorous sermon passage:

> [We see that] there are no works of supererogation; that we can never do more than our duty; seeing all we have is not our own, but God's; all we can do is due to Him. We have not received this or that, or many things only, but everything from Him: therefore, everything is His due. He that gives us all, must needs have a right to all: so that if we pay Him anything less than all, we cannot be faithful stewards. And considering, "every man shall receive his own reward, according to his own labor," we cannot be wise stewards unless we labor to the uttermost of our power; not leaving anything undone which we possibly can do, but putting forth all our strength.[1]

But this is only half of the answer, and this answer is such that, alone, half of it tells not half of the truth but no truth at all. For as the whole of Christian tradition is at pains to express, Christian faith does not begin with human beings: not with their condition or their actions, not with their duties or with the often pathetic character of their performance of them. Rather, Christian faith begins with and rests wholly upon what God has done: freely, preemptively, gratuitously, with no thinkable antecedent but God's sovereign mercy. The gospel is the news, good beyond all understanding, nearly beyond all believing, that "while we were yet sinners, Christ died for us" (Rom. 5:8). And everything, *everything* else—the conduct of Christians as well as their confession—comes from and depends upon the ability to receive that word. To his credit, Wesley can express this side of the paradox with equal passion and power:

> Thou ungodly one, who hearest or readest these words! Thou vile, helpless, miserable sinner! I charge thee before God the Judge of all: go straight unto Him, with all thy ungodliness. . . . Who art thou, that now seest and feelest both thine inward and outward ungodliness? Thou art the man! I want thee for my Lord! I challenge thee for a child of God by faith! The Lord hath need of thee. Thou who feelest thou art just fit for hell, art just fit to advance His glory; the glory of His free grace, justifying the ungodly

and him that worketh not. O come quickly! Believe in the Lord Jesus, and thou, even thou, art reconciled to God.[2]

I have used examples from Wesley's preaching because they are rhetorically clear and emphatic, and thus they serve to make their respective points compactly and unmistakably. But though he is at once an heir of high church Anglicanism and the inadvertent founder of an influential branch of Protestantism, in doctrinal content Wesley is anything but original. Apart from copious quotations from Scripture, he cites an eclectic range of sources from patristic to medieval to classical Reformation texts, and his theology is notable only for its synthesis of elements gathered from across the broadest spectrum of historic Christian thought. His insistence upon the pure initiative of divine grace is no idiosyncrasy but is fundamental to theologies, Catholic and Protestant, Eastern and Western alike.

What this means is that Christian life does not and cannot have obligation as its deepest root. Instead, the life of faith is entirely responsive, springing from gratitude rather than duty. Its obedience is an expression of the love awakened by God's love, born of a desire to please and not to grieve such a Lover. It is the celebration of a reconciliation already accomplished and not the condition of that reconciliation, part of the wedding feast and not the courtship. Do not misunderstand: real faith prompts real transformation; and faithfulness, obedience, the active love of God and neighbor, are all inseparable from the life of Christians. Martin Luther himself was quick to say that any supposed Christian not occupied in acts of love was simply a person without faith.[3] But such acts are offered to God like the ring of the bridegroom is offered to the bride, not to win acceptance but in token of a love already secure. Only when this essential priority of grace is grasped is one rid of the endless and insatiable anxiety about how much is enough, and only thus can one be freed from the obsessive self-interest that pervades and corrupts all efforts to satisfy God. I have done nothing so far but restate the Pauline insight, central to the Reformation, that salvation is the gift of God, received by faith, and not the consequence of works. This is the other piece of the answer to what God requires of us: "nothing at all."

But if this paradoxical point is hard to keep hold of in general, it is harder yet when we try to address the special topic we usually call stewardship. In fact, that term, a relatively recent coinage but one with deep biblical roots, may be part of the problem. It is, of course, very useful for illuminating the "everything" half of what God requires in the use of resources, material and otherwise. Historically speaking, the steward was not an owner of any kind, but merely a servant who had no claim on the assets over which he had control. In fact, most of the time stewards were themselves slaves, and the goods they managed belonged to a master to whom they were utterly accountable. Consider the cautionary tale in Luke 12:42–48. In it, Jesus warns of the master's imminent return and describes the fate that awaits the steward found to have neglected the household and squandered the resources in his charge. English Bibles usually translate this as something like "he will be severely punished." In fact, what the Greek says literally is "he will be cut in two"!

But by itself the metaphor of the steward is not very helpful for displaying the other side, the insistence of the gospel that *all* is gift, that God's grace is offered without condition. It misses something key, which is that, in the overarching narrative of the gospel, one becomes a servant only in becoming a son or daughter, one to whom it is truly said, "All that I have is yours" (Luke 15:31). It obscures the fact that the slave of Christ (as the early Christians delighted to call themselves) is the one set free from sin, death, and hell by a welcome so boundless and unconstrained that the only possible response is joyful self-abandonment. To be thus overcome by the goodness of God is, yes, to be "beholden," as my Southern relatives would say, properly to be "obliged" and to owe a response. But much more deeply, and much more crucially, it is to be drawn into that goodness: to fall in love with grace and thus to delight in sharing its work. All true love makes one generous, because generosity is as natural to fullness as stinginess is to want.

In such a state of abundance and security, giving is not a lessening of that fullness but the very overflowing of its joy. It is a gift and not a duty. For an example of dancing on the edge of this knife, of holding together both obligation and liberty, one need only turn to the second letter to the Corinthians, to Paul's artfully constructed appeal for funds for the church in Jerusalem.

> 8:1 We make known to you, brothers and sisters, the grace of God which has been given in the churches of Macedonia:
> 2 that in the midst of a great trial of suffering, the fullness of their joy and the depth of their poverty overflowed into the wealth of their openheartedness
> 3 that [they gave] according to their ability, I testify, and beyond their ability, of their own choice,

4 fervently begging of us the favor of sharing in the ministry to the saints,

5 and not just as we hoped, but first gave themselves to the Lord and to us by God's will.

6 As a result, we have asked Titus so that, as he had already begun, so also he should complete this [act of] grace among you.

7 But as in every way you are full—of faith and of speech and of knowledge and of all diligence and of love toward us—see that you are full also of this grace.

8 I say this not as a command, but as using the diligence of others to try the genuineness of your love as well.

9 For you know the grace of our Lord Jesus Christ, that for your sake he being rich became poor, in order that by his poverty you might become rich.

10 And I give you an opinion in this: for it is best for you, who last year began not only to do this but to desire it, [11] now to complete what you began, so that your eagerness in desiring it may be matched by your finishing it out of what you have.

12 For if the eagerness is there, it is acceptable according to what one has, not what one has not.

13 Not that there should be ease to others and suffering to you, but that out of equality [14] your present fullness should supply their lack, in order that their fullness may supply your lack, so that there may be equality.

15 As it is written: "The one [who gathered] much had no excess, and the one [who gathered] little had no lack."

[AUTHOR'S TRANSLATION]

It is important to bear in mind that Paul is here writing to Gentiles accustomed to being scorned by Jews as unclean—in fact, to natives of a city renowned for its vices. Writing to Corinth on behalf of Jerusalem is a little like writing to the denizens of Las Vegas on behalf of Salt Lake City; these are not natural allies. And that, of course, is half of Paul's point. The collection for Jerusalem is not just a practical necessity: it is a sort of visual aid, a material demonstration of the fact that "the cross of Christ has broken down the dividing wall of hostility" (Eph. 2:11) and made all distinctions moot. It is, if you will pardon the anachronism, a kind of sacrament, the "outward and visible sign of an inward and spiritual grace," which is the unity of the church effected by Christ.

This is the reason that, from Paul's point of view, the circumstance of want in Jerusalem is itself a gift; it is an occasion to manifest what God has done. Both need and response, both giver and receiver, have their place in the encompassing story of God's overwhelming generosity, which has made debtors and magnates of us all. But here Paul walks a delicate line. To live out this reality by sharing material resources is not simply an option that one might decline, but neither, Paul is careful to say, is it a command. He calls it a *Xaris*, a word that unites the ideas of gift, grace, favor, and blessing.

It is the *Xaris* of God given in impoverished Macedonia that opens the chapter, and the word recurs five times in these fifteen verses (1, 4, 6, 7, 9). Paul uses it to describe not only the gift of the Macedonians but the collection itself, their opportunity to participate in it, and the divine grace that prompts and finds expression in their generosity. Paul writes, then, in a mood more of celebration than of admonition, offering the Macedonian example of openheartedness to prompt the Corinthians to show the same graciousness, giving evidence by a tangible sign of their love for one another that they have received God's mercy.

But it is not the example of Macedonia that undergirds the church's practice of sharing, and Paul reminds Corinth of the final measure of giving in a perfectly balanced sentence, the centerpiece of this passage and one of the rare occasions on which Paul's Greek rises to elegance: "For you know the grace of our Lord Jesus Christ, that for your sake he being rich became poor in order that you, by his poverty, might be made rich" (2 Cor. 8:9). And here is the key and the very heart of the paradox. Those who know this grace can lay no claim on anything, having received all, beyond any possibility of reckoning the debt, and so all is owed. But what they know *is* grace, the free gift of God, which stands above all matters of debt and reckoning, a realm in which nothing is demanded—and nothing can be held back. Only those who know the wealth of which Paul speaks, who live with the daily experience of being filled to overflowing with every needful thing, can receive the advice Paul ultimately gives, which is that they give according to their desire: "It is best for you ... to complete what you began, so that your eagerness in desiring may be matched by your finishing it."

Three and a half centuries later, St. Augustine will put it succinctly: "Love, and do what you will."[4] But Augustine had long since discovered to his sorrow that love itself could not be decided upon, arrived at by reason, like the conclusion of a syllogism. It must rather be evoked, awakened in the heart as delight and gratitude. Love so awakened overflows into giving and service as a kind of participation in God's own life in the world, for God is among us as one who serves, and meets us there as nowhere else on earth. Such participation can only be a matter of liberty, and it is as an act of freedom that it constitutes a blessing equally for giver and recipient, and a service acceptable to God. Only thus does it flow toward what Paul takes to be the natural aim of sharing in the church, that all needs are met, and all equally.

But all of this only brings the problem home more pointedly: How can the puzzle of free but dutiful giving be solved? How can the practice of giving be inculcated and sustained? Indeed, how can it be given the centrality and seriousness it has in Scripture, without the communities that undertake it falling into the twin traps of scrupulosity and condescension? I am tempted to conclude that it cannot (as witness the clumsiness of my effort even to articulate the tension) and to abandon the effort. But the longer I spend on this topic, the longer I live with the texts that constitute the Christian theological tradition on wealth, the more I am persuaded that we must find a way to communicate this central paradox of grace or else fall silent, knowing that nothing else one might say can be the truth apart from this: those to whom much has been given are not so much *expected* as *invited* to give much, and in doing so to enter into the overflowing goodness of God. And it is not just that a biblical theology of stewardship will be faulty if it lacks this grounding in liberty and joy. It is also that it will have no lasting power to form the life and practice of the religious communities it serves.

As teachers and preachers and interpreters of a tradition, we have a responsibility to convey that tradition with clarity and passion and forthrightness, to transmit its deep suspicion about wealth as a hindrance to the gospel, a temptation to idolatry, an occasion of injustice. We must be prepared to voice its fiercest challenges and to confront them together: "If you have the means of worldly life and shut your heart against your brother in need, how does the love of God live in you?" (1 John 3:17). But by itself, I am convinced, this will not be enough. However accurate our exegesis, however cogent our arguments about our responsibilities to one another, no one will be won by them to the kind of extravagant and costly giving that Paul describes.

Likewise, while it is easy to make American Christians feel guilty about their spiraling consumption in the face of the world's dire need, no one will ever be brought by that guilt to the fullness and freedom that makes generosity a way of life. Do not mistake me: as an ethicist, I believe in guilt and think we would certainly be worse off, not better, without it. Moreover, to have a sense of sin, a "fear of the Lord" in its original meaning, is already to be called into the presence of grace. But no one comes to God simply by fleeing sin, or purely in fear of judgment.

In the end, it is not what we flee but what we are drawn to that is decisive. St. Francis did not shed his clothing in the town square of Assisi and take up a life of holy poverty in order to escape his inheritance and the social position that went with it, nor did he do it to avoid God's wrath. He did it to embrace, without encumbrances, the love of God with which he had become intoxicated. And we will shed our own encumbrances for the same reason or not at all. So, awkward though it may be to say in an academic article, what Christians need is nothing less than to fall in love again, to be awakened once more to the power and beauty of God's grace as that is known in Jesus Christ, so that they can join in the exultation that closes Paul's appeal: "Thanks be to God for his inexpressible gift!" From such wells alone will spring a genuinely free giving and a Christian practice of stewardship.

Yet it remains that no argument ever made can cause anyone to love, and no logic can bring forth gratitude. Nor is moral exhortation much help. It is true enough to say that gratitude can be owed, and there are many circumstances in which not to feel it is a moral offense, a failure of justice. Yet it is the very soul of generosity that nothing, including thanks, is required in return. Thus, gratefulness cannot be required without being destroyed, for the very thing one is grateful for is the liberty of the gift. Gratitude comes only without constraint, and then it is itself a gift, a grace of its own that evokes a new and distinct blessing for both giver and recipient.

But if not by argument or admonition, then how is gratitude to be kindled and renewed when even our prayers of thanksgiving have devolved into matter-of-fact acknowledgment without gladness or power? I will tell you outright that I have no answer of my own, but I do have some clues that I have cribbed from the pages of other people's books or learned from the observation of other people's virtue. I want to share those with you and to say a little about the implications of all this for stewardship education and formation in the church.

In a volume about the ethics of personal relationships, Margaret Farley argues that love arises from vision, welling up unbidden in the heart when we see the beloved in truth.[5] Under the spell of that vision, we need no prompting to do the deeds of love; indeed, we can hardly be kept from doing them. But, she warns, any number of things can cloud the vision, obscure it, and distract us from it, including the deadening round of duties and habits that are the ordinary daily expression of love. Those who love are eager and extravagant in making promises, as a thousand love songs attest; yet it is not long before the promises begin to bind and chafe, to replace the freedom and delight that gave rise to them with routine and obligation. Renewal requires a pause in the busyness, what Farley calls a kind of "attentive relaxation of the heart,"[6] which allows us to see again the reality of the one we love and thus to recover our joy in the ordinary presence and service of the beloved.

All this is true of our human love for spouses and children, for colleagues and friends, but it is true as well of our love for God. This may be why earlier generations devised not only the regular daily and weekly round of worship but also the feasts and festivals of the Christian year. They serve to break believers out of their routines and confront them once more with the astonishment of manger and cross and empty tomb, and thus to startle them into seeing once more what is there at all times. And as with love, so also with gratitude: just as we lose the capacity to see those whom we love, we also lose, over time, the capacity to notice the gifts that surround us, and so to take joy in them. In particular, it is hard for anyone to remain aware of the abiding wonder of God's grace precisely because it is the starting point, the ground from which all human being sets out. But without such an awareness, gratitude can be owed but not felt. Our debts are acknowledged in a kind of numb recognition but without the rush of joy and confidence that real gladness would bring. Thus, we experience emptiness and hunger in the midst of God's plenty, and we are, God help us, too impoverished to be generous.

It sounds simpleminded to say it, but I have come to believe that what Christians need in order to renew the springs of stewardship is nothing so much as to hear the gospel again. The church is often accused of preaching to the choir, but in truth I suspect it is the choir that most needs the preaching and most rarely hears it. Theologians are so busy trying to work out the systems of Christian thought and figure out the implications of Christian convictions that they forget how deeply and how continually we need to be nourished and re-converted by our own most basic proclamation. Those of us who are seasoned in the faith might learn something from the fact that much of the surviving correspondence of Paul, like many of the sermons and stories of Jesus preserved in the Gospels, have at their center no abstruse and difficult theological construction, but a thousand variations on the one theme: that God was in Christ reconciling the world to Godself, not counting trespasses (2 Cor. 5:19), but coming to seek and save the lost (Luke 19:10), who are and always will be none other than all of us.

Hard as it sometimes may be to believe the gospel, it is harder still to live with the truth of it. The gospel requires us to accept a verdict that condemns all our best efforts and makes nonsense of our dearest illusions about ourselves. It obliges us to accept not acquittal but pardon. It means learning to live at peace with a permanent indebtedness, and it is hard on our prized self-esteem to draw daily sustenance from a mercy that is forever undeserved, forever ours by gift and not by right. More difficult yet is the painful discipline of forgiveness imposed upon those who cannot bear the justice of God and thus are on impossible ground when they demand justice from one another. But all of Christian life has its intelligibility and its importance only in this: that it bears witness to the truth of the gospel.

The foregoing discussion suggests two things for Christian theologians who are thinking about nurturing the practice of giving. One is that Christian preaching and teaching about stewardship cannot be separated at any point from the ever-renewed proclamation of God's mercy revealed in the life, death, and resurrection of Jesus Christ. Thus, stewardship education will always look like basic evangelism and like the beginning of every Christian catechism, except that the converts and the catechumens will always be all of us. The other is that formation for stewardship will be identical with spiritual formation generally, for stewardship has the same wellspring as all forms of holiness: simply the knowledge and love of God. We who profess that God is the origin of every good should not be surprised to find that the practice of giving in the church cannot survive cut off from its source, from the practice of the presence of God. If, as Paul assumes, Christian giving is a *Xaris*, a kind of participation in the blessing of God bestowed upon giver and recipient, then it is only natural that it be dependent on what Christian tradition calls "the ordinary means of grace." These are just the stuff of our ongoing life with God in prayer and worship, in mutual care and mutual accountability, in the sacraments and the study of Scripture and the singing of hymns. Whatever crisis we may now confront in Christian giving is just a late symptom of a more fundamental crisis in Christian nurture. It is there that it must be addressed, and for reasons incalculably more important than the mere financial health of our religious institutions. Without a deep renewal of basic Christian formation, even our ailing institutions may outlast the living faith that gave birth to them.

But there is a danger in this account. Linking the practice of giving to gratitude and holiness may suggest a motive too rarefied and rare, and thus give us an excuse to wait for the character we need before giving—waiting until we detect no admixture of guilt or anxiety, no tincture of pride or condescension or resentment to compromise our charity. It may be that freedom has to be learned, partly by being practiced before it fully exists. Circular as it may seem, it appears there is no way to learn to be generous without being generous beforehand, just as there is no way to learn to play the piano without sitting down to practice playing it before you know how. This is why we make small children share their toys long before they have the least interest in their playmates' satisfaction, long before they have learned to take pleasure in the pleasure of another; we hope to form the behavior while we wait for the motive to develop. And that may not be all bad. Indeed, it may well be that we cannot know the sweetness of the shared life into which God invites us until we have taken the beginning steps that will allow us to meet and know Christ in those we serve. To make that point persuasive, I am going to recount a little history. It is none other than the story of the man whose preaching on what is and is not required of us by God I quoted at the start of this chapter. His example is instructive, because John Wesley started out as far as anyone could be from the model of free giving that I have been taking as normative.

When Wesley was a young man at Oxford, his brother Charles and four other young men asked him to lead their Bible study. He led them in a study of the Scriptures and other devotional books as part of an effort to develop holiness of life. These earnest young men encountered the words of Matthew 25:45: those who did not feed the hungry, clothe the naked, visit the sick and the imprisoned, had passed Christ by in the street and thus were at peril of their souls. By precept and invitation, by example and preaching and pointed narrative, Christ had enjoined the care of those in need. So John Wesley and those under his informal leadership, seeking to please (or perhaps at least to appease) God and acting in the straightforward fashion of obedience, went out to "preach good news to the poor" (Luke 4:19).

What they saw led them to set about securing food and medicine, education and decent living conditions for a group of families who were among the victims of England's Industrial Revolution. They did it not as a matter of social engineering, or social work, or even social ethics. They were simply heeding a basic imperative of the gospel, believing that to refuse was to court judgment. They came to instruct people in the basic tenets of Christian faith and the norms of Christian life. The crucial thing was that they went to their hearers. They did not wait for some sinner to come to a Bible study at Oxford, nor did they send a bus to bring these folks into a more respectable part of town. They went themselves, week in and week out, into the homes of the poor, into the workhouses that offered the meanest subsistence to the desperate, into the few and impoverished schools that existed for the children of the lower classes. It was this steady contact and firsthand exposure that educated Wesley about the grinding misery of the poor, that awakened him to the underside of the economic transformation then going on in England.

In the succeeding years, Wesley's understanding of the faith would change; his account of grace, his preaching, and his teaching would all undergo substantial transformation. The one thing that would remain constant was his involvement with the poor. This took multiple forms: there was the distribution, always in person, of food staples, medicine, clothing, blankets, and fuel. The sick were not only visited but physically cared for. The Methodists brought books and instruction in everything from hygiene to history into homes as well as founding and staffing schools for the children of the poor long before the establishment of public education. The list goes on and on, making modern Methodists like me feel both exhausted and guilty.[7] But it is not the good works that are Wesley's chief legacy. It is what happened to him in the doing of them.

It was the barest obedience to Christ's command that brought Wesley into constant contact with the poor and abandoned, and it was the struggle against the injustices he encountered that kept him there. But it is clear in his sermons, letters, and journals that it was compassion, the gift of suffering with, that came to animate his work and to give it the character of grace. Wesley saw with his own eyes the squalor and despair that filled England's slums, held with his own arms the children who died of hunger, put his own fingers into the wounds of the poor whom he nursed. He found that he could not bear to turn his back on these or even to separate himself from them by providing himself with anything beyond what was needful to sustain his work. He lived on 28 pounds a year—for a sense of scale, when Wesley was 82, he spent a Christmas day in London begging for the poor to buy them food and heating fuel, and collected 200 pounds. In his advancing age, some admonished him to eat better food and live in more comfortable surroundings and even to dress as befitted a clergyman. To those friends he wrote, "If you saw with your own eyes what I have seen—fathers working from light to dark and coming home to the sound of children crying for what they had not to give—could you lay out money in ornaments or superfluities?"[8]

Wesley, I daresay, began his work with the poor with all the prejudices, all the anxieties, all the distaste born of the eighteenth-century gentleman's ignorance of the struggles of the destitute. These would probably have been exacerbated by class bias and an uneasy conscience, which always tends to make us hate those who show us our guilt. Wesley's understanding of poverty, and with it his theology, his faith, and his character, were transformed by his own steady experience until he frankly preferred the poor (about whom he had no illusions). He wrote, after a preaching visit to a prosperous church, "How hard it is to be shallow enough for a polite audience!"[9] Wesley had read—as all Christians have—that Jesus Christ was to be found among the poor, that he could find and serve him by keeping company with the least of his brothers. He went and found it to be true. Thus it was that he came to recognize material sharing with the poor as itself a means of grace.

As Christians talk about the practice of stewardship, wrestle with the predicament of their wealth, and think about how they are to respond to the gospel's insistence on caring for the poor without compromising the grace and liberty of Christian existence, there is much in the history of the church to suggest that they need simply to stumble out there and do it. They will sometimes get it wrong, no doubt. They will say and do and think the wrong thing, I am sure. But they will be there. And they will learn. And if history is any teacher, the practice itself will make them better at it, better in their thinking as well as in their doing. The actual undertaking of care will generate both thought and character, both theology and charity. We may be persuaded in our heads that the opportunity to share God's life by giving is itself a gift, something we might, like the Macedonians, fitly entreat as a favor. But we cannot receive the gift it offers unless, some way or other, we begin.

For all these reasons, I suspect that, if we search for answers to the religious problems in giving only through analysis, only by thinking it through one more time, only by drafting articles and books like the present one, we will confront finally a fundamental limitation. Although the critical work of scholarship is essential to the vitality of religious communities, analysis by itself cannot serve as a channel of the grace that comes in doing. In the end, those of us who not only study the texts and traditions of communities of faith but bear those traditions and are nourished by them must find our way to the truth partly through practice, through the lived life in which alone the tensions are dissolved and the perplexities of giving as a religious discipline give way to the life-giving power of giving as a means of grace.

NOTES

1. John Wesley, "The Good Steward," in *The Bicentennial Edition of the Works of John Wesley*, Frank Baker, gen. ed. (Nashville, Tenn.: Abingdon Press, 1984–2003), 2:297; cited hereafter as *Works*.

2. Wesley, "Justification by Faith," *Works* 1:198–99.

3. Martin Luther, "Preface to the Epistle of St. Paul to the Romans," John Dillenberger, ed., *Martin Luther: Selections from His Writings* (New York: Doubleday, 1961), 24.

4. Augustine, "Seventh Homily on the First Epistle of St. John," in *Nicene and Post-Nicene Fathers*, ed. P. Schaff (New York: Scribner and Sons, 1903), 7:504.

5. Margaret Farley, *Personal Commitments: Beginning, Keeping, Changing* (San Francisco: Harper and Row, 1986), 54–66.

6. Ibid., 58ff.

7. For an excellent and compact summary, see Manfred Marquardt, *John Wesley's Social Ethics: Praxis and Principles* (Nashville, Tenn.: Abingdon Press, 1992).

8. *Works* 20:445.

9. *Works* 22:288.

A Catholic Theology
of Philanthropy

EDWARD VACEK, S.J.

[God] who dwells in me does his works. . . . [T]he one who
believes in me will also do the works that I do and, in fact, will
do greater works than these.

—JOHN 14:10–12

This essay probes the connection between God and philanthropy in America. There are multiple historical studies, sociological accounts, and exhortational reflections on philanthropy. Surprisingly, however, there are few theological works on it.[1] What follows is my attempt to connect the experience of Christian life with the practice of philanthropy.[2] It will also, I hope, be of use to other traditions since we all share, in however diverse ways, our humanity, the world, and the divine.

FUNDAMENTAL VISION

The basic theological vision I propose can be stated quite simply: God acts in history through creatures. Correlatively, creatures participate in God's action in our world (see Failer, chapter 3 in this volume). This connection, on God's part, is the activity of love; on our part, it can and should be a cooperative activity of love. Philanthropy is one way of cooperating. Let me develop these points.

GOD IS LOVE

Much depends on the image of God that we have. Religions, particularly the polytheistic religions, offer an enormously rich and colorful array of images. Philosophers add their own understandings. This is no idle conversation, since our spiritualities depend on our images of God. For example, if one believes in a sovereign God who punishes sinful people with diseases, then it would be ungodly for a philanthropy to fund research to cure those diseases.

I will be proposing a very different image of God, an image that quite commonly has been neglected or subordinated in the Western tradition. It is the image put forth in a biblical one-liner: "*God is love*" (1 John 4:8). This image underlies the gospel's claim that God so loved the world that God "*gave*" the Son (John 3:16). Similarly, St. Paul writes of "the Son of God, who *loved* me and *gave* himself for me" (Gal. 2:20). This gift seals a new covenant between God and us (Luke 22:20; 1 Cor. 11:25), a covenant characterized by the two Jewish love commandments (Deut. 6:5; Lev. 19:18) that Jesus unites (Matt. 22:37–40).

As I have argued elsewhere,[3] this image of God as love provides a much better starting point for Christian moral life than either of its two closest alternatives: the God who, as sovereign, is central in divine commandment theories, or the God who, as Creator, is central in natural law theories.[4] This Johannine image of God makes love for God a more fundamental religious activity than either faith, with its emphasis on the word, or hope, with its emphasis on the eschaton (1 Cor. 13:13). This understanding of God as love and ourselves as lovers of God provides the starting point of this essay.

COMMUNITY WITH GOD

The basic religious relationship between God and human beings, I have argued elsewhere,[5] is one that can be described schematically: (1) God loves us; (2) we accept God's love; (3) we love God in return; (4) we form community with God; (5) we cooperate with God. Let me draw out four implications.

First, this theology of philanthropy does not begin with love for the neighbor or with gratitude for the gifts we have received. Rather, it begins with God's love for us, disclosed in Jesus Christ but also in daily life. Through the eyes of faith, we Christians can and should see and name *God's* love in the multitudinous events of our lives, such as the kindness of a fellow employee or the availability of clean water.[6] More fundamentally, we can and should see our very lives as a basic expression of God's love for us. From a theological point of view, we can and should see that the "movement" of our own love is itself bound up with the Holy Spirit. God is the beckoning horizon that attracts some of us to promote renewable energy sources. God is the challenging horizon that moves others of us to fight against ovarian cancer; that is, in resisting this and other evils, we have what Edward Schillebeeckx calls a "negative contrast experience," an awareness that these evils are contrary to God's love and therefore are to be resisted.

Second, the proper response to the experience of being loved by God is to love God in return. An essential "step" is missing if we say, "God loves us and therefore we should love our neighbor." If a husband professes love for his wife, and her reply is to promise to take care of their children, something is missing. Jesus' first great commandment should not, as all too often happens, be reduced to the second.[7] Loving our neighbors is not a substitute for loving God. Unfortunately, we limited humans often love and act without any accompanying sense of God. Contrary to secular opinion, we are moral failures when we do not have an active relationship with God.[8]

Third, a theology of philanthropy does not begin with isolated individuals who, through free choice, decide to help others in need. American individualism has many strengths, but it is only a half-truth. The other "half" is that both by nature and by God's grace we are "belongers." We are members of a family, of a country, and of a covenant with God long before we choose to be such. Like a child, we are born into God's family prior to any choice on our part. We can fulfill in greater or lesser degrees this pre-established communal relationship. Indeed, we can reject it. But it still claims us. Christoph Schwöbel puts these points well: "Human beings are indeed set within a structure of relationship which they have not constituted, but which is constitutive for their being. . . . This structure . . . confronts us with the obligation of shaping these relationships: we are related in order to relate."[9]

Fourth, lovers share life. To the degree they are able, they do things together. Their shared activity adds a new dimension to their individual efforts. "What" they do, and not just their motive, is different. Two friends who go to see a movie together are doing something different from two other people who happen to sit next to one another in the movie theater. The first pair is sharing an activity as part of their friendship; the other two are not. For a theology of philanthropy, the most fundamental "sharing" is cooperation between God and us in giving and receiving. As Pope Benedict XVI wrote: "Love of God leads to participation in the justice and generosity of God towards others."[10]

Our cooperation with God does not follow the sort of "logic" that characterizes individual transactions. If, at least for the purpose of discussing philanthropy, we set aside "miracles," then we discover a strange mathematics. Stated cryptically, 100 percent plus 100 percent equals 100 percent, and 100 percent plus nothing makes nothing. Stated more clearly, theologians such as Aquinas or Calvin argue that the work we do is wholly ours and wholly God's.[11] Without God we can do nothing, but also without us what the Spirit wants to do through us will not happen. In this context, then, the activity of donors is enormously important. The work they accomplish is of great significance not just to recipients but also to God. Without donors' cooperation, God fails in God's effort to bring about good through them.

Needless to say, many donors, Christian and otherwise, are oblivious to the religious dimension of their action. In fact, if they are atheists, they would deny that they are cooperating with God. Still, a theology of philanthropy understands that their activity is itself an invitation from God to share in God's attitudes toward good and evil.

In brief, I have tried to establish a theological framework that connects God and philanthropy. I've resisted the leap most theologians make when they jump from God's gift to our moral obligations. For example, Luke Timothy Johnson writes, "Since faith sees our selves as gifted . . . the logic of faith is to share that gift with others."[12] No explanation is given for this "logic." The more plausible conclusion would be that since faith sees our selves as gifted, faith leads us to give thanks to God and to enjoy the gifts we have been given. Thus, I have not taken the common path to connecting the two great commandments, namely, that we should love our neighbor because the sovereign God has commanded us to do so. I also have not used as my starting point the argument that the creator God has so made us that, if we want to attain our fulfillment, we must give to others. Instead, by starting with "God is love," I have tried to show how God's love for us and our love for God lead to love for our neighbors. Let me now turn to what I mean by "love."

LOVE

The Greek roots of the word *philanthropy*, of course, mean "love of humans." Aquinas similarly locates the very meaning of acts of philanthropy in love: "Love has the nature of a first gift, through which all free gifts are given."[13] In this part of my essay, I consider the meaning of love and three kinds of love.

NATURE OF LOVE

Though often named, love is rarely defined or even well described. Summarizing what I have written elsewhere, let me say that love is an emotion through which we participate in someone or something in such a way that we are inclined to the realization of its greater good.[14] That definition, of course, pales in comparison to the experience of love, but it is serviceable. I want to highlight a few of its features with reference to philanthropy.

Love involves emotion.[15] It is not just benevolence (to will the good) or beneficence (to do the good). Put simply, we have to care about those we help. We have to "like" the people we love, even if our liking is only an affective appreciation of their humanity. Moreover, as an emotion, love is a form of perception that is correlative to value. That is, it "sees" recipients under the aspect of their value/disvalue qualities. Thus, to be truly an act of philanthropy, an act must involve some kind of affection for recipients and be focused on what is good or bad about them. Lastly, although this essay concentrates, though not exclusively so, on love for persons, we can also love animals, foods, mountains, ideals such as world peace, and so forth. Importantly, humanitarian love may be the motivation behind philanthropic activity that is devoted to changing unjust social structures (see Bangert, chapter 4 in this volume).

Philanthropy, if it is a form of love, is also a kind of participation. The word *participation* tries to account for two essential features that need to be held in tension: unity and difference. Put simply, participation means "unity-in-difference." The unity is made possible by difference, and the difference is accented by the unity. Those who are needy in terms of time, talent, or treasure meet those who are rich in these goods. Together, they can create a better world or, at least, a less-bad world. Their union is not properly described as "identification" since the parties retain their own identity. Rich people do not suddenly become scientists just because they support a scientific project; scientists do not become good businesswomen just because they are supported by such entrepreneurs. Rather, their unity is made possible by their differences. But reciprocally, their cooperation enables them to be more distinctly who they are. Similarly, God becomes, if I might use this strange expression, more distinctly God in cooperating with us, and we become more who we most fundamentally are in cooperating with God. That is, God becomes, in and through us, our creator, redeemer, and sanctifier; and we become more fully redeemed and sanctified creatures.

The third feature of love relevant to philanthropy is that it is directed to the realization of the good. This might seem self-evident, but it deserves some clarification. The most basic point is that love promotes the flourishing of the beloved. Rather than making the recipient a "dependent," Leon Kass rightly argues, "the exercise of compassion-rightly-practiced is centrally concerned with enabling the recipient to become more willing and able to choose better and to accept responsibility in the future."[16] Rather than humiliating a fellow human being, gifts to persons must enable them to better appreciate their dignity as children of God and thus their worthiness to receive gifts. To be directed to the good of the recipient does not mean that love will always be successful. It can be misguided or ineffective.[17] But, as Kant might point out, the moral goodness of an act of philanthropy does not depend on whether it succeeds. If one fails, one still has acted in a morally good way. Even God all too frequently is not successful.

The fourth feature is that love is directed to any "object" that is, or that can become, good. For the philanthropist, this includes, in quite different ways, individual human beings, communities, institutions, ideals, and so on. Love must also be directed to those whom Leon Kass calls the "foolish brother" and the "naturally unlovable."[18] St. Paul insisted that God loved us "while we were still sinners" (Rom. 5:8). God did not wait until we overcame our sins and deserved salvation. In terms of one strand of theology, we are by creation good and loveable; in terms of another strand of theology, God loves us even when we are foolish or sinful. Philanthropists can participate in this love.

KINDS OF LOVE

There is a further set of clarifications about love needed for a theology of philanthropy. Commonly, theologians and philosophers use three different Greek words for love: *agape, eros,* and *philia.*[19] Unfortunately, there is little or no agreement on what these terms mean. For example, Plato held that eros brings us to God, while in the minds of some Christians, eros brings us to the gutter. I distinguish among these three by one simple criterion: for whose sake are we loving?

I use *agape* when we love for the sake of the beloved. Although agape is often taken to be the distinctively Christian love, Aristotle called attention to it long before Christ.[20] Similarly, Rabbi Moses Maimonides described the highest degree of love in the following way: "The donor gives in such a way as to enable someone unknown to him to become self-sufficient; the beneficiary does not learn the name of the donor and loses no self-respect."[21] Love in this form is highly likely to be "for the sake of" the recipient; that is, it is agape.[22] On the other hand, it is also likely to be the love in which there is the least personal unity between the donor and recipient.

I use *eros* when we love for our own sake. Eros is a genuine love in that it affectively affirms its beloved. It does so, however, on the condition that the good of the beloved redounds to the good of the lover. Because of this, sexual love is usually thought of as eros. We also should have an eros love for God, since we find fulfillment in loving God that can be gotten in no other way. Biblically, that fulfillment has been pictured as banquets in heaven, and its opposite as fires in hell.

I use *philia* when we love for the sake of a community we belong to. In philia, we act for the sake of the union we have with others. We not only give and receive, we also belong. For example, we come to a Sunday service not only to give thanks (agape), not only to receive God's Word and blessing (eros), but also to enact our communion with God and with other believers. We gather—to use an early Christian phrase—as "friends of God,"[23] or—to use another venerable phrase—as brothers and sisters of Christ. We exercise philia when our actions are manifestations of our belonging to God and to one another.

There are occasional times and places for pure agape. There are vastly more occasions for a vibrant eros. There are a great variety of relationships within which we exercise philia. Usually, we have mixed loves,[24] with one or the other kind of love being at the forefront. Our philia relationships of friendships and families are especially full of such mixtures. Many institutions that people support, such as the hospitals described by Katz (chapter 9) and Failer (chapter 3), were founded to express and promote philia relationships. The biblical God who invites us into a covenant also manifests all of these loves.[25] In what follows, I try to show the place of all three loves in a theology of philanthropy.

PHILANTHROPY

As I began my research on a theology of philanthropy, I ran into two surprising obstacles. The first is that there is enormous ambiguity about just what counts as philanthropy.[26] The second is that the theological literature on philanthropy is extraordinarily thin. In this part of my essay, I give a rough description of philanthropy, and in the following I will reflect on the role of religion in philanthropy.

EXPANSIVE TERM

The contemporary meaning of philanthropy, with overtones of development offices and mass mailings, is a relatively new phenomenon. Philanthropy has been undergoing considerable evolution over the past century. Partly due to this change, there is no stable meaning for the term. In most contexts, what is important is the philanthropic gift, not the label.[27] We need not decide whether giving food to a starving beggar is, as some say, a philanthropic act, while others say it is a matter of charity, and still others say it is an act of justice.[28]

The root meaning of philanthropy, love of human beings, points in the right direction but is far too inclusive.[29] For example, since our children are human beings, we could say that a mother's love for her child is philanthropy. Similarly, it is correct to insist, as some do, that philanthropy aims at a "melioration of the human condition,"[30] but most morally good activities do this. Brushing our own teeth improves the human condition, but it is not "philanthropy." Another oft-cited characteristic is that philanthropy must be directed not to private concerns but rather to the "public good."[31] This characteristic also does useful but still very rough service, because the wall between public and private is so porous. Creating a family is a great public good, indeed, the foundation of society. But few think of a family as a philanthropy. Similarly, painting the picket fence around our home may add more beauty to the neighborhood than painting a wire fence around a nearby park, but the first would likely be called a private good, while the second would be a "public good."

Without pretending to provide a definition, I will use the word *philanthropy* restrictively to refer to the coordinated donation of goods from one or more persons who care to promote some non-private good. This coordination frequently takes place through an institution set up to collect and channel the goods. The goods are donated in that they are not required by government or by a commercial transaction. These donations include money, services, and association.[32] The goods promoted range, on the human level, from well-fare needs (minimum necessities) to well-being goals (human flourishing). On the subhuman level, the goods promoted include, for example, protection of animals or the preservation of a coral reef. For simplicity sake, I most commonly refer not to "time" or "talent" but to "treasure."

The term "religious giving" can refer either to the religious activity of giving or to that giving which goes to explicitly religious enterprises. While Rooney (chapter 1) concentrates on the second meaning, I, like Schervish (chapter 7), use the term in the first sense. As I shall later observe, a question can be raised about whether much giving to religious organizations is properly philanthropy.

DEEDS AND ACTS

In considering the giving of gifts, we do well to make a distinction between "philanthropic deeds" and "acts of philanthropy." This distinction can be made clearer by considering a parallel distinction between "loving deeds" and "acts of love." The phrases ordinarily are synonyms, so I admit to using them stipulatively. Suppose that a young woman is paid to take care of a wealthy man's children. Since she is paid so well, she makes an extra effort so that these children are very well cared for. Suppose, however, that she really doesn't like these "spoiled brats." If so, then she does "loving deeds" for them, but not "acts of love." On a bad day, she might even be tempted to strangle these urchins, but she treats them gently and playfully because she doesn't want to lose her job.

With this parallel in mind, we may distinguish between "philanthropic deeds" and "acts of philanthropy." The distinction turns on the possibility that we can do good deeds for reasons that are unrelated to those goods. That is, we may contribute to philanthropy, thereby doing philanthropic deeds, but our reasons may be quite unrelated to a desire to act philanthropically. Studies show that people donate for many reasons unrelated to philanthropy. One person gives out of guilt for legally inherited, but unearned, wealth.[33] A second gives due to social pressure. A third volunteers at a children's hospital because she is lonely, and a fourth volunteers on weekends to build up his résumé. Each person is doing a philanthropic deed; however, none of them are doing "acts of philanthropy" unless they are also motivated by some kind of love for the human beings (or other recipients) they help.

At first glance, this distinction is irrelevant to anyone except the donors themselves. Those who manage a philanthropic enterprise often neither can nor need to find out why donors give.[34] Their primary role is to connect donor and recipient and to ensure that good is done for the recipient.[35] They do not inquire about motivations not only because this might limit donations but especially because the donor's gift is still a philanthropic deed no matter what motivates it.

Still, matters are not so simple. Philanthropy managers must also be at least somewhat concerned for the agent of philanthropy and not just focused on the philanthropic deed. Clearly, if the donor were *non compos mentis*, the manager would ordinarily be wrong to take the gift, no matter how much good could be done with it. The same could be said of money that was stolen or coerced. While it is very difficult, and indeed often an invasion of privacy, for the manager to pry into the motives of the donor, some inquiry may be morally required, at least if there is any question that in doing good for the recipients one would be facilitating the dehumanization or sin of the donor. Managers must want not only to help donors avoid sin but also to help them act in a morally virtuous way (see Schervish, chapter 7). Thus, out of consideration for the good that giving does for the donor, a philanthropic institution might accept gifts that, on balance, contribute little to its goals. For example, a philanthropy might accept a $5.00 gift, knowing full well that the solicitation and thank-you letter cost $6.00.

RELIGION AND PHILANTHROPY

It might seem obvious that Christian faith would promote the kinds of good works that philanthropies do. But as is common in life, matters are not so neat. Scripture itself has been used to stifle the philanthropic impulse. Ripe for promoting self-interest by the rich is the parable in which Jesus says that those who invest wisely will be given even more, while those who do not invest will be deprived even of what little they have been given. As Johnson observes, "Scripture's frequent directions concerning possessions . . . are so bewilderingly diverse and even contradictory that virtually any practice with respect to money and the stuff it buys and the boxes for storing the stuff can find biblical support somewhere."[36]

It is not surprising, then, that religion's critics have found much to be critical about. When Marx decried religion as the "opium of the masses," he was pointing to the way religion supported the economic status quo. "Liberation theology" in the twentieth century was born in reaction to long-standing Christian teaching that urged people to seek the things of heaven and to make no effort to improve the things of this earth.[37] In the Protestant tradition, Martin Luther likewise denounced those who tried to promote equality between the classes.[38] Calvin's theology suggested that the possession of riches was a sign of God's favor, while a lack of wealth was a sign of God's disfavor.[39] And, although Wesley's triad of "Gain all you can, save all you can, give all you can" surely did support philanthropy, the literal practice of its third injunction would have hindered its impoverished hearers from climbing out of their poverty.

Still many, perhaps most, religious persons who give to philanthropy think of themselves as at least partially motivated by their faith commitments. What theologians have failed to provide them, however, is a plausible theology of philanthropy. This must be remedied.

As we have seen, those who welcome God's love are moved to respond by forming a communal relationship with God. As part of that relationship, they want to cooperate with God in what God is doing. Since the Christian tradition holds that what God is doing is—to use broad strokes—creating, sustaining, redeeming, fulfilling, and sanctifying creation, then

Christians who love God will cooperate with God in these activities.[40] As David Smith insists: "Christian tradition puts the issue starkly: God gives; those who identify themselves with God's cause must also give."[41] My earlier analysis sets the framework for explaining why we "must also give."

We finite humans, of course, cooperate in extremely small ways. Still, we can and should think of ourselves as created co-creators, sustained co-sustainers, redeemed co-redeemers, and so forth. As God did for Abram (Gen. 12:2–3), God not only blesses us but also makes us to be a blessing to others. This vision of Christian life renews one important strand in the history of theology. Following Augustine and his war against Pelagianism, theology often emphasized a "one-sided or unilateral initiative of God toward humanity." There is another strand—central to this essay—that insists on a twofold relation. This second strand "emphasizes the co-workership between covenantal partners."[42] We are "God's fellow workers" (1 Cor. 3:9; 1 Thess. 3:2).[43]

God acts not only through individuals but also through communities and institutions. For example, the church "is the medium and instrument of God's creative and re-creative action in constituting and reconstituting identity and dignity. The church's acts therefore must be sacramental in the most radical sense of becoming iconic for the action of God."[44] God sanctifies through churches, but God also builds mountain trails through Sierra Clubs and creates new forms of life through university labs.

This is the crux of this essay: God works in and through philanthropies. Seen from a theological perspective, philanthropies are institutions through which human beings cooperate with God. The Spirit of God accomplishes divine goals through the conjoined efforts of those who participate in philanthropic work, whether as donors, as managers, or as recipients. The Spirit does not "use" human beings but instead invites them to cooperate (see Wheeler, chapter 5 in this volume). The Holy Spirit does not want them to be passive but expects them to make their own distinctive contribution to this cooperative action. Through them, God engages in ongoing action in the world.

Is it necessary, then, to believe in this God before one might be inspired to be a benefactor? Clearly not. All humans can, and most do, develop some degree of the virtue of generosity. As Miroslav Volf comments, "We *are* givers because we were made that way." Selfishness, he adds, cuts against this natural grain: "We are at odds with ourselves."[45] David Smith points out that Aristotle held up for highest esteem the great-souled person who "did not think that one could live the good life by simply looking out for oneself. Rather, he thought, the good life required using one's resources to benefit one's community."[46] Indeed, this pagan philosopher opined that it would not make much sense to want possessions if one could not thereby share them with friends and community.[47] Building on this natural generosity, there is also a graced virtue called "charity." In other words, the atheist's philanthropic acts are naturally good acts, while the believer's acts are additionally acts of graced charity.[48]

Is faith, then, irrelevant or incidental to philanthropy? Two quite different answers should be given. On the one hand, the deeds we do are separate from the motives we have. Thus, it is not necessary that those who are, in fact, cooperating with God be themselves believers. That is, atheistic or agnostic philanthropists cooperate with God, whether they want to or not, whenever their work properly overcomes evil and promotes what is good. For example, an atheist might contribute to the Jesuit Refugee Service, not for religious reasons but because her parents were once refugees. She cooperates with God, who wants to "redeem the captives," even if she does not imagine that she is cooperating. Conversely, those who believe they are cooperating with God may not, in fact, be doing so. For example, a Muslim might donate to a family charity in Iraq, not knowing that, contrary to her own personal beliefs, the money will be used to encourage suicide bombers.

On the other hand, it does make a difference when we know what we are doing. In fact, the "what" is itself transformed. The person of faith realizes that she and God together are installing sewers in Guatemala. That is, the person of faith realizes that what she and God are doing is enacting their relationship. Their co-activity flows from and in turn contributes to their philia relationship. It does so in a way that is over and above the good work achieved. Since "what we are doing" takes its meaning in part from the intentions of the agents, wanting to cooperate with God adds a philia meaning to the good worldly activity we are engaged in. While we can de facto cooperate with someone we do not know or love, there is a new and richer meaning when we are acting together with the One we know and love. In sum, God loves, and out of that love God wants to overcome evil and to promote the good. We who love God want to cooperate in God's work.

SPIRITUAL AND MATERIAL GIVING

The highest gifts we can give are spiritual gifts. The donor is not diminished but increased by the giving of a spiritual gift. Teachers learn as they

teach. Those who love grow in the capacity to love. In general, the exercise of a spiritual virtue increases that virtue, while the lack of its exercise
leads to its diminishment. In Jesus' paradoxical phrase, those who lose their
lives gain them, while those who save their lives lose them (Matt. 10:39).

When people think of philanthropy, however, they are more likely to
focus on giving material gifts, especially gifts of money. Nevertheless, these
material gifts can and should also be forms of self-giving. As Johnson
observes, "The way we dispose of our possessions is the symbol of our spiritual commitments, just as the disposition of our bodies enacts the desires
of our heart."[49] Unfortunately, the self-giving character of donating money/
material is obscured by a contrast that the Christian tradition makes between being and having. The valid insight of this contrast is that a poor
person is not less valuable because she does not have many possessions.
The mistake, however, is the way this contrast denies the experiential fact
that we are in part constituted by our material possessions.[50] As a parallel,
I might note that I both "am" and "have" my body. My arm is really me,
but if I lose the arm I have, I am still me. So also, in lesser ways, I both am
and have my possessions.[51] We feel personally violated when one of these
appendages of our selves is harmed or stolen, especially when such things
are close to our selves, such as our home or our lecture notes or our son's
bronzed baby shoes. If our "having" were not part of our being, then giving of what we have could not rightly be experienced as self-giving.

Perhaps surprisingly, one thing we have that can be quite distant from
who we are is money. Of course, money often represents many personal
matters that are quite close to our selves: security, self-sufficiency, status,
freedom, and so forth. But as Marx might say, money is abstract in the
sense that it is nearly nothing in itself and it can stand for nearly anything.
$10,000 represents two season tickets to the opera, and it represents two
irrigation wells for a Rwandan village. To the degree that people already
have what money represents—and of course many people seem never to
be able to be secure about their status, freedom, power, and so forth—to
that degree they can give away a considerable amount of money without
significant loss to their person, that is, without a sense of having made
a significant self-gift. Jesus' comparison of several rich people's large
donations with the widow's small coins illustrates this difference: "All of
them have contributed out of their abundance, but she out of her poverty
has put in all she had to live on" (Luke 21:4). The implication is that the
widow is the one who made the truly deep gift of herself (cf. Bangert,
chapter 4).

When material giving is truly a self-gift, it expands or transforms the donor; that is, it has a spiritual effect on the donor.[52] In giving, we participate in larger enterprises than the conduct of our own personal or immediate life. We belong to a larger sphere that entices and challenges us in otherwise unavailable ways. If that sphere is noble, we are ennobled by our participation. If that sphere is dehumanizing *but* we share in God's uplifting effort to ameliorate that condition, we are divinized.[53] We also, typically, participate in a larger community of givers. Frumkin insightfully observes, "The very act of giving can and should be understood as a core civil society activity, which contributes both to the formation of social capital and to the functioning of democracy."[54] Giving is an important way of sharing in the life of the community, especially the church, so much so that, as Mary Oates observes, "Those who do not give in accord with their means . . . are not full participants in its life."[55] Johnson draws an appropriate conclusion: "For Christians, this means that the faithful sharing of possessions is not simply a matter of individual faith but must express the faith of the community as well."[56]

SELF-INTEREST

Most of what I have written thus far is irrelevant, according to Alan Buchanan. In his view, "the dominant theory of donation has shifted from characterizing giving as an altruistic act to characterizing it as a self-interested bargain."[57]

EGOISM

This shift corresponds to the proposals of many contemporary sociobiologists, economists, and psychologists, who tell us that all evolutionary behaviors, rational choices, and affections are necessarily aimed at promoting our own self-interest.[58] These theorists do not deny that others may also benefit by our deeds. But, they insist, we should be honest that the one for whose sake we act is our own self. Thus, some psychologists explain giving as a way of avoiding aggression (giving before "they" take); others postulate that giving is always motivated by some personal goal such as gaining heaven or creating a memorial for oneself. Furthermore, some educational specialists postulate that "all prosocial behavior is motivated by some form of self-benefit," and many economists think that those who act altruistically are "silly, foolish, or simply guilty of poor judgment."[59] These views are even supported by research that claims givers have seven kinds of motives: (1), guilt, (2) recognition, (3) self-preservation and fear,

(4) tax rewards, (5) obligation, (6) pride or self-respect, and (7) religious, spiritual, or philosophical beliefs.[60] Only the last seems altruistic (see Bangert, chapter 4).

To Christian theology, these claims about egoistic motives are counterintuitive and tell a vastly incomplete story. These theorists sell us only a half-ticket, or rather they pawn off a ticket stub, which is what remains after the more important part of our motivation has been detached. In response to them, three points should be made.

The first point is that such views often contain an elemental confusion between "having an interest in something" and "self-interest."[61] For example, Jon Van Til mistakenly tries to demonstrate the centrality of self-interest when he observes that people seek rewards such as a name on a building or a desired social reform.[62] These two goals are very different. The first is sought as "good for me," and the second is sought as good-in-itself. If a donor has a great interest in reforming education in Uganda, her interest is in the cause itself, not in her own self. To act for goals of one's choosing is not the same as to choose one's self as goal.

The second point is to acknowledge that we always or almost always act with mixed motives.[63] After Freud and his many successors, we know that whenever we act there are motives either outside or only on the periphery of our consciousness. If we have at least some significant concern for the beneficiary, we can still say that our philanthropic deed is not simply a self-interested pursuit. St. Paul preached philanthropy, and the motives he offered were quite mixed. He urged the Philippians to look, not to their own interests, but to the interest of others (Phil. 2:1–8); and the reason he offers is that they thereby imitate Christ. On the other hand, in his second letter to the Corinthians, he appealed to their pride, to their sense of competition, and to their interest in his not being humiliated if they failed in generosity (2 Cor. 8–9).[64] These latter motives do not automatically purge the more altruistic motives behind their gift. There is a legitimate love of self, and this self-interest can itself facilitate genuine concern for others. Sadly, many Christian writers conflate self-love and selfishness, which does exclude concern for others. Rather, self-love can quite appropriately be one Christian motive for doing philanthropic deeds. In fact, the New Testament encourages self-concern by promising to those who do good works that they will themselves be rewarded by God (Matt. 6:1–4).

The third point is that—contrary to the claims of the above theorists—most of us have had important and formative experiences when we did sacrifice ourselves for another's sake. We enacted an almost pure agape. For Christians, the paradigmatic example is Jesus. We say he died to save humanity from its sins (however one understands this teaching); we do not think that what Jesus was really doing was promoting his own self-interest. Similarly, at one point St. Paul writes that it would be more in his own self-interest for him to die and be in heaven with Christ, but he chooses to continue his missionary work because that is better for others (Phil. 1:23).

In brief, it is important to keep in mind "for whose sake" we are acting. Philanthropy may—and indeed, in some sense, always will—benefit the donor. However, if it is given solely for the purpose of benefiting the donor, then it is a philanthropic deed but not an act of philanthropy. If it is also given out of love for the recipient, then to that extent it is an act of philanthropy.

SATISFACTION

While some theorists argue that all philanthropy is self-interested, some theologians insist that philanthropy not only can but must be a purely agapic matter, stripped of all self-interest. They argue that the presence of any satisfaction in giving or any expectation of getting a response will pollute philanthropy.[65] This "purist" view of philanthropy is mistaken in at least two ways.

It is a common mistake to infer from the satisfaction we derive from giving that we must be acting "for our own sakes." To the contrary, our actions are deficient to the degree that there is no sense of satisfaction. Satisfaction is our nature's way of indicating that we are properly enacting some capacity of our selves. Thus we should expect this satisfaction. Doubtless, some acts of philanthropy are difficult because they involve considerable sacrifice on our part or because we have not yet developed a habit of generosity.[66] But just as a well-trained runner enjoys running, so too, when we have developed a practice of philanthropy, we will enjoy being generous. Living virtuously is satisfying.

Second, as relational beings, we can and often should hope for a response from those we benefit.[67] Friends do not give to one another at Christmas in order to get a return. Rather, they give as part of their ongoing friendship. Still, that friendship itself creates an expectation of some response. The theological approach I have been taking makes the same point: God gives gifts, in part, to develop a covenant or friendship with us. God expects us to respond to these expressions of love, not just by obeying commandments, but by a return love. As Stephen Webb observes:

"Against the idealism of the theologians, most Christians do tend to think of God's love as involved in a process that entails some form of reciprocity."[68] Benefactors deserve at least a "thank you."

OBLIGATORY, VOLUNTARY, AND VOCATIONAL

Acts of philanthropy are obligatory, yet voluntary.[69] They are obligatory in two ways: the needs of others and the need to be a giver.

The needs of others, as Richard De George notes, create an "obligation to help . . . to the extent that we can do so." This side of the Parousia, there will always be some people in great need. The weak version of this obligation says that one must "help others in serious need to the extent that one can do so with little or moderate costs to oneself. A stronger version says that one must do so even at great expense to oneself, although one does not have to make oneself worse off than the person or persons one is helping."[70] The strongest version, modeled on Jesus, who gave his life for sinners, requires at times that one helps others even when this makes one worse off.

We are by nature givers,[71] so giving to others is not only graced co-operation with God's love for and in us but also a fulfillment of that nature. Aquinas observed that, to the degree we experience our own genuine goodness, we will want to share with others. We use our freedom to consent to this natural movement toward sharing. But what if one is poor? One religious teacher cleverly recommended that one poor person should give to another poor person some small item, which the second person then gives back, so that both can thereby fulfill their duty to be givers and experience the benefits of giving.[72] This sage recognized that giving is necessary for growing. Those who don't give, shrivel. We see this insight in the strange reason that Ephesians 4:28 gives for why thieves should stop stealing and get a job. The text does not recommend this because it is the honest thing to do. Rather, it urges them to labor "so as to have something to share with the needy."

"Voluntary" does not mean arbitrary or without reason. Philanthropic managers respect donors' freedom when they try to make a "compelling" case for a donation. If, to take a different kind of example, someone offered to pay for our dream cruise to the Bahamas, we might say, "What else could I do but accept? I had no choice!" Freedom is deepened, not taken away, by persuasive reasons. Frequently, our obligation to give will feel like an opportunity rather than an obligation (Cf. Bangert, chapter 4). If the goal is attractive or if we have already developed the virtue of generosity, we likely will experience joy in giving. A sense of "duty" or a need to exert extra effort arises chiefly when we are only minimally virtuous or when, as is also common, we experience inner conflict among competing obligations.

Not infrequently—indeed, usually—we have many competing obligations to fulfill. Prudence then must be exercised. Even so, prudence ought not to dampen too much the way love moves us to be generous.[73] God's love as manifest in Jesus Christ was far more excessive than prudent. With the crucifixion in mind, the author of Ephesians exhorts: "Therefore be imitators of God, as beloved children, and live in love, as Christ loved us and gave himself up for us, a fragrant offering and sacrifice to God" (5:1–2). Even so, donors often must choose among various worthy causes. As Johnson wisely comments, "Between faith professed and faith enacted, therefore, lies discernment. . . . [Faith] must discern in the constantly altering face of real life the appropriate way."[74] Discernment, in a theological sense, requires not only a good analysis of the needs and opportunities of various people in the world. It also requires a sense of what befits our unique relationship with God, that is, our vocation (see Schervish, chapter 7).

Many things that are good in themselves are not consistent with who we are with God. While God may want to bring about all good, God does not want to do all good through us. If I am an excellent Spanish teacher, then it is likely that God does not want me to become a research chemist. It rarely, if ever, is our vocation to do the "most important thing possible." Rather, it may be that our own pet project or our own peculiar interest is exactly what God wants to pursue through us.[75] God often guides us through these personal attractions and repulsions, which vary over time. As Johnson comments: "The response of faith is never once for all, but is a lifelong series of responses to a God who constantly moves ahead of us."[76]

APPROPRIATE RECIPIENTS

The beneficiaries of our gifts range from the most concrete to the most abstract and from the most personally related to those with whom we share only a common humanity (or even creaturehood). On one end of the spectrum, we have the mother who donates blood to assist her child's surgery; on the other end, we have people like Warren Buffet, who seems to have said: "Bill and Melinda Gates, here's thirty billion dollars; do some good with it." Some philanthropists legitimately have what might be called a Kantian mindset. They want to help humanity or creation; only secondarily do they want to help particular human beings or creatures. In

Christian theology, the foundation for this approach is a set of claims: God has made all creatures good; God has given all persons extraordinary dignity; and God wants us to participate in developing the goodness of God's creation.[77]

Much philanthropy, however, is far more targeted. Even appeals to help distant people often are accompanied by a picture of some starving child with an empty rice bowl.[78] There is some warrant in theology for giving to those we are more closely related to, for example, to poor people in one's neighborhood rather than to poorer people in a distant land. Such discernment can be complex, as when Siddiqui (chapter 2 in this volume) observes that the maxim "Charity begins at home" means that he, an American, has a primary obligation to the poor in Pakistan, his family's country of origin. Because we are relational beings, we must participate in the lives of others; because we are finite, we can participate only in an attenuated way in groups that are distant from our daily lives; because we are unique, we need to participate in a few "special relationships" that allow particular aspects of ourselves, especially intimate aspects, to come forth. For example, a father has more obligations to his daughter than to the daughter of an unknown family in China. God cares for different aspects of us through these various kinds of relationships.

This variation in recipients mirrors God's relation to our fellow human beings. On one end of the spectrum, God loves all human beings just as human beings. On the other end, God has a special relationship with each human being, so much so that Aquinas argued that God loves some people more than others. Similarly, Jesus is said to have died for all human beings. Still, he cured people only in a tiny region of the world; he preached to a small number, explaining what he meant to an even smaller number; and he had a special affection for the disciple John. These special relationships raise both a theoretical and an ethical issue.

The theoretical issue is whether special relationships can be properly called recipients of philanthropy. Gifts to our children are not philanthropic. Similarly, donations to our local church, synagogue, mosque, or temple for its religious worship and upkeep may not be philanthropic. These donations look rather like membership dues paid to one's nonprofit country club.[79] A church or mosque, it seems to me, is a philanthropic recipient only if one gives to it as a way of supporting the institution beyond the way it contributes to one's own self, for example, by compensating for noncontributing members or by funding care for people outside its own community.

The ethical issue with "special relationships" arises when, as often happens, philanthropic gifts seem, prima facie, to be contrary to social justice. The largest quantity of philanthropic giving in the United States sustains or increases social inequality. The corporation that donates to the opera benefits the rich far more than the poor. The tax break given to those in the highest income bracket allows the wealthy to donate money to Harvard's thirty-five billion dollar endowment, money that otherwise might be used by the government to support a community college that serves recent immigrants.[80] The individual who donates a new copy of the Torah to her wealthy synagogue is not using that money to help a poor mosque across the tracks. Thus, there is a moral obligation for donors to discern who or what is the morally appropriate focus for their gifts (see Schervish, chapter 7).

INSTITUTION

When examining philanthropy, we have to keep in mind not only the donors and the ultimate beneficiaries but also mediating institutions such as UNICEF or the Red Cross. Thus, as a final consideration, I want to glance at the institutional side of philanthropy. More and more philanthropic activity is being bureaucratized. Oates has charted certain changes in religious philanthropy from the nineteenth to the twenty-first centuries. What were initially decentralized groups of poor and middle-class Christians responding to local needs grew eventually into much more efficient and effective bureaucracies. This development created what she describes as a paradox in Christian philanthropy. "By adopting secular standards in organization and fundraising, and by relying heavily on extra-ecclesial funding, it has vastly expanded its capacity to assist the poor and to offer high-quality services. Yet in critical ways these strategies compete with primary religious values."[81] Among such values is the personal interaction between donor and recipient. Such personal contact is not developed, or not developed as well, when donations are mediated through philanthropic institutions.[82]

To be sure, arrangements are occasionally made so that the very wealthy can make such personal contacts. But the small donor most frequently will not have that contact. When people speak disparagingly of "just writing a check," they are not disdainful of the good being done. Rather, they point to the affective emptiness that stems from lack of personal contact. Because money is abstract, writing a check to the telephone company and writing a check to a philanthropy begins to feel similar.

As philanthropy becomes ever more institutionalized, how can this need for personal involvement be satisfied? William May suggests that "we may be moving into a period in which we need to sustain two types of social organization." On one end of the spectrum, in addition to government and corporations, we need major philanthropies. These large philanthropies may be corporately endowed, like the Lilly Endowment; or, like the Catholic Refugee Service, they may be supported by many thousands of otherwise unrelated donors. On the other end of the spectrum, May suggests, we also need small-scale, informal, spontaneous communities that keep the spirit of personal involvement alive.[83] At this end of the scale we find a battered women's shelter sponsored by a small parish or the local chapter of Habitat for Humanity.

Peter Frumkin points to another way in which personal involvement can and should be increased. He notes that, with the rise of large public philanthropies, the "private values, commitments, passions, and perspectives of individual donors are slowly overwhelmed by more agnostic, uncontroversial, and acceptable procedural values of professional staff."[84] Thus, there is a need for philanthropies that facilitate the particular goals and passions of unique donors. Without the latter, many ethically important though unpopular causes will go unsupported and unrealized. Through them, on the other hand, donor involvement can increase.

CONCLUSION

As population has grown, as the concerns of the world become everyone's concerns, as human life grows ever more complex, as wealth increases both in the amount owned and in the number of owners (see Schervish, chapter 7), the practice of philanthropy has had to change. It will continue to do so. This essay has tried to help givers be aware of theological resources that can guide that change.

I have rooted philanthropy in the virtue of love. What is still needed is greater clarity about how love works within institutions.[85] I have insisted on the essential connection for a Christian between God's action and that of the believer. What is also needed is greater clarity about how God uses institutions to achieve God's goals. I have indicated how self-transcendence and self-interest affect the practice of philanthropy. What is also needed is clarity about how institutional practices modify this transcendence and interest. Christians regularly pray, "Thy kingdom come." Our acts of philanthropy are ways we practice what we pray.

NOTES

1. William McManus, "Stewardship and Almsgiving in the Roman Catholic Tradition," in *Faith and Philanthropy in America: Exploring the Role of Religion in America's Voluntary Sector,* ed. Robert Wuthnow et al. (San Francisco: Jossey-Bass, 1990), 117–19; Risto Saarinen, *God and the Gift: An Ecumenical Theology of Giving* (Collegeville, Minn.: Liturgical Press, 2005), 2.

2. I use a phenomenological or experiential approach. Robyn Horner, in *Rethinking God as Gift: Marion, Derrida, and the Limits of Phenomenology* (New York: Fordham University Press, 2001), 19, describes phenomenology as the effort to pay exacting attention to what is given in consciousness and to how it is given, or, put more simply, to what we experience and to how we come to have that experience.

3. Edward Vacek, S.J., "Divine-Command, Natural-Law, and Mutual-Love Ethics," *Theological Studies* 57 (1996): 633–53. In chapter 7 of this volume, Schervish argues that, at least for wealthy donors, God the admonisher also may inhibit donations.

4. Doubtless, each of these images of God, since they have been so much a part of Christian tradition, protects an essential dimension of the Christian life. Something similar can be said for less well-known images of God, such as rock, mother, lord, or husband.

5. Edward Vacek, S.J., *Love, Human and Divine: The Heart of Christian Life* (Washington, D.C.: Georgetown University Press, 1994), 116–56.

6. For a study of gratitude, see Edward Vacek, S.J., "Gifts, God, Generosity, and Gratitude," in *Spirituality and Moral Theology: Essays from a Pastoral Perspective*, ed. James Keating (New York: Paulist Press, 2000), 81–125.

7. Edward Vacek, S.J., "The Eclipse of Love for God," *America* 174 (March 9, 1996): 13–16.

8. Edward Vacek, S.J., "Love for God—Is It Obligatory?" *Annual of the Society of Christian Ethics* (1996): 221–47.

9. Christoph Schwöbel, "Recovering Human Dignity," in *God and Human Dignity*, ed. R. Kendall Soulen and Linda Woodhead (Grand Rapids, Mich.: Eerdmans, 2006), 47.

10. Benedict XVI, "On Christian Hope," #28, at www.vatican.va/holy_father/benedict_xvi/encyclicals/documents/hf_ben-xvi_enc_20071130_spe-salvi_en.html.

11. Edward Vacek, S.J., "Inquiring after God when Working," in *Inquiring after God: Classic and Contemporary Readings*, ed. Ellen Charry (Malden, Mass.: Blackwell, 2000), 89–107.

12. Luke Timothy Johnson, "The Life of Faith and the Faithful Use of Possessions," Thomas H. Lake Lecture (April 6, 2006), 4.

13. Thomas Aquinas, *Summa Theologica*, trans. Fathers of the English Dominican Province (Westminster, Md.: Christian Classics, 1948), I:38.2.

14. Vacek, *Love, Human and Divine*, 34–70.

15. On the meaning of emotion, see Vacek, *Love, Human and Divine*, 1–33.

16. Leon Kass, "Am I My Foolish Brother's Keeper?" *Ethics of Giving and Receiving: Am I My Foolish Brother's Keeper?* ed. William May and A. Lewis Soens Jr. (Dallas, Tex.: Southern Methodist University, 2000), 11.

17. Jon Van Til, "Defining Philanthropy," *Critical Issues in American Philanthropy: Strengthening Theory and Practice*, ed. Jon Van Til et al. (San Francisco: Jossey-Bass, 1990), 27.

18. Kass, "Am I My Foolish Brother's Keeper?" 3.

19. Vacek, *Love, Human and Divine*, 157–318.

20. Aristotle, *Nicomachean Ethics*, trans. H. Rackham, Loeb Classical Library (Cambridge, Mass.: Harvard University Press, 1926), 483; cited in Miroslav Volf, *Free of Charge: Giving and Forgiving in a Culture Stripped of Grace* (Grand Rapids, Mich.: Zondervan, 2005), 11.

21. Moses Maimonides, Mishneh Torah, 10:7–15, cited by David Hammack, "Donors, Intermediaries, and Beneficiaries: The Changing Dynamics of American Nonprofit Organizations, in *Good Intentions: Moral Obstacles and Opportunities*, ed. David H. Smith (Bloomington: Indiana University Press, 2005), 185.

22. In my judgment, however, agape is not the highest form of love, and, as I shall later argue, it is not the best basis for philanthropy. God cannot and does not want to practice exclusively this sort of love. The biblical God, upon whom we depend, fosters our self-sufficiency but also knows us and wants to be known and loved by us. Nevertheless, agape has a venerable place in philanthropy.

23. Gilbert Meilaender, *Friendship* (Notre Dame, Ind.: University of Notre Dame Press, 1981), 2.

24. For how emotions are central to morality, see Edward Vacek, S.J., "The Emotions of Care in Health Care," in *Medicine and the Ethics of Care*, ed. Diane Fritz Cates and Paul Lauritzen (Washington, D.C.: Georgetown University Press, 2001), 105–40; and "Passions and Principles," *Milltown Studies* 52 (Winter 2003): 67–94.

25. Vacek, "Gifts, God, Generosity, and Gratitude," 82–84.

26. For example, see David Smith, "Introduction: Doing Good," in *Good Intentions: Moral Obstacles and Opportunities*, ed. David H. Smith (Bloomington: Indiana University Press, 2005), 6–7.

27. Of course, we should seek greater precision to the degree that pragmatic purposes require it. For example, those who develop the tax code need to specify what is and what is not philanthropy.

28. For example, Gerald Freund writes: "There is, however, a fundamental distinction between charity and philanthropy. Funds used for life's essentials, such as food, clothing, shelter, health care, family emergencies, are classified as charity. . . . Philanthropy is distinguished from charity because it has a creative edge. Its purpose is to produce something that does not already exist or to enhance through special recognition and change something that does." See Gerald Freund, *Narcissism and Philanthropy: Ideas and Talent Denied* (New York: Viking, 1996), 13. On the other hand, most histories indicate that one central form of philanthropy in the past (and in the present) is this very work of "charity."

29. Some descriptions may be too restrictive. Should the definition of philanthropy exclude astronomy projects, preservation of wilderness areas, or the prevention of cruelty to animals, since these are not in any obvious way forms of love for humanity?

30. Van Til, "Defining Philanthropy," 20, 32.

31. See "Public Good," http://en.wikipedia.org/wiki/Public_good; see also Van Til, "Defining Philanthropy," 33; Siddiqui, chapter 2 of this volume.

32. Van Til, "Defining Philanthropy," 20, 21, 34.

33. Norman Stryker, "Expunging the Guilt of Unmerited Wealth," in *Gospels of Wealth: How the Rich Portray Their Lives*, ed. Paul Schervish et al. (Westport, Conn.: Praeger, 1994), 111–26. The guilt can also be communal; see Janna Thompson,

"Collective Responsibility for Historic Injustices," *Midwest Studies in Philosophy* 30 (2006): 154–67.

34. In focusing on motive, I proceed differently from authors like Robert Wuthnow, who set aside human intentions, focusing on the deed rather than "love of humanity"; see "Faith and Giving: From Christian Charity to Spiritual Practice" (Indianapolis: Center on Philanthropy at Indiana University, 2004), 4.

35. Peter Frumkin, *Strategic Giving: The Art and Science of Philanthropy* (Chicago: University of Chicago Press, 2006), 376. Again, it exceeds the scope of this essay to take up the responsibility that a philanthropy has to ensure that the recipient uses the gift well, which might include recipient obligations of gratitude and the like.

36. Johnson, "The Life of Faith and the Faithful Use of Possessions," 1.

37. Edward Vacek, S.J., "Work," in *The New Dictionary of Theology*, ed. Joseph Komonchak et al. (Wilmington, Del.: Michael Glazier, 1987), 1098–105; and Vacek, "Inquiring after God when Working," 89–107.

38. David Wagner, *What's Love Got to Do with It?* (New York: New Press, 2000), 78.

39. John Calvin, "Commentary on the Psalms," in Charry, *Inquiring after God: Classic and Contemporary Readings*, 83–86.

40. Edward Vacek, S.J., "John Paul II and Cooperation with God," *Annual of the Society of Christian Ethics* (1990): 81–108.

41. David Smith, "Help or Respect: Priorities for Nonprofit Boards," in May and Soens, *Ethics of Giving and Receiving*, 61.

42. H. Russel Botman, "Covenantal Anthropology: Three Discourses of Human Dignity," in Soulen and Woodhead, *God and Human Dignity*, 84.

43. Benedict XVI, "On Christian Hope," # 35.

44. Schwöbel, "Recovering Human Dignity," 57.

45. Volf, *Free of Charge*, 60. See also Wheeler, chapter 6 in this volume.

46. Smith, "Help or Respect," 61.

47. Aristotle, *Nicomachean Ethics*, 1155a, in *Basic Works of Aristotle*, ed. Richard McKeon (New York: Random House, 1941), 1058.

48. Wuthnow, "Faith and Giving," 12.

49. Johnson, "The Life of Faith and the Faithful Use of Possessions," 6.

50. I disagree, therefore, with the many others who say that we are stewards who, by definition, do not own our own possessions: what we do not own, we cannot give away (cf. Bangert, chapter 4 of this volume). Curiously, as Dempsey (chapter 8) suggests, this theology de-emphasizes trust in God and pictures us as bursars or comptrollers.

51. See Edward Vacek, S.J., "God's Gifts and Our Moral Lives," in *Method and Catholic Moral Theology: The Ongoing Reconstruction*, ed. Todd Salzman (Omaha, Neb.: Creighton University, 1999), 116–17.

52. James Joseph, "Building a Foundation for Faith and Family Philanthropy," in *Faith and Philanthropy: Grace, Gratitude, and Generosity, National Center Journal*, 4 (Washington, D.C.: National Center for Family Philanthropy, 2001), 12; also Stephen Webb, *The Gifting God: A Trinitarian Ethics of Excess* (New York: Oxford University Press, 1996), 124.

53. The dangers of "compassion burnout" or even worse are real, since in addition to the generous love that animates us in such service other aspects of ourselves can be dragged down by the dehumanizing conditions in which we may immerse ourselves.

54. Frumkin, *Strategic Giving*, 375.

55. Mary J. Oates, *Catholic Philanthropic Tradition in America* (Bloomington: Indiana University Press, 1995), 165.

56. Johnson, "The Life of Faith and the Faithful Use of Possessions," 7.

57. Allen Buchanan, "The Language of Fund Raising," in *The Ethics of Asking: Dilemmas in Higher Education Fund Raising*, ed. Deni Elliott (Baltimore, Md.: Johns Hopkins University Press, 1995), 51–52. Similarly, Derrida argues that it is impossible to genuinely give a free gift; see Wing-Chi Ki, "Gift Theory and the Book of Job," *Theological Studies* 67 (2006): 734.

58. Don Browning, "Human Dignity, Human Complexity, and Human Goods," in *God and Human Dignity*, 305–9; see also Robert Solomon, *The Passions* (Garden City, N.Y.: Anchor, 1977), 99; however, it should be noted that Solomon later retracted his view that all emotions are primordially self-interested; see "Lecture XIX *The Passions: Philosophy and the Intelligence of Emotions* (audiocassette by The Teaching Company, 2006).

59. Gary Sapp, "The Psychology of Religious Compassion," in *Compassionate Ministry*, ed. Gary Sapp (Birmingham, Ala.: Religious Education, 1993), 82.

60. Deni Elliott, *The Kindness of Strangers: Philanthropy and Higher Education* (New York: Rowman and Littlefield, 2006), 53–54. See also Roy Menninger, "Observations on the Psychology of Giving and Receiving Money," in *Ethics of Giving and Receiving*, 207–9; Robert Wuthnow, "Improving Our Understanding of Religion and Giving: Key Issues for Research," in *Faith and Philanthropy in America*, 272; Sapp, "Psychology of Religious Compassion," 85–94.

61. Keith Green, "Aquinas's Argument against Self-Hatred," *Journal of Religious Ethics* 35 (2007): 130–31.

62. Van Til, "Defining Philanthropy," 30.

63. Menninger, "Observations on the Psychology of Giving and Receiving Money," 209. Still, philanthropies ought to be aware that offering incentives to donors can, in fact, impede generosity when an act that is mainly motivated by its intrinsic goodness becomes compromised by the prospect of reward. Barry Schwartz, "Money for Nothing," www./nytimes.com/2007/07/02/opinion/02schwartz.html?th&emc=th.

64. Volf, *Free of Charge*, 65–66.

65. Horner, *Rethinking God as Gift*, 4.

66. Kass, "Am I My Foolish Brother's Keeper?" 10, fails to see that philanthropic deeds can be both self-sacrificing and self-fulfilling, though in different senses.

67. See Chi Ki, "Gift Theory and the Book of Job," 729.

68. Webb, *Gifting God*, 127.

69. "We did not think of what we did for others as volunteering, because it was as much a moral imperative as an act of free will" (Joseph, "Building a Foundation for Faith and Family Philanthropy," 6). For another approach to this same tension, see Wheeler, chapter 5 in this volume. The mix of obligation and voluntariness on the part of the *recipient* presents another large set of considerations. See, Vacek, "Gifts, God, Generosity, and Gratitude," 101–18.

70. Richard De George, "Intellectual Property and Pharmaceutical Drugs: An Ethical Analysis," *Business Ethics Quarterly* 15 (2005): 554–59; needless to say, the obligation is modified by many factors, e.g., ability to give, proximity of recipient, urgency, etc.

71. Contemporary evolutionists have come to see the fallacies involved in understanding human beings as just the product of the "selfish gene." See, e.g., Stephen Pinker, "The Moral Instinct," *New York Times Magazine*, January 13, 2008.

72. Elliot Dorff, "Nonprofits and Morals: Jewish Perspectives and Methods for Resolving Some Commonly Occurring Moral Issues," in *Good Intentions*, ed. David H. Smith, 121.

73. Webb, *Gifting God*, 141.

74. Johnson, "The Life of Faith and the Faithful Use of Possessions," 5.

75. Ibid., 6.

76. Ibid.

77. Leon Kass reflects the opposite view of Christian life: "For unlike our natural loves, which are inspired by the beautiful or the virtuous, Christian love is unconditional and unmerited. Indeed, it stands out for its capacity to love the naturally unlovable—not only the poor, the weak, the deformed, and crazed, but even the wicked and vicious" ("Am I My Foolish Brother's Keeper?" 3).

78. Abstract statistical appeals can even hinder generosity; see "To Increase Charitable Donations, Appeal to the Heart—Not the Head," http://knowledge.wharton .upenn.edu/article.cfm?articleid=1767; Nicholas Kristof, "Save the Darfur Puppy," http://select.nytimes.com/2007/05/10/opinion/10kristof.html?th&emc=th.

79. Rob Reich, "Philanthropy and Its Uneasy Relation to Equality," *Philosophy and Public Policy Quarterly* 26 (Summer/Fall 2006): 21–22.

80. Ibid., 17–26.

81. Oates, *Catholic Philanthropic Tradition in America*, 174–75. See www.philanthropy .iupui.edu/Research/WorkingPapers/reconciling_religious_giving_estimates.pdf, and www.eco.utexas.edu/~stuntz/charity1006.pdf.

82. Elliott, *Kindness of Strangers*, 29–46.

83. William F. May, introduction to *Ethics of Giving and Receiving*, ed. May and Soens, xxvii.

84. Frumkin, *Strategic Giving*, 372.

85. See, for example, Edward Vacek, S.J., "Contemporary Ethics and Scheler's Phenomenology of Community," *Philosophy Today* 35 (Summer 1991): 161–74.

Religious Discernment of Philanthropic Decisions in the Age of Affluence

PAUL G. SCHERVISH ————————————————————————

My focus here will be on a *religious discernment process* as a guide for wealth holders in the allocation of their wealth. The hope is that religious discernment—as a key element of religious giving—will shape the spiritual horizons of wealth and philanthropy to the same extent that findings on the ongoing wealth transfer are shaping the material horizons.[1] Providing a religious discernment process is the key ingredient missing from current efforts to expand philanthropy among wealth holders. Implementing a methodology of financial planning and fundraising that is spiritually oriented as well as donor-oriented will create a more respectful and engaging path toward charitable decision making and financial morality in general. The effect will be a *discerned philanthropy*, one that is more highly motivated, personally meaningful, financially magnanimous, socially effective, and culturally formative.

In the first section of the chapter, I review the material and cultural conditions brought about by today's burgeoning financial capacity. The unprecedented nature of these conditions calls for a process of religious discernment that is capable of guiding the use of vast material resources as a tool for deeper purposes. In the second section, I propose that the goal of a discernment process is to develop a moral biography of wealth, and I indicate what makes a moral biography spiritual and religious. In the third section, I identify care of others and the exercise of friendship love as the end of a moral biography. In the fourth section, I discuss the need of wealth holders for a discernment approach in applying their resources to achieve desired ends. In the fifth section, I set out one general approach to discernment whereby, in a context of spiritual or religious reflection, people clarify their philanthropic resources and aspirations, and implement them as a form of discerned philanthropy. In the conclusion, I summarize my argument and suggest the implications for a new spirituality of financial life.

MATERIAL AND CULTURAL CONTEXT
MATERIAL CONTEST

Several distinct forces affecting wealth holders are changing the meaning and practice of wealth allocation. Over the past two decades, the Center on Wealth and Philanthropy (CWP) at Boston College has identified and analyzed these new forces. In particular, our analysis of the ongoing $41 trillion transfer of wealth (measured in 1998 dollars) has changed the way many fundraisers, charities, and financial professionals approach their work.[2] We estimate that over the next five decades, in *2007 dollars*, an unprecedented $52 to $173 trillion in wealth transfer will occur—despite recent economic downturns—and that this will produce between $2.5 and $10.5 trillion in charitable bequests. In a separate projection for the same period, we estimate that lifetime giving will provide an additional $19.4 to $53.3 trillion in charitable contributions. Taken together, charitable bequests and lifetime giving will range from $22 to $64 trillion, with between 52 and 65 percent of this amount being contributed by households with $1 million or more in net worth. Given the fact that the real annual rate of growth in wealth between 1950 and 2006 (including nine recessions) has been over 3.3 percent, there is every reason to expect that the actual wealth transfer and amount of total charitable giving will be closer to the upper estimates than to the lower ones. Over the 25 years from 1980 to 2005, the real annual rate of growth in individual charitable giving has averaged 3.34 percent, and the growth in charitable bequests has averaged 5.09 percent.

CULTURAL CONTEXT

As bountiful as the foregoing projections are, they are based conservatively on current dispositions toward philanthropy. They do not take into account the potential that, under certain identifiable conditions, wealth holders—indeed, the population at large—are likely to become more charitably inclined in the future. It is already clear that charitable giving is spurred by material and spiritual wherewithal.[3] As I discuss in this chapter, I believe philanthropy will be advanced even further to the extent that individuals participate in a process of discernment by which they identify their financial capacity and clarify their personal aspirations.

Today, increasing numbers of individuals are approaching, achieving, or even exceeding their financial goals with respect to their material needs and are doing so at younger and younger ages. A level of affluence that heretofore was the province of a scattering of rulers, generals, merchants, and industrialists has come to characterize whole cultures. Never before have questions like the following, of how to align broad material choice with spiritual character, been placed before such a large segment of the population:

- How can wealth become a tool to achieve the deeper purposes of life, including charitable giving, when acquiring more wealth or augmenting one's standard of living have ceased to be of high importance?
- How can religious discernment help individuals choose and carry out those deeper purposes for the use of their resources?

If wealth holders address the foregoing issues in a conscientious manner, they will increase the probability that something will occur that has never before been possible in history: *a level of wealth that the world has never seen before will accomplish what the world has never been able to do before—to solve so many of its pressing needs for so many of its people.*

THE MORAL BIOGRAPHY OF WEALTH AS A SPIRITUAL AND RELIGIOUS CALLING
MORAL BIOGRAPHY

What I am suggesting here, as a means for aligning material choice with spiritual character, is that wealth holders develop a moral biography. The term *moral biography* refers to the way we conscientiously apply a moral compass to the use of our personal capacity. Moral compass is the array of purposes or aspirations to which we devote our capacity. Personal capacity is simply the set of resources—financial, intellectual, and physical—that we have at our disposal to accomplish our goals. What distinguishes a moral biography of *wealth* is not merely the existence of great financial, intellectual, physical, creative, or personality capacity, but the presence of a moral compass that contains the nobler aims of life for which wealth—and one's other capacities—serve as instruments, that is, to combine prosperity and purpose in a spiritually fulfilling, culturally formative, and socially consequential way.

Much about the essence of a moral biography can be found in Aristotle's *Nicomachean Ethics*. Aristotle reasons that the goal of life is happiness, and that happiness is achieved by closing the gap between where we are and where we want to be. We close this gap by making wise choices, that is, by combining the freedom to choose among a range of alternatives (a matter of personal capacity) with the virtue of practical wisdom (a matter of moral compass)—that is, by living a moral biography.

In more contemporary terms, a moral biography is the daily story of how we, as choosing agents, conscientiously strive to close the gap between where we are today (*genesis*) and where we want to be (*telesis*). Genesis is the set of chosen and unchosen constraints, resources, knowledge, feelings, and values that we bring to our choices—for example, a happy or homeless childhood, a prospering or failing business, a confident or hesitant personality, an affluent or modest financial condition. Telesis is about aspiration; it is the constellation of possibilities, hopes, needs, desires, and interests that mobilize us to transform our past and shape our future.

If genesis is about the past, and telesis is about the future, agency is about what we do in the present. Agency derives from the Latin *agere*, meaning "to do" or "to act." Agency in a moral biography is revealed in the sequence of wise choices that we implement to close the gap between where we are and where we want to be.

THE MORAL BIOGRAPHY OF WEALTH

The difference between a moral biography and a moral biography of wealth is that wealth holders are endowed with such great material capacity that they must work out a moral compass that is as complex and consequential as their capacity. Great capacity, if it is to be in the service of good, must gain its bearing from an especially discerning and wise moral compass. In terms of capacity, wealth holders are not just agents, but hyper-agents. Their wealth makes them world builders. While agents seek to *find* the best place for themselves within existing alternatives, hyper-agents, when they choose, are *founders* of the institutional framework within which they and others live and work. What takes a social, political, or philanthropic movement for agents to accomplish, hyper-agents can accomplish relatively single-handedly. They can design their houses from the ground up, create the jobs and businesses within which they work, tailor-make their clothes and vacations, endow their children, create foundations, and initiate new philanthropic directions.

Just as wealth provides a capacity of great possibilities, it calls for a moral compass wise enough to guide great expectations. Those who have achieved or are close to achieving financial security can have what they want in the material realm and can strive to fulfill their psychological and spiritual needs. Great capacity does not guarantee a conscientious moral compass, but it opens the door to a more responsible one. Those for whom acquiring more wealth is no longer of high importance can choose to develop a moral compass that includes discerning a proper scale of consumption, an appropriate inheritance for their children, a path of personal development, and a strategy for business and investment. But today more than ever before, a moral compass of wealth has come to include, for many, an aspiration to more fully and freely devote their time, talent, and treasure to the philanthropic causes they care about.

SPIRITUAL AND RELIGIOUS MORAL BIOGRAPHIES

Thus far I have used the term *moral* biography to refer to how individuals implement their unique combination of capacities and purposes. I do not use the term "moral" in the narrow sense of ethical precepts or philosophical principles. My use follows that of Emile Durkheim, for whom it means a normative orientation or direction by a full range of formal and informal *mores*—the horizon of laws, customs, and conscience that direct daily practice. What Durkheim does not recognize is the reality of genuine spiritual or religious life in the way today's believers would understand that reality.

In defining the spiritual or religious dimensions of a moral biography, the first thing to note is that there is a close affinity between what may be considered spiritual and what may be designated as religious. Life's questions posed and answered in personal or philosophical language are often indicative of, or answered in terms of, the respondents' religious horizons. By spirituality, I mean the array of deeply seated thoughts, feelings, and actions that individuals pursue in the light of their ultimate origin, ultimate destiny, and ultimate depth. By religiosity, I add to the definition of spirituality the orientation to *devote worship* to the source of their ultimate origin, ultimate destiny, and ultimate depth—that is, as Rudolf Otto says, to *bow their head to the numinous*. According to Otto, such worshipful relation to the numinous entails the experience of awesome dependence and attractive engagement with the holy, even if not explicitly enshrouded with religious terminology. As such, a spiritual moral biography is one lived in the light of ultimate genesis, telesis, and depth. A religious moral biography is one that adds the aspects of worship, for instance, of a divine presence, an ontological being, an ultimate force, or a personal God.

Today it is important to remain open to what constitutes the spiritual or religious experience and language of a moral biography of wealth. For each era, a fresh experience and language of the spiritual or of the Divine needs to emerge. One way they are emerging is through the wealth holders. As wealth holders learn the particulars of their moral biographies through the process of religious discernment, they and those who study and work with them will gradually formulate a constellation of elements for a contemporary experience and language of the Divine.

CARE AND FRIENDSHIP LOVE:
THE PURPOSE OF A MORAL BIOGRAPHY

Thus far I have discussed the material and cultural context of today's wealth holders, the nature of a moral biography, what is distinctive about a moral biography of wealth, and the aspects that make a moral biography of wealth spiritual or religious. Continuing this move from the general to the particular, the next question is: What is the proper content of a moral biography? If the intersection of capacity and purpose constitutes the general framework of a moral biography, what is the *content* that connects capacity and purpose? In all areas of life, but particularly relevant to a moral biography of wealth engaged in charitable giving, the practical content is care and friendship love.

Jesuit philosopher and theologian Jules Toner formulates a notion of care grounded in a phenomenological analysis of *radical love*. Toner defines radical love as the affection by which a lover "affirms the beloved for the beloved's self (as a radical end) . . . [and] by which the lover affectively identifies with the loved one's personal being, by which in some sense the lover is the beloved affectively."[4] If love is the affection of identifying with another as a radical end, care is the practical or implemental aspect of love. As Toner insists, care is love directed at meeting the true needs of others. Figuring out just what the true needs of others are is never easy. But it is always the right question.

We can come upon the deeper content of philanthropy from a second direction. We do this by exploring the root meaning of *philanthropy*, which comes from the Greek words *philia* and *anthropos*—concepts developed ages before the world had any notion that doing good or being financially virtuous was tied to what today we call the nonprofit sector. The two terms in combination are almost always translated simply as "love of humankind." No special attention is given to the particular kind of love connoted by *philia*, although we get a hint of the root meaning when we call *Phila*delphia the City of Brotherly Love.

For Aristotle, *philia*, or friendship love, extends out in concentric circles from the family to the entire species. *Philia* originates in the parent-child bond and becomes expanded to the species in *philanthropeia*. Friendship love is a relation of mutual nourishment that leads to the flourishing of both parties. Just as generosity finds its root in *genus*, the origin of *philia* is connected to *species*. Thus, friendship love implies that, as people mature, mutual nourishment extends to the entire species.

"A friend is another self." "Friends share one soul in two bodies." "One friend loves the other for the other's own sake." Aristotle used these phrases when speaking of the kind of friendship that brings individuals together for mutual benefit. The best friendship is the friendship that inspires all parties to develop their virtues and become more fully their true selves.

It is these profound notions of care and friendship that define the responsibility of all moral biographies and all moral biographies of wealth: we are to meet the true needs of others as we enter into expanding horizons of mutual nourishment. Through discernment, wealth holders heighten their alignment to care and friendship love and choose how to implement them.

DISCERNMENT AND THE NEEDS OF WEALTH HOLDERS

Having affirmed the general content of a moral biography to be care and friendship love, I now elaborate aspects of the discernment process by which that general moral content can become specified for individuals through an inductive spiritual process.

THE NEEDS OF WEALTH HOLDERS

The discernment approach focuses first on the needs of wealth holders. Wealth holders need: (1) to clarify how to apply their resources to achieve a deeper effectiveness and significance in their own life and in the lives of the beneficiaries, and (2) to disentangle themselves from pressure by financial advisors, charities, and financial institutions, whose primary aim is to obtain the use of the wealth holders' assets. The discernment approach is more akin to marketing than to sales strategies. While the goal of a sales strategy is to get people to do what the seller wants them to do, the goal of a marketing strategy is to provide the opportunity for people to choose among an array of options to meet their needs. In the case of wealth holders, a critical need is to clarify and carry out a self-chosen moral purpose for the use of their wealth.

The distinctive trait of wealth holders is that they enjoy the fullest range of choice in selecting and fulfilling who they want to become and what they want to do for themselves, their families, and the world around them. Wealth holders who have achieved or are approaching financial security do not need to own more money. Rather, they need to discern how to make wise choices in the use of their wealth. They need to define their capacities, clarify their moral purposes, and implement the combination of the two in a way that creates a moral biography of wealth for them and an enhanced moral biography for their beneficiaries.

EXISTING APPROACHES

Over the past several years, many new initiatives have been undertaken to expand charitable giving. In a widely circulated report, Dan Siegel and Jenny Yancey of the Donor Initiative Project review "the state of donor education today and a leadership agenda for the road ahead."[5] In 2003 they identified 172 for-profit and nonprofit organizations that participate in some form of donor education to encourage philanthropy. Since that time, the number of donor education programs has expanded. For instance, there has been a dramatic increase in philanthropic advisement programs in financial institutions and independent financial advisement firms. Siegel and Yancey conclude that, despite the abundance of such programs, donor education remains largely a "cottage industry." It is relatively unsystematic, generally works with those who are already connected to the philanthropic world, and does not yet possess a method that attracts the participation of business-oriented wealth holders or generates a consistently positive outcome.

My interviews with wealth holders, financial professionals, and development officers reveal an additional reason for this lack of success. Many of the current programs use a counterproductive "admonishment" approach to donor motivation, as my interviewees attest.[6] This approach seeks to spur philanthropy by setting charitable quotas and admonishing individuals implicitly, if not explicitly, about not giving enough to the right causes at the right time and in the right way. Wealth holders are determined and self-possessed agents who are resistant to being pushed into financial decisions, especially those that are deemed to be voluntary and to have a special personal significance. Many people give regularly and generously, and some form a habitual philanthropic identity that many hope will become more universal. But many wealth holders admit to being stalled at the margins of philanthropy and will not be moved by a hectoring tone. No matter how amiably it is framed, the admonishment model is incapable of generating a culture of self-motivated charitable giving.

NEW DIRECTIONS

Our research shows that it is not innate selfishness or lack of generosity that curtails greater charitable involvement among wealth holders. Nor is it the technical or organizational complexities of implementing a philanthropic strategy. Rather, the curtailment is due to wealth holders' lack of clarity about their financial potential and their charitable aspirations.

I believe that wealth holders (1) have a greater desire for a discernment process than is currently appreciated, (2) find the admonishment model personally offensive and financially simplistic, and (3) would welcome a refined and accessible discernment process for clarifying their philanthropic potential and purposes. Yancey and Siegel support this assessment: "Many organizations that service donors, whether financial or philanthropic, lack either the inclination or skill set to engage donors in the very personal learning journey to assess their own values—what Paul Schervish at Boston College calls 'the discernment process.'"[7] Promoting and developing a discernment process will address the "tremendous shortage of donor educators highly skilled and trained in both the hard and the soft sides of philanthropic education and advising."[8] In addition, the discernment process will appeal to a wider range of wealth holders, especially the self-determined entrepreneurs, executives, and professionals who look to philanthropy as both a field of active financial engagement and a venue for expressing and deepening spiritual life.

DISCERNMENT AS A PROCESS OF GUIDANCE

People of means need to see more clearly through the fog that descends upon them when their task shifts from accumulating to allocating wealth. They need the new spiritual teaching and learning that is developing, in large part, outside formal religious settings. It often springs from the teaching and learning that are guided by a reflective discernment process. Such reflection can occur either through solitary contemplation or through conversation with one's spouse and family, one's pastor, or, increasingly, with financial professionals. Such discernment leads wealth holders to allocate their wealth in accord with what they perceive to be the most effective, significant, and generous way.

The leading motif revolving around discernment and discerned giving is that the responsibilities of philanthropy are best understood and generated, not as deriving from abstract principle or imposed duty alone, but as growing from a spirituality of care. In order not to return to a reliance on deductive precepts, there must be a process of conscientious decision making by which individuals chart what needs to be done and their place in doing it. In the process of discernment, which was originally proposed by Ignatius Loyola, the founder of the Jesuit religious order, and subsequently fleshed out by others, individuals discover their duty, not by eliminating predilections and desires, but by discovering them at a deeper level. According to Jesuit theologian Michael Buckley (1973), discernment is most explicitly and regularly carried out as an encounter with the Absolute; but it is also a process that is relevant for all who are seeking guidance for important decision making.[9] In both its religious and nonreligious contexts, then, discernment is a spiritually attuned process by which individuals review and decide upon the conditions and directions of their decision making.

DISCERNMENT

Figures 1 and 2 outline the key concepts and relationships for applying discerned decision making to the meaning and practice of philanthropy. The term *discern* derives from the Latin *cernere*, "to sift," and *dis*, "apart." The process is thus one of archeological exploration in which the discrete aspects of life are unearthed, sifted through, and ordered into meaningful patterns and purposeful decisions. It is a process of self-reflection, often aided by the questioning and direction of an advisor, by which individuals clarify and make decisions. The discernment process requires a *via negativa*, or an unlearning of the obstacles to voluntary virtue and generosity. It also requires a *via positiva*, or a learning of the aspirations and purposes that spur voluntary virtue and generosity.

Although the discernment process eschews imposing dictates, it does not eliminate duty. Rather, the discernment model allows duty to be self-discovered in an environment of liberty and inspiration, and hence to be more wholeheartedly pursued and sustained. Liberty is material and psychological freedom from unfounded assumptions, fears, and anxieties; inspiration is the array of desires and aspirations that motivate a commitment.

Discernment is a mediating variable in the model of charitable giving in the sense that it influences the way other variables have their effects. In regard to charitable giving, the discernment process first helps individuals

Figure 1
Charitable Giving as a Social Relation of Care

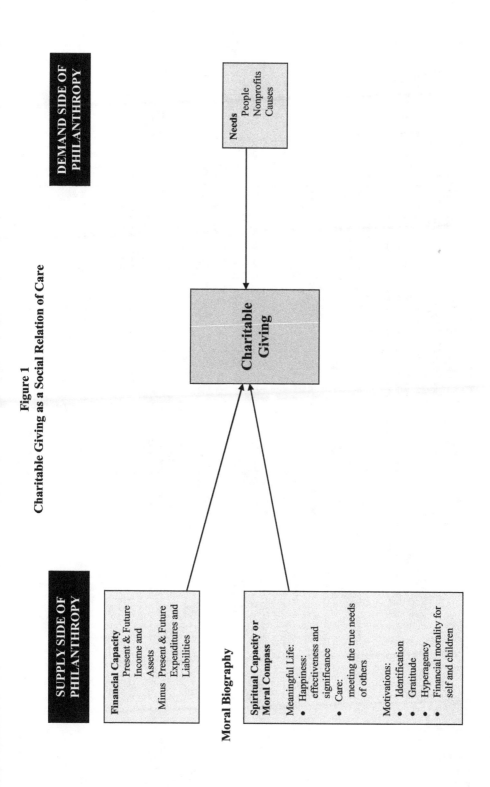

Figure 2
Discerned Philanthropy

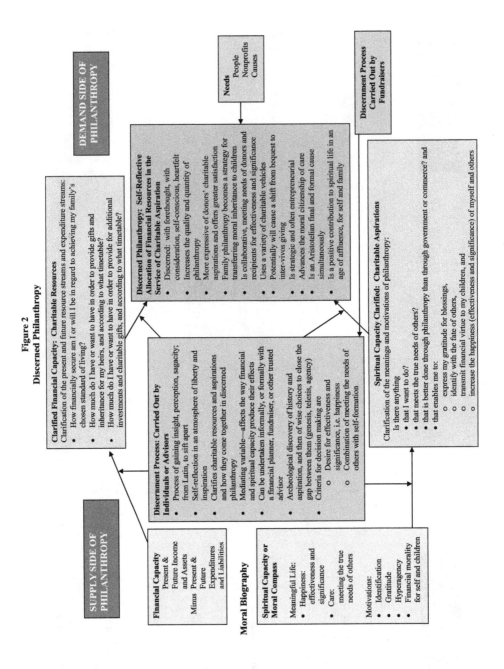

SUPPLY SIDE OF PHILANTHROPY

Financial Capacity
Present & Future Income and Assets
Minus
Present & Future Expenditures and Liabilities

Moral Biography

Spiritual Capacity or Moral Compass

Meaningful Life:
- Happiness: effectiveness and significance
- Care: meeting the true needs of others

Motivations:
- Identification
- Gratitude
- Hyperagency
- Financial morality for self and children

DEMAND SIDE OF PHILANTHROPY

Needs
People
Nonprofits
Causes

Discernment Process Carried Out by Fundraisers

Clarified Financial Capacity: Charitable Resources
Clarification of the present and future resource streams and expenditure streams:
- How financially secure am I or will I be in regard to achieving my family's chosen standard of living?
- How much do I have or want to have in order to provide gifts and inheritance for my heirs, and according to what timetable?
- How much do I have or want to have in order to provide for additional investments and charitable gifts, and according to what timetable?

Discerned Philanthropy: Self-Reflective Allocation of Financial Resources in the Service of Charitable Aspiration
- Discerned: with forethought, with consideration, self-conscious, heartfelt
- Increases the quality and quantity of philanthropy
- More expressive of donors' charitable aspirations and offers greater satisfaction
- Family philanthropy becomes a strategy for transferring moral inheritance to children
- Is collaborative, meeting needs of donors and recipients for effectiveness and significance
- Uses a variety of charitable vehicles
- Potentially will cause a shift from bequest to inter-vivos giving
- Is strategic and often entrepreneurial
- Advances the moral citizenship of care
- Is an Aristotelian final and formal cause simultaneously
- Is a positive contribution to spiritual life in an age of affluence, for self and family

Discernment Process: Carried Out by Individuals or Advisors
- Process of gaining insight, perception, sagacity; from Latin, to sift apart
- Self-reflection in an atmosphere of liberty and inspiration
- Clarifies charitable resources and aspirations and how they come together in discerned philanthropy
- Mediating variable—affects the way financial and spiritual capacity produce their effects
- Can be undertaken informally, or formally with a financial planner, fundraiser, or other trusted advisor
- Archeological discovery of history and aspiration, and then of wise choices to close the gap between them (genesis, telesis, agency)
- Criteria for decision making are
  - Desire for effectiveness and significance, i.e. happiness
  - Combination of meeting the needs of others with self-formation

Spiritual Capacity Clarified: Charitable Aspirations
Clarification of the meanings and motivations of philanthropy:
Is there anything
- that I want to do?
- that meets the true needs of others?
- that is better done through philanthropy than through government or commerce? and
- that enables me to:
  - express my gratitude for blessings,
  - identify with the fate of others,
  - transmit financial virtue to my children, and
  - increase the happiness (effectiveness and significance) of myself and others

clarify what they have to give (arrow 1, fig. 2) and their meanings and motivations for giving (arrow 2, fig. 2). Then, combining individuals' understanding of what they have to give with their meanings and motivations for giving, it helps them decide upon and implement what we call *discerned philanthropy* (arrows 3 and 4, fig. 2). When advisors and counselors, hired or chosen by the donor, assist in discernment, it takes place on the supply or donor-side of the philanthropic relationship. When fundraisers and charity professionals assist in discernment, it takes place on the demand side of philanthropy. Neither supply-side-led nor demand-side-led discernment necessarily produces a more propitious charitable decision. However, on the demand side, fundraisers often feel such pressure to garner support for their causes that they need to be especially attentive to ensure that liberty and inspiration—and hence the integrity of any decision, including the decision not to make a gift—are preserved throughout the discernment process.

DISCERNMENT OF FINANCES, ASPIRATIONS, AND PHILANTHROPY

Although discernment is a process of decision-making in all realms of our extraordinary and ordinary choices, I here focus on discernment as it applies especially to philanthropic giving. Discernment is a unified and recursive process touching on all aspects of a decision at the same time. But for clarity of exposition and to suggest how it can be an orderly method, I distinguish three realms and phases where it comes into play to meet the needs of wealth holders:

- clarification of their general financial capacity and charitable resources

- clarification of their broader moral purposes and charitable aspirations

- clarification of how to forge charitable resources and charitable aspirations into specific philanthropic practices.

Figure 1 illustrates the understanding of philanthropy as a social relation of care connecting the supply of resources to the demand of needs. On the demand side are the needs of ultimate beneficiaries, which are enunciated to donors by the media, by associates, and in the person of fundraisers and other representatives of intermediary charitable organizations that serve beneficiaries. On the supply side, donors combine their material resources with their personal meanings, aspirations, and motives to provide donations that meet the needs of beneficiaries through the instrumentality of charitable organizations.

Figure 2 indicates the key concepts and relationships that I will now explore in more depth. Once again, the model distinguishes between the supply and demand sides of philanthropy. Although demand-side factors are integral to philanthropic decision making, our primary focus is on supply-side variables and on the use of discernment by donors or by their advisors.

THE DEMAND SIDE: NEEDS AND THE USE OF THE DISCERNMENT PROCESS IN FUNDRAISING

The demand side of needs is a prominent consideration in the discernment process of donors as they clarify their financial and spiritual capacities and bring them together in shaping a specific or general philanthropic plan. The demand side of philanthropy—the effectiveness of nonprofit organizations in meeting the needs of beneficiaries or the organizational dynamics of nonprofit management, board relations, and so forth—will not be part of our research. However, there are two aspects of the demand side that do come into our next phase of research: (1) how the *needs* of ultimate beneficiaries and the causes and charities that serve these beneficiaries enter into the decision-making process of donors, and (2) the use of the discernment process in fundraising.

THE SUPPLY SIDE: CAPACITY AND MORAL COMPASS COMBINING TO FORGE A MORAL BIOGRAPHY OF PHILANTHROPY

The combination of financial capacity and moral compass, or spiritual capacity, forms the moral biography of philanthropic giving. In the following sections I elaborate what is generally involved in clarifying how financial capacity becomes translated into charitable resources, how general hopes and desires come to be specified as charitable aspirations, and how charitable resources and aspirations become combined to implement sometimes a specific philanthropic gift and at other times a broader philanthropic strategy.

CLARIFYING MATERIAL CAPACITY AND CHARITABLE RESOURCES

Financial capacity is the level of financial resources that individuals command at a particular point in time. Charitable resources are the subset of financial resources that individuals view as available for charitable purposes.

The formal discernment process comes into play as part of a technically informed methodology carried out with a trained financial professional of one's choice. The goal is for wealth holders to grasp (1) a conservatively defined stream of present and future financial resources; (2) a liberally defined stream of present and future expenditures to support the standard of living they desire for themselves, their family, and other heirs; and (3) a stream of excess resources potentially available for philanthropy. The discernment approach ensures that all information important for subsequent decisions emerges from insights that wealth holders themselves formulate about how long and in what way they want to continue to accumulate wealth; how financially secure they are in regard to providing the standard of living they want for themselves and their heirs; how much and when they wish to provide gifts and bequests to their heirs; and how much and when they want to provide for additional investments, business formation, and charitable giving.

Ultimately, discerned financial capacity entails clarifying whether, given their level of resources and desired standard of living, donors are at the point in their lives of (1) *financial dependence*—still in the accumulation phase and not yet at a level of financial security to confidently think about disbursement of resources other than for self and family; (2) *financial independence*—able to shift their focus partially or wholly to allocation decisions; or (3) *financial transcendence*—able to focus on their wealth as a tool with which they can shape the world, including through substantial entrepreneurial philanthropy.

In this way, potential charitable resources are determined inductively from the bottom up. Usually, but not necessarily, personal, business, and family considerations are addressed first; what remains is a trusted *minimal* amount available for philanthropy. An informal polling of financial and estate planners indicates that, for the very wealthy, this remaining amount tends to be greater than individuals conceived it to be before they clarified their resource and expense streams. At the same time, the amount first designated for philanthropy tends to be lower than the amount they eventually allocate because over time they realize that their original assessment underestimated their resource stream, overestimated their expense stream, and underestimated the accomplishment and satisfaction of their charitable giving.

CLARIFYING MORAL COMPASS AND
CHARITABLE ASPIRATIONS

Spiritual capacity is the inclinations that animate individuals both to pursue their ultimate life goal (happiness, union with God, service, and so forth) and to care for self and others as the path to that ultimate goal. By meeting the true needs of others through financial care, donors increase their own effectiveness and significance (or happiness) as well as that of others, thereby closing the gap between where they are in their lives and where they want to be. The inclinations that animate individuals to care for others include identifying with the fate of others, expressing gratitude for blessings, being active agents in shaping and not just supporting the organizational aspects of care, and fashioning a positive path of financial morality for themselves and their children. In sum, moral compass is the constellation of meanings, motivations, aspirations, and responsibilities that directs individuals in the use of their material capacities.

Discernment helps individuals uncover the ideas, emotions, and activities that shaped their moral compass in the past and helps them identify the moral bearings and purposes that they wish to advance now and into the future. It offers the opportunity to examine the major turning points in life, the people and circumstances that shaped them, the hurts and happinesses that ensued, and an agenda for the future.

Just as charitable resources are a subset of general financial capacity, charitable aspirations are a subset of one's broader moral compass. In identifying charitable aspirations, discernment focuses on clarifying what one wishes to do voluntarily so as to address the needs of others personally and directly rather than through business or government. Unlike the admonishment model that requires assent to expectations, the discernment model invites consideration of questions like the following:
Is there anything you want to do with your wealth

- that meets the true needs of others?

- that you can do better through philanthropy than through business or government?

- that enables you to identify with the fate of others and to express gratitude for the blessings you have received?

- that will help you fashion a financial morality for yourself and your family?

- that will achieve greater happiness in the form of effectiveness and significance for yourself and others?

As with financial discernment, discernment of aspirations is an ongoing process that generates new insights in light of subsequent experience. As such, charitable aspirations are the outcome of a process of discernment in which spiritual capacity is clarified. As a result of discerning spiritual capacity, individuals figure out which, if any, endeavors of financial care they want to pursue to experience in a deeper way the unity of love of God, love of self, and love of neighbor—or in my terms, the unity of the moral biography of God, self, and neighbor.

DISCERNED PHILANTHROPY:
CLARIFYING CHARITABLE ENDEAVORS

The next step in the application of the discernment model is to select specific philanthropic endeavors and ascertain how to carry them out. Discernment at this stage is about practical execution, since donors have already deliberated about what they would like to do and whether they have the resources to do it. Discerned philanthropy is the outcome of the process of discernment by which an individual applies a conscientiously decided-upon level of financial resources to implement a conscientiously decided-upon aspiration to care. Discernment can be useful for donors across the economic spectrum, since there are no essential elements of discerned philanthropy other than that it be self-reflective. Nonetheless, when we consider discerned philanthropy, several—and sometimes all— of the characteristics indicated in figure 2 are manifest.

The most general outcome of discerned philanthropy is that it tends to result in an increase in the quality and quantity of individual gifts and charitable giving in general. A quantitative increase in giving is not a *defining* element of discerned philanthropy, but it is likely to occur over time because self-reflection provides donors with a better appreciation of their financial capacity and of the importance of charitable needs in relation to their own needs. More likely, however, is that the philanthropy that emerges from discernment will be as much a formative activity for the donor as it for the beneficiary. Such philanthropy is a biographical event of character and vocation. It derives from a personal history of identifications, gratitude, blessings, and troubles and is destined toward a final end of care for self and others.

My early research identified several giving strategies that most wealth holders mix and match, depending upon the circumstance.[10] A giving strategy is a way of thinking, feeling, and acting to achieve a complex set of purposes involving self, family, and the needs of others. As such, each strategy requires a decision about the size of a gift, the recipient, the timing, and the giving vehicle. Each strategy also requires a decision about the kind of personal engagement one desires. In a *contributory strategy*, donors limit their engagement to making a financial contribution. In an *entrepreneurial strategy*, donors fund and carry out a charitable endeavor that they conceive and manage. In a *consumption strategy*, which can have either contributory or entrepreneurial components, donors direct funds toward institutions and causes that have benefited them or their families, such as schools, hospitals, churches, and performing arts organizations.

No matter what specific strategy wealth holders undertake, either in general or for a specific contribution, there is a sense in which all discerned philanthropy tends to be entrepreneurial. That is, it is self-directed, at least in disposition, even when not also in actual practice. This means that it is sufficiently thought through and planned as to often result in either new philanthropic initiatives or new directions in existing ones. But even when it is not explicitly innovative, it is entrepreneurial in the sense that it is self-consciously expressive of an entrepreneurial disposition of the donor to be a producer of effective outcomes.

Another characteristic of discerned philanthropy is that it is not tied to any particular charitable vehicle, nor is it particularly tax-driven; instead, it is the donor's biography that orients the financial and moral content and the timing of substantial giving. The element of "planning" in discerned giving is more holistic than the term "planned giving" usually implies. Planned giving technically refers to the charitable vehicles that are connected to trusts, bequests, and other mechanisms related to financial events that occur at the death of the donor. Discerned giving does include this type of "planned giving," but also includes any mode of giving that comes under the broader definition of "planning" as a process in which donors purposefully chart and time their giving in light of their life's purpose. As such, discerned giving includes conventionally defined planned giving as well as any form of inter vivos gifts, both outright and pledged that are carried out as a self-reflective translation of financial capacity into charitable gifts. Discerned philanthropy, then, is a financial and biographical event that produces a collaborative relationship that meets the needs of both donors and recipients for effectiveness and significance.

While financial gifts flow to meet the needs of recipients for happiness and to close the gap between their history and their aspirations, moral and spiritual gifts flow to the donors as a result of charitable giving that fulfills their true needs for happiness. This flow of mutual benefits, in turn, advances a more caring society characterized by a moral citizenship of care. By a moral citizenship of care I mean the array of privileges and responsibilities that express a conscious aspiration of citizens to freely attend to the true needs of others in a self-chosen manner. Although the moral citizenship of financial care has always been part of an ascetic way of life, it is an especially valuable element of spiritual life in an age of affluence. As personal and social wealth expands the horizon of choice for individuals, it becomes increasingly important that we develop a positive spirituality for affluent living and for making wise choices among the obstacles and opportunities of affluence.

ARCHEOLOGICAL DISCUSSIONS AND CONVERSATIONS

The major mechanism for carrying out discernment about capacity and aspiration is archeological conversation. Because it is not easy for wealth holders to decipher the moral compass that will guide their great capacity, we hear much from them about the turmoil, worry, and dilemmas they face in regard to how their riches shape the moral biographies of themselves, their children, and those they affect in business and in philanthropy. Acquiring great wealth, it turns out, is the beginning, not the end, of a moral biography of wealth. As a result, there is a growing need for a process of conscientious self-reflection by which wealth holders discern how to complement the growth in their material quantity of choice with a commensurate growth in the spiritual quality of choice.

Of course, individuals and their families can carry out this process of clarification informally and without the assistance of others. But most wealth holders will benefit from engaging in what I call an extended archeological conversation with their trusted advisors, including development professionals. As I describe below, there is a special role for gatherings of wealth holders in which archeological conversations will occur away from the agendas of financial and development professionals. Such conversations follow the principle that archeology precedes architecture, that self-discovery comes before defining and implementing a financial or estate plan. The methodology of archeological conversation can be easily taught to professionals (retreat directors, spiritual directors, etc.) working with wealth holders.

These archeological facilitators would help wealth holders to uncover the ideas, emotions, and activities that shaped their moral biography in the past and to identify the moral bearings and purposes that they wish to advance now and into the future. These facilitators and counselors will offer wealth holders the opportunity to examine the major turning points in life, the people and circumstances that shaped them, the hurts and happinesses that ensued, and an agenda for the future. In an archeological conversation, wealth holders discern their capacities, clarify their moral purposes, and combine the two in a way that creates a moral biography of wealth for themselves, their children, and others throughout the world for whom they care. When this process of discernment is carried out with no hidden agendas and with the purpose of helping wealth holders uncover their true aspirations, a deeper commitment to philanthropy invariably ensues.

CONCLUSION

In this chapter I have proposed that an important aspect of "religious giving" is a spiritual and religious process of discernment. In my thinking, all giving that is chosen and implemented through reflection on ultimate origins and ultimate goals is religious. Religious giving is not limited to contributions that go to congregations or religiously affiliated organizations. Religious giving occurs whenever individuals, while abiding in the presence of God flowing through them, freely develop down-to-earth and competent choices about the resources they possess and the wise purposes for which they seek to use those resources.

The broadest context for this is the material growth in wealth and the cultural and spiritual questions this poses. Most generally, these questions revolve around how to carry out a moral biography of wealth in our contemporary era. This means becoming attuned to the aspirations of care and friendship love, which link us to others through gratitude for blessings and identification with the fate of others. Individuals who harbor these dispositions are those whom Ignatius Loyola says are "going from good to better in their lives." Such souls, which include the majority of us, are then encouraged to chart the particular details of their wealth allocation with liberty and inspiration. They do not *deductively* obey the mandates of traditions, ideologies, or theologies. They *inductively* "seek and find," "taste and see" what they are to do in their own time, place, and circumstances.

For those going from good to better, discernment results in finding the will of God, not in what is the hardest or most sanctioned thing to do, but in the most inspiring thing to do.

We have arrived at a historical turning point in the accumulation and allocation of wealth that has the potential to increase philanthropy not just among those with substantial wealth but also among the highly affluent. Developing and implementing a discernment process will address the needs of individuals to find the deeper prospects and purposes of their wealth. It will also contribute to the mutual benefit of donors, charities, and beneficiaries. To the extent that individuals are guided to and through a process of conscientious self-clarification about their material capacity and moral purposes, philanthropy will emerge as an ever more familiar way to be "economically purposive for others even after it has ceased to be reasonable for oneself."[11] Spiritual discernment has the promise to make the early twenty-first century the first era in which the conscientious allocation of extraordinary wealth for the care of others becomes an ordinary path of financial spirituality.

NOTES

1. John J. Havens and Paul G. Schervish, *Millionaires and the Millennium: New Estimates of the Forthcoming Wealth Transfer and the Prospects for a Golden Age of Philanthropy*, Social Welfare Research Institute (now the Center on Wealth and Philanthropy), Boston College. Report released October 19, 1999.

2. John J. Havens and Paul G. Schervish, *Why the $41 Trillion Wealth Transfer Estimate Is Still Valid: A Review of Challenges and Questions*, Social Welfare Research Institute (now the Center on Wealth and Philanthropy), Boston College, January 6, 2003.

3. Paul G. Schervish and John J. Havens, "The Mind of the Millionaire: Findings from a National Survey on Wealth with Responsibility," *New Directions for Philanthropic Fundraising: Taking Fundraising Seriously*, ed. Eugene R. Tempel, no. 32 (Summer 2001): 75–107.

4. Jules Toner, *The Experience of Love* (Washington, D.C.: Corpus Books, 1968), 183.

5. Dan Siegel and Jenny Yancey, "Philanthropy's Forgotten Resource? Engaging the Individual Donor: The State of Donor Education Today and A Leadership Agenda for the Road Ahead, The Donor Education Initiative," 2003, p. 44, at www.newvisionsprd.org.

6. Paul G. Schervish and John J. Havens, "The New Physics of Philanthropy: The Supply-Side Vectors of Charitable Giving—Part 2: The Spiritual Side of the Supply Side," *CASE International Journal of Higher Education Advancement* 2, no. 3 (March 2002): 221–41.

7. Siegel and Yancey, "Philanthropy's Forgotten Resource?" 44.

8. Ibid.

9. Michael J. Buckley, "The Structure of the Rules for the Discernment of Spirits," *The Way*, Suppl. 20 (Autumn 1973): 20–37.

10. Paul G. Schervish and Andrew Herman, *Empowerment and Beneficence: Strategies of Living and Giving Among the Wealthy*, Final Report: The Study on Wealth and Philanthropy, Social Welfare Research Institute (now the Center on Wealth and Philanthropy), Boston College, July 1988.

11. John Maynard Keynes, "Economic Possibilities for Our Grandchildren," in *Essays in Persuasion* (London: Macmillan and Co., 1933), 372.

Consumer Debt and Christian Money Management: Messages from the Large U.S. Denominations

PAULA R. DEMPSEY

Religious giving is naturally a core concern of denominations and religious organizations not only for the survival of these institutions but also for the spiritual development of their members. One would expect, therefore, that the problem of consumer debt, which is growing among all demographic groups, would be a major denominational concern.[1] Thus, it is striking how little public discourse from major Christian denominations deals with consumer debt in the context of faithful living, despite the fact that people with a burden of debt obviously have less money available to give to religious organizations (see Rooney, chapter 1 of this volume) or to engage in low-paying ministries:

> Denominations sponsoring traditional missionary appointments find their candidate pool shrinking, as candidates must be largely debt-free to serve in subsistence settings. . . . Loans provide a hidden incentive to pursue higher-paying forms of ministry. (Ruger, Miller, and Early 2005, 35)

This chapter examines the ways in which debt is framed in the publications of large Christian denominations in the United States and proposes that balancing the individualistic, prescriptive approach, which these publications tend to stress, with a structural, descriptive approach could help to build more robust religious identities around the subject of money. Rather than focusing on debt as a matter of individual sin, I would ask denominations and other religious bodies teaching about money management to consider the following:

1. What are faithful individual and social responses to financial risks, such as health crises or job loss, for people struggling with existing mortgages, student loans, and credit card debt?

2. How can religious leaders confront the powerful and complex role of financial institutions in marketing debt, particularly to those with limited means to repay?

3. How can communities of faith overcome the wall of privacy that surrounds money troubles in order to support their members spiritually and practically?

4. In what ways may Christians interpret teachings about the forgiveness of debt from the perspective of both borrower and lender?

In my view, denominations that attend to the financial realities of members' lives and provide ways for them to understand debt from a Christian perspective will be more effective in shaping everyday decisions about money, including decisions about faithful giving. Ideally, decisions about taking on and getting out of debt will be introduced as part of a larger discernment process surrounding personal finances in a spiritual context. However, the existing denominational teachings about debt fail believers by focusing only on individual shortcomings that might lead to indebtedness. Paul Schervish (chapter 7 in this volume) contends that the admonishment approach is ineffective in leading the wealthiest among us to give, and I would argue that an approach of individual censure is also ineffective for those holding negative assets.

After describing what existing denominational teachings have to say about debt, I will address ways in which denominational and other religious leaders can do more to provide believers with the information and religious grounding they need to discern appropriate levels of debt as one aspect of money management in a spiritual context.

EXISTING TEACHINGS ON DEBT

My research examined the ways large, national Christian denominations in the United States address beliefs and practices about money (Dempsey 2006). I analyzed 302 texts on financial topics published from 1995 to 2004 by thirty-one denominations and other national religious bodies of more than 400,000 members in 2002 (see appendix). In official denominational pronouncements, books, magazine articles, pamphlets, and Web sites, these national bodies encourage—and sometimes admonish—their

TABLE 8.1. NUMBER OF REFERENCES TO DEBT IN
PUBLICATIONS ABOUT MONEY MANAGEMENT FROM LARGE
U.S. DENOMINATIONS (1995–2004)

Denomination	Debt References	% of Total
Southern Baptist Convention	50	43%
Seventh-day Adventist	16	14%
Latter-day Saints	15	13%
Assemblies of God	6	5%
Wisconsin Evangelical Lutheran Synod	6	5%
Evangelical Lutheran Church in America	5	4%
Roman Catholic Church	4	3%
Christian Churches (Churches of Christ)	2	2%
Church of God (Cleveland, Tenn.)	2	2%
Jehovah's Witnesses	2	2%
United Methodist Church	2	2%
African Methodist Episcopal	1	1%
Churches of Christ	1	1%
Church of God in Christ	1	1%
Episcopal Church	1	1%
Church of the Nazarene	1	1%
National Baptist Convention, USA	1	1%
Salvation Army	1	1%
TOTAL	117	

Note: Denominations that did not mention debt in publications about money management: American Baptist, African Methodist Episcopal Zion, Baptist Bible Fellowship International, Christian Methodist Episcopal, Disciples of Christ, Greek Orthodox Archdiocese of America, Lutheran Church Missouri Synod, National Baptist Convention of America, Inc., National Missionary Baptist Convention of America, Pentecostal Assemblies of the World, Presbyterian Church-USA, United Churches of Christ.

members to see money and possessions as ultimately being owned by God, while recognizing their responsibility to care for themselves, their families, and others in need. Only 117 of these texts, representing eighteen of the thirty-one denominations, mentioned the issue of debt. These 117 texts include 700 references[2] to the causes, consequences, and solutions for indebtedness (see table 8.1). This chapter analyzes the teachings of those eighteen denominations on the subject of debt. The bulk of the teachings (70%) come from just three denominations: one in the conservative mainstream (Southern Baptist Convention) and two with unorthodox theologies (Latter-day Saints and Seventh-day Adventist). Although these three groups have radically different structures and theological traditions, they have produced publications with strikingly similar themes. They all teach that trust in God's providence, accompanied by rigorous attention to proper use of money, will lead to financial stability and personal freedom.

Although not included in this study, messages about debt from nondenominational megachurches and parachurch organizations either reinforce existing denominational perspectives (Crown Financial Ministries is cited as a resource by the American Baptist, Southern Baptist, and Seventh-day Adventist denominations) or offer contrasting and innovative approaches (Willow Creek Association's Good $ense Ministry is not cited by any of the thirty-one denominations). More recent explorations suggest growing interest in these nondenominational and parachurch programs by other denominations (Byassee 2007).

Those few denominations that focus on debt portray financial stability as a result of faithful Christian practice. Taken as a whole, teachings about debt over the past decade emphasize an *individual* locus of control in which sin and deficient spirituality are the focus, rather than a *social* locus of control in which the larger financial structure is the focus (see table 8.2). (In no case do these teachings claim a basis in empirical observation.)

The most common cause of debt mentioned in these 117 documents (21% of coding references) is the desire for material goods and services that are not necessities. This is usually framed as the failure to distinguish between needs (which God will always provide) and wants:

> Before beginning the budgeting process, it is important to distinguish between wants and needs. Realistic, workable budgets result when couples agree to provide carefully for their needs and to exercise self-discipline and patience as they seek to provide for some of their wants. (Latter-Day Saints level 2)
>
> A written plan is important for everyone, but it's an absolute necessity for those in financial debt. And for God's people, a written plan is crucial, because most Christians have lost the point of reference between needs, wants and desires. (Southern Baptist Convention level 2)

The Jehovah's Witnesses and the Southern Baptist Convention note that the Bible lists only food and clothing as needs: "If we have food and

TABLE 8.2. CAUSES OF DEBT IN PUBLICATIONS FROM
18 LARGE U.S. CHRISTIAN DENOMINATIONS
(202 REFERENCES IN 117 DOCUMENTS)

Cause	% of references
Desire for non-necessities	21%
Sins (greed, pride, vanity, etc.)	20%
Indebtedness as a way of life	14%
Mismanagement of credit cards	10%
Aggressive marketing of credit cards	8%
Lack of trust in God's providence	6%
Psychological maladjustment	6%
Illness, disability, job loss, divorce	5%
Lack of financial skills	5%
Temptation by the devil	3%
Recession, unemployment	1%

Note: Total is not equal to 100%, due to rounding.

clothing, we will be content with these" (1 Tim. 6:8, NRSV). However, other texts acknowledge a broader range of needs associated with middle-class identity: house, car, college education, vacations, and medical insurance.[3] These texts affirm that God can be trusted to provide necessities to the faithful. Christians must recognize, however, that "needs" can become "wants" if they involve choices about quality: e.g., steak versus hamburger or a new car versus a used car.

After the inability to distinguish wants from needs, the most common cause of debt (20%) is excessive spending as a result of greed, pride, vanity, envy, selfishness, covetousness, and other sins:

> Debt is seldom the real problem; it is symptomatic of another problem, such as greed, poor self-image, self-indulgence, impatience, or lack of self-discipline. (Church of God, Cleveland, Tenn., level 2)
>
> Greed and selfishness: Many families live beyond their means. They are unwilling to live in, drive, or wear what they can really afford. (Seventh-day Adventist level 2)

Some of these texts point to the growing cultural acceptance of debt as a way of life (14% of coding references about causes of debt), which is portrayed in some texts as a cultural degradation of early twentieth-century values:

> We live in a society of declining morals and ethics. Bankruptcy and Chapter 11 proceedings are being used by many as a means of avoiding rightful obligations. But just because it has become a way of life for many is no reason for a Christian to follow this pathway. The Christian must live by a higher code. (Assemblies of God level 1)

> Irresponsible indebtedness is a national scandal at present in our society. This is generally true of our nation's leaders and citizens alike. (Wisconsin Evangelical Lutheran Synod level 2)

Other causes of debt in these documents are the inability to control credit card spending (10%), which is closely related to the more general lack of financial skills (5%). A few references (8%) point to financial industry practices such as (1) aggressive marketing of credit cards, especially to youth; (2) low minimum payments leading to extended borrowing periods at high interest rates; (3) automatic overdraft protection on checking accounts, which is marketed as a service but in fact charges high interest; and (4) equity stripping by predatory home financing firms. However, with one exception (in a text about college student borrowing from the Evangelical Lutheran Church in America), these publications expect individuals to understand the profit motive of consumer credit companies and protect themselves from such practices. As a Southern Baptist Convention writer puts it:

> [Financial institutions] are in it for the money. There's nothing wrong with that, per se—I am quite fond of the capitalistic free-enterprise system myself. Still, I want to arm you with the knowledge you need to make the choice that is right for you so you can participate with this industry in a reasoned way. Then if the powerful industry snatches a lot of your hard-earned money, you will at least know that it happened by your choice, not theirs. (Southern Baptist Convention level 2)

This illustrates the moral neutrality accorded to corporations, in contrast to the sin of greed attributed to individuals operating in the same economic system.

Other failings of individuals that are causes for debt include lack of trust in God's providence (6%), psychological problems prompting excessive spending (6%), and temptation by Satan (3%). Individual misfortunes outside the borrower's control, such as medical emergencies or job loss, comprise only 5% of the references to the causes of debt. More commonly, these denominational teachings deny that misfortune is a cause of indebtedness:

> Relatively few families crash and burn financially because of a medical catastrophe, a bad business investment, or because they are swindled. (Southern Baptist Convention level 2)
>
> But rarely do financial troubles come from those kinds of disasters. Most come from unwise management. (Wisconsin Evangelical Lutheran Synod level 2)

Still less common is linking individual debt to broader economic circumstances such as recession or unemployment (1% of references to debt), and even here individual planning is portrayed as the solution:

> The only control one has is keeping expenditures within one's income—in fact, within 90 percent of income, for God has a claim on the 10 percent tithe. . . . (Assemblies of God level 1)

Given the emphasis on the individual's responsibility for debt, it makes sense that denominations frame the solution as being within the individual's control as well (see table 8.3).

The major suggestions are to reduce spending (20%) and to follow a budget (18%). Taking these actions requires a shift in attitude (10%), also assumed to be within individual control. The publications provide many helpful tips on how to save money, not only by eliminating large luxuries like driving a new car and small ones like restaurant meals, "daily lattes" at Starbucks, expensive bath products, and dry cleaning, but also by monitoring spending on necessities, such as health care, through self-discipline.

The link to tithing is another significant element for a few churches in solving the problem of debt (8% of the references to debt solutions). Large U.S. denominations steer away from framing the tithe as a guarantee of prosperity on a reciprocal basis with God, but the 18 denominations that focus on debt imply a supernatural benefit from tithing:

> We believe that the road to financial solvency is longer without tithing than it is with tithing. God honors those who make His money the first priority in their budgeting and spending. (Assemblies of God level 1)
>
> The Lord only asks for 10% of what we make. This is the first check I write each week, and it seems like we have extra money to pay on bills. He will bless you—just try Him. (Latter-day Saints level 2)
>
> Giving exposes my finances to God's supernatural intervention. (Southern Baptist Convention level 2)

TABLE 8.3. SOLUTIONS FOR DEBT IN PUBLICATIONS FROM
18 LARGE U.S. CHRISTIAN DENOMINATIONS
(348 REFERENCES IN 117 DOCUMENTS)

Reduce spending	20%
Follow a budget	18%
Change attitude	10%
Tithe	8%
Start saving regularly	7%
Prepay debts	7%
Manage credit cards	6%
Pray	5%
Get credit counseling	5%
Sell assets	3%
Rolling payoff	3%
10-10-80 (give 10%, save 10%, spend 80%)	2%
Part-time job	2%
Be accountable to other Christians	1%
Get help from the church	1%
Reduce college costs	1%

Note: Total is not equal to 100%, due to rounding.

From that day forward I gave God the first 10 percent of what He gave me, and He has always provided. Within 18 months of working hard, tithing first, and learning to become a wise steward, I became debt-free. (Seventh-day Adventist level 2)

NEW POSSIBILITIES FOR TEACHINGS ABOUT DEBT

My research on these denominational publications reveals the need for a different perspective in denominational messages about money management. Denominational publications implicitly address a middle-class audience by taking for granted core elements of middle-class status: a house and mortgage, a car, a college degree, a job with health benefits (or at least the possibility of finding such a job), and college-bound children. For many believers, clergy as well as laypeople, *having* a house and a college education is part and parcel of *being* a middle-class (read "normal," "average," "typical") American (Johnson 2006).

However, denominational messages about money that tacitly support this assumption and do not present alternative possibilities are unlikely to reach or to motivate people who are struggling to maintain this way of life in a context of slowing income growth and rapidly rising costs of housing, health care, and education (Warren and Tyagi 2003; Weller 2007b). My goal is to stimulate discussion across a wider range of economic and theological perspectives by encouraging a broader group of denominations to focus on debt in publications about Christian money management. People need a positive and uplifting message from their religious leaders, one that is rooted in their own faith tradition and hermeneutical stance toward Scripture.

Rather than focusing only on debt as a personal failing, I see new possibilities in teachings that will: (1) develop faithful individual and social responses to financial risks such as health crises or job loss, (2) examine the role of financial institutions that aggressively market debt to those least able to repay, (3) find ways to talk about money troubles in spite of the wall of privacy that surrounds money in communities of faith, and (4) clarify the meaning of forgiveness of debt from the perspective of both borrowers and lenders.

DEVELOPING NEW RESPONSES TO FINANCIAL RISK

Existing denominational teachings about debt assert that the risks of job loss or health crises can be managed by virtuous self-discipline. In this view, debtors bear the sole responsibility for their indebtedness. Bankruptcy researchers Elizabeth Warren and Amelia Warren Tyagi call this approach the Myth of the Immoral Debtor. Warren and Tyagi argue that the narrative of individual responsibility makes people feel safer about their own financial situation and also reduces the motivation to change public policy:

> The Myth of the Immoral Debtor nourishes the unspoken idea that families who have lost their financial footing are a tainted group, some "other" who are different from the rest of us. If we can believe that those in serious trouble are morally suspect, then it is easier to glance away from the harsh dangers of everyday life. (Warren and Tyagi 2003, 89)

Maintaining savings for unexpected or recurring expenses should certainly be encouraged as central to financial stability. However, this individual strategy needs to be balanced by an understanding of our mutual vulnerability to economic risk. A survey of 1,771 people who filed for bankruptcy found that half cited medical causes for their financial difficulties

(Himmelstein et al. 2005). A study of trends in the *Survey of Consumer Finances* showed that "the run-up in debt is more a consequence of economic necessities than of profligate spending" (Weller 2007a). Few people can be prepared to meet major medical expenses or the consequences of mass layoffs in a regional industry.

Warren and Tyagi propose that because not all of the financial risks of everyday life are within individual control, government policies should provide a safety net for basic financial stability. I do not advocate shifting the entire responsibility for indebtedness to the wider social sphere. However, I do think it makes sense to acknowledge our shared exposure to everyday financial risk. The notion that people who have faith and follow a strict budget—"moral" money managers—are safe from financial catastrophe leads people to conceal money troubles rather than reaching out for help before it is too late. Depending on how a given denomination views such risks, public policy advocacy might be called for that would spread risk by improving health insurance or unemployment benefits. Or denominations might design programs such as revolving loan funds to allow for mutual aid among church members in times of crisis (Moore 2003, 150).

EXAMINING THE ROLE OF FINANCIAL INSTITUTIONS

U.S. denominations have neglected to confront the problem of greed in the way some financial institutions market credit. In contrast to existing denominational teachings, the historical condemnation of usury recognized that the profit motives of lenders is a key element in promoting indebtedness. Diane Ellis of the FDIC found that the Supreme Court's 1978 Marquette decision gave low-income borrowers unprecedented access to credit and ushered in a long-term rise in personal bankruptcy rates (Ellis 1998). Ellis argues that high interest rates provide a strong financial incentive to banks to offer credit to those with little or no means to repay, such as college students or borrowers recently emerging from bankruptcy. When banks choose to lend amounts far beyond what borrowers' incomes and assets allow them to repay, the banks have far more information about financial realities than do the borrowers. Their profits from high-risk loans compensate them for what they lose in defaults.

Denominations are right to call believers to be responsible for their decisions, but they must also consider whether this extends equally to institutional decision-makers who oversee loans. For some denominations, this will mean advocating for specific policies concerning marketing of debt, and for others it will mean more pronounced efforts to make believers aware of the reality of financial practices so they can protect themselves. At the very least, education is called for to help people understand the danger of relying on credit cards or home equity loans in tough times. Such education should include information refuting the common perception that banks do not offer more credit than the borrower can afford to repay.

FINDING WAYS TO TALK ABOUT MONEY

Denominations face an uphill climb when attempting to help believers integrate everyday financial decisions about giving, spending, borrowing, and saving into religious identity. One problem is that clergy and other religious leaders are not immune from financial problems or debt, and they might lack the background and skills to help others with money matters (Ronsvalle and Ronsvalle 1996, 143; Wuthnow 1994). In addition, the cultural emphasis on social equality within communities of faith makes it awkward to acknowledge economic disparities (Lynn 1999, 60). To effectively reach those in debt and offer financial practices that will be helpful to individual believers and the community, it is important for denominations to address explicitly the ways in which some forms of debt function as a means of keeping money troubles private and protecting the illusion of independence. The ability to borrow on a credit card at high interest rates means not having to ask a relative, neighbor, or community/religious organization for assistance. In this way individuals, even in otherwise supportive religious communities, may not become aware of the financial stress fellow church members experience.

CLARIFYING THE MEANING OF FORGIVENESS OF DEBT

Finally, it is striking how little attention denominations give to the theme of forgiveness of debts, given its scriptural prominence in the Lord's Prayer: "And forgive us our debts, as we also have forgiven our debtors" (Matt. 6:9–14, NRSV)[4] and in three parables. In the parable of the shrewd manager (Luke 16:1–9), a steward reduces the debts owed to his master to win favor with the debtors; in Matthew 18:23–25, a slave who refused to forgive the debts of the other slaves is handed over to be tortured; and in Luke 7:41–43, Jesus compares the forgiveness of grave sins to the canceling of a great debt. In these passages, the debtor is not merely forgiven on a spiritual level but is also no longer required to repay the creditor. However, the few large U.S. denominations that emphasize debt in their publications do not permit believers to accept forgiveness for actual debts, even those incurred before conversion and even when remitted under bankruptcy:

> Even if you had to declare bankruptcy someday, you would still make every effort to pay back each creditor in full. (Latter-day Saints level 2)
>
> If someone forces you into bankruptcy, you are legally, but not scripturally, released from the debts. You are still obliged to repay the loans unless the lender releases you from the debt. (Southern Baptist Convention level 2)
>
> Even if a Christian must declare bankruptcy, he will still seek to repay his debts as soon as possible, and to the full extent of his ability. (Wisconsin Evangelical Lutheran Synod level 2)

The denominations that talk about debt do not acknowledge the possibility of forgiveness of debt as a lived reality. The metaphor of forgiveness of debt in the Bible stories includes waiving the demand for repayment, giving a clean slate in a practical sense, and not just a spiritual one. The Roman Catholic and Episcopal churches are vocal and active in the area of debt forgiveness for developing nations but are relatively silent on the issue of personal bankruptcy.[5] How can religious organizations offer support to those whose debt cannot realistically be repaid? Is the forgiveness extended in the Lord's Prayer merely spiritual, or should Christians both give and receive forgiveness for actual debts? In many cases, this debt was taken on irresponsibly and, in many others, it was a result of the ordinary risk of life in a society in which access to credit is abundant, even for those with little means to repay. Gary Moore argues that the Bible is skeptical about the legitimacy of charging interest and the absolute moral obligation to repay loans (Moore 2003, 114–15). He reasons that giving is more appropriate than lending in cases of greatest need and that lenders should share risk with borrowers in circumstances beyond the borrowers' control: "A healthy balance of repayment when possible—and not simply convenient—but debt-forgiveness when debt is truly burdensome is what our modern bankruptcy laws and foreign policies regarding Third World debt should move toward" (118). Given the increase in personal bankruptcy, it is important for religious organizations to wrestle with the scriptural metaphor of forgiveness as relief from debt and to help believers find a faithful path forward after a financial crisis.

CONCLUSION

As mortgage foreclosures and other signs of financial distress increase, denominations and other religious organizations have a significant opportunity to expand the range of Christian messages about money management by balancing the individualistic perspective with a structural perspective. Any discussion of giving in a faith context requires understanding the relationship of the individual or household to larger financial issues in the religious community and in the overall economy. This chapter has argued that relating religious identities to financial realities calls for attention to new responses to financial risks, the role of financial institutions in rising debt levels, the silence and shame around money troubles, and interpretations of the forgiveness of debt. Addressing these financial realities will allow religious organizations to more effectively guide their members' everyday decisions about money, not the least of which are their decisions about religious giving.

APPENDIX:
DENOMINATIONS RANKED BY SIZE IN 2002

	1995	*2002*
Roman Catholic Church	60,190,605	66,407,105
Southern Baptist Convention	15,614,060	16,247,736
United Methodist Church	8,584,125	8,251,042
Church of God in Christ	N/A	5,499,875
Church of Jesus Christ of Latter-Day Saints	4,110,000	5,410,544
Evangelical Lutheran Church in America	5,119,048	5,038,006
National Baptist Convention, USA, Inc.	8,200,000	5,000,000
National Baptist Convention of America, Inc.	N/A	3,500,000
Presbyterian Church (USA)	3,698,136	3,407,329
Assemblies of God	2,324,615	2,687,366
Lutheran Church—Missouri Synod	2,596,927	2,512,714
African Methodist Episcopal Church	3,500,000	2,500,000
National Missionary Baptist Convention of America	N/A	2,500,000
Progressive National Baptist Convention, Inc.	N/A	2,500,000
Episcopal Church	2,504,628	2,333,628
Churches of Christ	N/A	1,500,000
Pentecostal Assemblies of the World, Inc.	1,000,000	1,500,000
American Baptist Churches in the U.S.A.	1,507,934	1,484,291

DENOMINATIONS RANKED BY SIZE IN 2002 *(continued)*

	1995	*2002*
African Methodist Episcopal Zion Church	1,230,842	1,430,795
United Church of Christ	1,501,310	1,330,985
Baptist Bible Fellowship International	1,500,000	1,200,000
Christian Churches and Churches of Christ	1,070,616	1,071,616
Jehovah's Witnesses	N/A	1,022,397
Church of God (Cleveland, Tenn.)	945,990	944,857
Seventh-day Adventist Church	775,349	918,882
Christian Methodist Episcopal Church	718,922	850,000
Christian Church (Disciples of Christ) in the United States and Canada	937,644	786,334
Church of the Nazarene	597,841	643,649
Salvation Army	443,246	454,982
Greek Orthodox Archdiocese of America	N/A	440,000
Wisconsin Evangelical Lutheran Synod	414,874	403,345

Note: Some of these bodies resist the term "denomination," which is used here for convenience.

Source: Office of Research, Evaluation and Planning of the National Council of the Churches of Christ in the U.S.A. *Yearbook of American and Canadian Churches* (Nashville, Tenn.: Abingdon Press, 2003).

NOTES

1. Americans are increasingly likely to devote a larger proportion of disposable income to servicing mortgages and consumer debt, growing from 11.85% in 1995 to 14.48% in 2006 (Federal Reserve Board 2007).

2. Sources for the quotations from these texts have been identified by their level of authority within the denomination. Level 1 documents are endorsed by the highest national body. Level 2 documents are teaching material published by the denomination in a book, magazine, or Web site. Level 3 documents are by authors or publishers claiming denominational affiliation.

3. Latter-day Saints, Church of the Nazarene, and Southern Baptist Convention present life insurance as a basic necessity: "Do not risk going for one day without health insurance!" (Southern Baptist Convention level 2). The Southern Baptist Convention also asserts individual responsibility for health insurance: "They let circumstances dictate their choice not to carry health insurance" (Southern Baptist Convention level 2).

4. This translation is commonly used in Presbyterian and other churches in the Reformed tradition, whereas other traditions use the terms *trespasses* or *sins*.

5. Warren and Tyagi note that a group of Catholics, Unitarians, and Jews wrote an open letter to Congress (February 28, 2001) speaking against personal bankruptcy reform because of its harsh impact on children and families. Another religious effort on behalf of borrowers in bankruptcy law was the Religious Liberty and Charitable Donation Protection Act (1998 S. 1255; 105S. 1244)—sponsored by the Southern Baptist Convention, Seventh-day Adventist, Evangelical Lutheran Church in America, Latter-day Saints, Catholic League for Religious and Civil Rights, and the National Association of Evangelicals—to prevent bankruptcy courts from forcing churches to return tithes from bankrupt members on the ground that they are fraudulent transfers.

REFERENCES

Byassee, Jason. 2007. "Counting the Cost: A Crusade against Consumer Debt." *Christian Century*, August 7, 18–22.

Dempsey, Paula. 2006. More Money Than God: U.S. Christian Teachings on Personal Finance. Ph.D. diss., Loyola University, Chicago.

Ellis, Diane. 1998. "The Effect of Consumer Interest Rate Deregulation on Credit Card Volumes, Charge-offs, and the Personal Bankruptcy Rate." *Bank Trends* 98, no. 5 (March).

Federal Reserve Board. "Household Debt Service and Financial Obligations Ratios." www.federalreserve.gov/Releases/housedebt/ (accessed November 7, 2007).

Himmelstein, David U., Elizabeth Warren, Deborah Thorne, and Steffie Woolhandler. 2005. "MarketWatch: Illness and Injury as Contributors to Bankruptcy." *Health Affairs*, February 2, 2005.

Johnson, Luke T. 2006. "The Life of Faith and the Faithful Use of Possessions." Thomas H. Lake Lecture, Lake Institute on Faith and Giving, Indianapolis, Ind., April 6.

Lynn, Robert Wood. 1999. "Why Give?" In *Financing American Religion*, ed. Mark Chaves and Sharon L. Miller, 55–65. Walnut Creek, Calif.: AltaMira Press.

Moore, Gary. 2003. *Faithful Finances 101: From the Poverty of Fear and Greed to the Riches of Spiritual Investing*. Philadelphia: Templeton Foundation Press.

Ronsvalle, John, and Sylvia Ronsvalle. 1996. *Behind the Stained Glass Windows: Money Dynamics in the Church*. Grand Rapids, Mich.: Baker Books.

Ruger, Anthony, Sharon L. Miller, and Kim Maphis Early. 2005. "The Gathering Storm: The Educational Debt of Theological Students." *Auburn Studies* 12 (September). New York: Auburn Theological Seminary.

Warren, Elizabeth, and Amelia Warren Tyagi. 2003. *The Two-income Trap: Why Middle-class Mothers and Fathers Are Going Broke*. New York: Basic Books.

Weller, Christian. 2007a. "Need or Want: What Explains the Run-up in Consumer Debt?" *Journal of Economic Issues* 41, no. 2 (June): 583–91.

———. 2007b. *Risks Rise for Middle Class: Economic Security Continues to Fall*. CAP Economic Policy Report. Washington, D.C.: Center for American Progress, Service Employees International Union. www.americanprogress.org/issues/2007/01/pdf/middle_class_indicators.pdf.

Wuthnow, Robert. 1994. *God and Mammon in America*. New York: Free Press.

9 Paging Dr. Shylock! Jewish Hospitals and the Prudent Reinvestment of Jewish Philanthropy

ROBERT A. KATZ ─────────────────────────

Tzedakah, or "righteousness" (imperfectly translated as "charity," from the Latin *caritas* or "love") refers mainly to providing aid to needy Jews and doing so as a matter of duty rather than choice. While the concept of *tzedakah* has deep roots in Judaism, it also reflects the experience of Jews as a discrete and insular minority living in a determinedly hostile environment.[1] Jews used philanthropy in the first instance to take care of fellow Jews: if they were not for themselves, who would be for them?[2] Jews also used their philanthropy to make their environment more hospitable for Jewish individuals to live and work and for Jews collectively to survive and flourish as a distinct community. This function of Jewish philanthropy (defined as giving from a Jewish perspective[3]) was especially evident in the Jewish hospital movement in the United States.

Between 1850 and 1955, Jewish communities in twenty-four U.S. cities founded general hospitals.[4] All but two opened after the Civil War, which marked the start of the most anti-Semitic period in American history (Kraut and Kraut 2007, 242–47; Dinnerstein 1994, 35). This conjunction was no coincidence. Jewish hospitals were an important part of the Jewish community's response to anti-Semitism. With names like "Jewish Hospital," "Mount Sinai," and "Beth Israel," they were the Jewish community's most identifiable and impressive philanthropy (Kutzik 1967, 306). Jews hoped that these institutions would help improve relations with non-Jews, counteract anti-Jewish stereotypes and prejudice, and provide enclaves from anti-Jewish discrimination. Jewish hospitals advanced these ends in many ways. They diminished the need for poor Jews to seek care from non-Jewish sources, which helped answer complaints that Jewish paupers were a burden on society. They publicized their nonsectarian intake policies, which weakened claims that Jews were clannish and only took care of their own. They also provided opportunities denied elsewhere for Jews in medicine to train, do research, and practice.

The decline of anti-Semitism in the United States after World War II eliminated the most immediate problems that Jewish hospitals were founded to address (Dinnerstein 1994, 150–51). Starting in the 1980s, changes in the hospital industry squeezed out many independent community-based hospitals, a class that included all Jewish hospitals. In the past quarter-century, roughly one-third of Jewish hospitals outside New York (which is *sui generis*) merged with non-Jewish systems. This move made these hospitals more competitive but surrendered control by members of the local Jewish community. Another one-third tried to remain both competitive and Jewish, and most succeeded. The last one-third sold their facilities, most often to for-profit systems, and used the proceeds to endow grant-making foundations. All of these foundations make at least some grants to Jewish organizations and causes.

Of these options, the sale of Jewish nonprofit hospitals to for-profit systems was the most controversial. This was especially the case when the sale proceeds were *not* used exclusively to serve the health care needs of the community at large—for example, by providing uncompensated care to poor, elderly, and other underserved populations. However, the interests of American Jewry were generally better served by funding programs that ensured its future as a distinct and vibrant community, such as those for Jewish education, religion, culture, and communal life. Applying the assets of Jewish hospitals to those ends also keeps faith with the deepest hopes of many who founded those institutions. These founders responded in their day to the most serious threat to the Jewish community's well-being—anti-Jewish hostility and discrimination. But Jewish hospitals cannot cure the current ills of American Jewry—assimilation, alienation, and indifference—which are internal, not external, threats.

RELIGIOUS, ETHNIC, AND PRAGMATIC RATIONALES FOR JEWISH HOSPITALS

The first Jewish hospitals in the United States were The Jewish Hospital in Cincinnati (1850) and Jews' Hospital in New York City (1855), now known as Mount Sinai Hospital. Like most hospitals of that era, they were intended for the sick poor; patients who could afford care were generally treated at home. Although these hospitals provided modest treatment at best, they could meet their patients' religious needs: kosher food, Sabbath and holiday observances, access to rabbis. At the same time, they protected patients from being exposed to proselytizing, which sometimes occurred at non-Jewish institutions.[5] They also were congenial to Jewish sensibilities in ways that are easier to joke about than to explain. A modern instance: Mr. Goldberg, a patient at Massachusetts General Hospital, asked to be transferred to Boston's Beth Israel Hospital, a less prestigious institution, for no apparent reason. "Was anything wrong at Mass General?" his physician asked. "No, everything was fine. I can't complain." "So why did you want to come to Beth Israel?" "Because here I *can* complain."

As its name suggests, Jews' Hospital in New York initially admitted only Jews, but it made exceptions for accident victims and emergencies (Aufses and Niss 2002, 2–3). This policy found support in the traditional Judaic concept of *tzedakah*, the giving of aid to the needy—and to Jewish needy in the first instance—as a matter of righteousness or justice.[6] In distributing charity, say rabbinic authorities, a donor should show preference for the needy members of his family over the poor in his community. These poor, in turn, have a greater claim to his resources than the poor of other cities, and so on (Taub 2001, 50–52). The traditionally insular focus of *tzedakah* points to a major difference between Christian and Judaic approaches to philanthropy. "Jewish morality," explains Walter Wurzburger,

> takes seriously the moral requirements arising from the particular features of a given historical situation, be they filial duties, obligations to benefactors, members of one's own family, community, or people. While some Christian moralists may contend that "Love thy neighbor as thyself" implies that, ideally, in matters involving concern for others, one should not discriminate between members of one's family and total strangers, since they are all equally entitled to our love, Jewish morality does not accept this basic premise. (1994, 95)

The sectarian admissions policy of Jews' Hospital also reflected the historically insular nature of Jewish communal life. Prior to their emancipation, European Jews lived in separate communities whose semiautonomy was recognized by the overarching authorities. In that setting, the duty to give *tzedakah* was not just a religious obligation; it was a legal duty that could be enforced by communal authorities—"the equivalent of a tax in today's society" (Dorff 2005, 132). The first Jewish communities in

America, explained Boris Bogen, "were small and homogeneous and consisted of individuals from the Old World, steeped in an atmosphere of which Jewish charity was an integral part." Given this history, "it was but reasonable that these communities should embody the same spirit and organize societies to *help their own*" (Bogen 1917, 2; emphasis added). In America, where the Jewish community lacked the legal power to tax, members nonetheless contributed to its safety net as a form of voluntary taxation (Telushkin 1991, 513).

In addition to religious duty and ethnic tradition, American Jews had pragmatic reasons to minimize the reliance of poor Jews on non-Jewish charities. They believed that "'taking care of their own' was an important factor in establishing and maintaining good relations between them and their neighbors" (Fiske 1902, 390). This belief was fostered by the chilly reception Jews received in 1654 from Peter Stuyvesant (c. 1612–1672), then governor of the Dutch colony of New Amsterdam (now New York). In that year, twenty-three Brazilian Jews arrived in New Amsterdam seeking refuge from the Portuguese Inquisition. Stuyvesant asked the colony's sponsor, the Dutch West India Company, for permission to expel them. They posed a threat, he claimed, not only because they were Jews ("hateful enemies and blasphemers of the name of Christ" who engaged in "usury and deceitful trading with Christians"), but also because of their drain on the colony's resources. Rejecting Stuyvesant's request, the company permitted the refugees to stay on condition that they "support their own poor" and not let them become a burden to it or the larger community. American Jews internalized their hosts' expectation of communal self-sufficiency as an imperative. The Jews' "sacred promise" to the larger society to take care of their own became known as "the Stuyvesant Pledge" (Kutzik 1967, 941).

In the mid-1800s, American Jews were sometimes extolled for the charity they practiced amongst themselves. In 1837, the Boston press declared that "the Jews love each other, and never refuse aid to a brother in distress." This was a continuing source of surprise to non-Jews. In 1860, a New York newspaper stated that "few of our citizens know [Jews] socially and all are too willing to believe Shylock their true type." To challenge this view, it pointed to Jewish charities in general and one in particular. "This city, also, contains a hospital, supported at the expense of the Jews, and as a proof of the liberality really existing among them, for which they are rarely credited" (Kutzik 1967, 292–93). In 1871, the *New York Times* ran another story on the same topic: "The general public knows comparatively little of the extent of Hebrew benevolence." This was partly because, it opined, "their good works are performed quietly among those of their own race and persuasion exclusively."[7]

Hospital care was "the only charity of consequence provided by non-Jews to Jews," according to Kutzik (1967, 307). Jewish hospitals helped maintain the perception that needy Jews did not burden the larger society. An 1837 Boston newspaper also declared that "a Jew has hardly ever been known to solicit alms" (Kutzik 1967, 292–93). American Jews largely succeeded in keeping poor Jews from stirring up public resentment until the 1880s, when Jews from Russia and Eastern Europe began immigrating in large numbers (Bogen 1917, 4). Still, the perception lingered. In 1902 an American historian wrote that the Stuyvesant Pledge "has been well fulfilled, for such a kind of person as a Jewish pauper has seldom been seen" (Fiske 1902, 390).

JEWISH HOSPITALS GENERATED GOOD WILL FOR THE JEWISH COMMUNITY

Although anti-Jewish prejudice and discrimination existed throughout American history, it was only during and after the Civil War that the United States became "a full-fledged anti-Semitic society" with pervasive and institutionalized bigotry, says Leonard Dinnerstein. The economic distress and political tensions that accompanied the Civil War "ignited vicious reactions to Jews" as Americans North and South "presumed [Jews] to be disloyal profiteers and blamed them as well for major societal problems" (1994, 30–31).

The most notorious incident occurred in December 1862, when Major General Ulysses S. Grant issued an order expelling all Jews from areas under his control, allegedly to counter the activities of smugglers and war profiteers, some of whom were Jews. President Abraham Lincoln later rescinded the order, but not before Union troops forced Jewish families— including "women at home and children at the breast"—from some towns in Tennessee. Grant's order, wrote the *New York Times*, "must have [to Jews] revived the history of their unfortunate people during the twelfth, thirteenth, and fourteenth centuries when England, France, and Austria successively followed each other in decrees against them of banishment and persecution."[8] Indeed.

In response to increased anti-Jewish hostility, American Jews increased the amount of philanthropy they gave to non-Jews. Jews' Hospital exemplified this trend. In 1862, its board volunteered to care for injured Union soldiers, an undertaking that generated positive press (Hirsh and Doherty 1952; Kutzik 1967). The beds at Jews' Hospital, reported the *New York Times*, "are not restricted to the use of the Jews," and its patients were shown great kindness by the hospital's "wealthy and sympathetic ladies," who furnished them delicacies, visits, readings, entertainment, and new and better tailored uniforms. The newspaper also reported that the soldiers' "spiritual needs are not overlooked, but met with that support which seems most genial."[9] This Mission to the Gentiles sought converts from anti-Semitism rather than to Judaism. In 1864, the board of Jews' Hospital decided to admit patients "of every religion or nationality." In 1866, it changed its name to "The Mount Sinai Hospital" to underscore this new policy (Hirsh and Doherty 1952, 44).

Also in 1866, Philadelphia's Jewish community opened a nonsectarian hospital that proclaimed this policy at its entrance: "The Hospital was erected by the voluntary contributions of the Israelites of Philadelphia, and is dedicated to the relief of the sick and wounded without regard to creed, color or nationality." A Philadelphia newspaper lavishly praised the new hospital:

> While taking a justifiable pride in its purely Jewish origins, the founders, with a broad and cosmopolitan charity worthy of all admiration and emulation, declare that its mission of kindness and love would be incomplete did it not embrace suffering humanity irrespective of all distinctions. Charity such as this is the crowning virtue of a citizen.[10]

After the Civil War, writes Alfred Kutzik, American Jews "universally accepted" the proposition that Jewish philanthropy to non-Jews was "the main antidote to anti-Semitism" (1962, 306). Jewish hospitals, writes Kutzik, "were the single most potent community relations component of Jewish philanthropy" (311). "With an imposing facility, huge budget, and commensurate fund-raising," a Jewish hospital was the "most identifiable and impressive Jewish philanthropy" in the area. By serving Jews and non-Jews alike, it "undercut the single substantial criticism of Jewish philanthropy, that Jews restricted their charity to Jews." A Jewish hospital also provided opportunities for non-Jews (as staff, patients, visitors, and attendees at fund-raising events) to interact with and form favorable impressions of Jews (306–8).

Opening the benefactions of Jewish charities to non-Jews to counteract anti-Semitism is consistent with Judaic concepts of *mipnei darkhei shalom* ("for the sake of the ways of peace") and *mipnei eivah* ("to prevent enmity").[11] Traditionally, rabbis invoked these concepts to justify ordinances that supplemented or modified biblical law on a range of subjects, including relations between Jews and non-Jews. Although biblical law did not expressly require *tzedakah* to non-Jews, traditional rabbinic authorities favored some such assistance "for the sake of peace" and "to prevent enmity." A passage in the Talmud reads: "One supports poor non-Jews together with poor Israelites, and one visits sick non-Jews together with sick Israelites, and one buries dead non-Jews as one buries dead Israelites on account of the ways of peace."[12]

The notion of giving for the sake of peace reflects the marginal and precarious situation of Jews in those times when society segregated them into semiautonomous polities. Jews and non-Jews were each expected to take care of their own. This explains why one Judaic authority holds that *darkhei shalom* "only applies when the non-Jew *asks* for Jewish aid. If the non-Jew does not request Jewish aid and does not expect it, there is no obligation to volunteer a contribution because *there are sufficient non-Jews who can support those causes.*"[13] According to one medieval source, ordinances for *darkhei shalom* giving "were in effect only when the Jewish society in some sense depended upon the goodwill of the non-Jewish world" and could be suspended "in situations where Jews had no ground to fear the reaction of the non-Jewish world."[14] Such a time may be far off, believed modern Judaic scholar Moshe Feinstein, who argued that Jewish doctors should be permitted to violate the Sabbath in order to treat non-Jews:

> All must appreciate that a [Jewish doctor's refusal to treat a non-Jew on the Sabbath] would now be totally unacceptable in every country known to us. . . . [The contrary view] is surely not in consonance with the current social condition. . . . If it should be reported that a Jewish physician refuses to treat a non-Jew on the Sabbath while he does treat his fellow Jews, true animosity (*eivah*) will result to the great detriment of the Jewish inhabitants.[15]

Some Judaic authorities—most notably Moses Maimonides (1138–1204)—held that charity to non-Jews expressed more than Jewish self-interest. He wrote that "the Sages *commanded* us to visit the sick of the pagans to promote the ways of peace"—as opposed to simply permitting or suggesting such activity. As proof text, he quoted Psalm 145:9: "As it is said: 'God is good to all and His compassion extends to all His creatures.'" In this way, writes Walter Wurzburger, Maimonides sought to "mak[e] it clear that the prescribed practices [mandating philanthropy to non-Jews] represent vital components of the religious imperative to engage in *imitatio Dei*" (1994, 50–51).

Darkhei shalom giving is inherently pragmatic, although it may also contain touches of the transcendent. In order for Jewish philanthropy to counter anti-Jewish hostility, the beneficiaries must know that their benefactors are Jews. Contrast this with Maimonides' view that giving in secret is the second highest level of *tzedakah*. In such giving, the benefactor "does not know to whom he gives, nor does the recipient know his benefactor."[16] Giving to non-Jews "for the sake of peace" requires publicity in a way that giving to fellow Jews "for the sake of Heaven" does not.

After the Civil War, *darkhei shalom* concerns may have influenced Jewish hospitals to admit non-Jews. According to one historian, "the community relations objective of [the non-sectarian admissions] policy of Jewish hospitals was conscious and in line with the Jewish teaching that *for the sake of peace* all those who are sick should be visited, not only one's own."[17] Directors of Jewish hospitals did not justify the policy on this ground in public. In an era of rising anti-Semitism, American Jews sought to prove that Judaism enjoined philanthropy that was (as a Philadelphia newspaper wrote) "broad and cosmopolitan," "worthy of all admiration and emulation," and "embrace[d] suffering humanity irrespective of all distinctions." Or as Antonio says of Shylock, "The Hebrew will turn Christian: he grows kind."[18]

JEWISH HOSPITALS PROVIDED ENCLAVES FROM ANTI-JEWISH DISCRIMINATION

In 1870, there were approximately 200,000 Jews in the United States. Between 1880 and 1921, an estimated 2.25 million Jews—mostly poor, Yiddish-speaking, and observant—immigrated to the United States. Jewish communities responded by expanding their safety nets. Between 1880 and 1920, the number of cities with Jewish general hospitals more than doubled (Kraut and Kraut 2007, 242–47).

During this period, Christian anti-Semitism was reinforced by the new racial science of eugenics, which linked Jewish ethnicity with such characteristics as weakness, passivity, aggression, and manipulativeness (Praglin 2007, 36). Jews came to be seen as "moral cripples with warped souls who emanated from an inferior racial stock" (Dinnerstein 1994, 59). During the 1920s, Congress passed immigration laws that restricted immigration to Anglo-Saxons, Aryans, and Nordics. Jews were the special target of these laws because "more than any other Caucasian group, Jews were perceived as inimical to the American way of Life" (77).

In the face of racial anti-Semitism, Jewish philanthropy could do relatively little to counter anti-Jewish prejudice. During these years, writes Dinnerstein, "many Jews of German origin tried every method to impress their Gentile peers," including "donat[ing] huge sums of money to favorite Gentile charities like museums, libraries, and universities. . . . But they were never accepted by those they tried to emulate" (1994, 92). Dinnerstein concludes that "no behavioral modifications would lessen antisemitism nor could any particular acts significantly impress Christians who did not like Jews" (54). In 1898, a Jewish newspaper in St. Louis advised Jews to "desist from their endeavor of pleasing Christians more than themselves" (54).

Anti-Jewish prejudice could affect the quality of medical care that Jews received. At Massachusetts General, staff members typically assumed that a Jewish immigrant's life had less social value than a native-born American's (Praglin 2007, 34). Writing in 1910, a distinguished Boston physician confessed that, when presented with a Jewish male patient,

> the chances are ten to one that I shall look out of my eyes and see, *not* Abraham Cohen, but a *Jew*; not the clear outlines of this unique sufferer, but the vague misty composite photography of all the hundreds of Jews who in the past ten years have shuffled up to me with bent back and deprecating eyes, and taken their seats upon this stool to tell their story. I see a Jew—a nervous, complaining, whimpering Jew—with his beard upon his chest and the inevitable dirty black frockcoat flapping about his knees. I do not see *this* man at all. I merge him in the hazy background of the average Jew. (Kraut and Kraut 2007, 4–5)

Care such as this could be hazardous to Jews' health. When immigrants *kvetched* about fatigue, headaches, pain, constipation, or apprehension, some doctors diagnosed them with "Hebraic Debility" or "jew-neurasthenia" (Linenthal 1992, 19–20; Praglin 2007, 36).

For recent immigrants, Jewish hospitals provided some shelter from the consequences of prejudice. At these institutions, the patients' observances and mannerisms were accepted "without indifference or hostility" (Solomon 1961). They "could pour their hearts out to [the doctors] without an interpreter," which itself could be "powerful medicine."[19] They were also more likely to follow instructions given in their native tongue.

In the 1920s Jewish immigration virtually ceased, but anti-Semitism did not. Its focus shifted to the children of Jewish immigrants, who "came of age with great expectations for their futures in America" (Wegner 2007,

199). To some Protestant elites, the rising generation of Jews threatened to overrun their exclusive realms of schooling, employment, housing, and recreation, and so diminish the "American" and Christian character of these institutions (Dinnerstein 1994, 78–79). Jews seeking careers in medicine and other fields faced new hurdles. Colleges and medical schools imposed quotas to limit the number of Jews admitted. From 1920 to 1940, the enrollment of Jewish students in Columbia University's medical school dropped from 47 percent to 6.5 percent (Wegner 2007, 158). The University of Pittsburgh's medical school enforced a 10 percent quota so strictly that one year it admitted 9.5 Jews for a class of 95 students—the half-student took courses on a half-time basis (Bleier et al. 1997). To help screen out Jews, schools required an applicant to submit a photograph and answer questions about his religion or "racial origin," his parents' place of birth, his mother's maiden name, and any changes to his own name (Kraut and Kraut 2007, 118).

Anti-Semitism in the medical establishment was more nuanced than elsewhere. Jewish medical students were objectionable, it was claimed, because of their manner and style, as opposed to their race or religion. They were aggressive, asocial, unstable, and disagreeable—traits that were out of place in a profession that valued gentility. Moreover, quotas were good for Jews, it was alleged, because they averted the backlash that would occur if medical schools admitted them in large numbers (Kraut and Kraut 2007, 118–20).

Anti-Jewish discrimination did not stop at medical school admissions. Non-Jewish hospitals denied internships and residencies to Jewish medical school graduates, hampering their ability to specialize. This, in turn, made it harder for Jews to engage in medical research or obtain faculty appointments at medical schools (Kraut and Kraut 2007, 119). Non-Jewish hospitals denied staff privileges to Jewish practitioners, which meant they could not admit or treat patients at those facilities. "Without access to hospital beds and facilities to practice first-rate medicine, it became impossible [for these practitioners] to efficiently treat ill patients" (Lyon 1995, 10). When a Jewish physician had patients who needed hospital care, he had to refer them to a non-Jewish colleague.

After Jewish immigration ended, "the need for Jewish hospitals became far greater for Jewish doctors than it was for Jewish patients" (Lyon 1995, 33). As Jews became more Americanized, they felt more comfortable staying at non-Jewish institutions (Rosner 1986, 319). According to a survey taken in the 1930s, one-half to two-thirds of Jewish patients were receiving care at general hospitals under public, proprietary, Christian, or nonsectarian auspices (Lurie 1961, 448). The situation was much different for Jewish physicians. As a doctor from Pittsburgh explained, "Patients might be more comfortable in a Jewish atmosphere and perhaps more trusting in the absolute integrity of the kosher tray, but they had options. We didn't."[20] Discrimination in the medical establishment gave American Jews new reasons to support Jewish hospitals, and they responded.[21] From 1920 to 1960, Jewish federations—the fundraising umbrella groups in Jewish communities—allocated approximately 25 percent of their local grants to Jewish hospitals (Ginzberg and Rogatz 1961, 130; Lurie 1961, 318). During most of the 1960s, Jewish hospitals continued to receive the single largest allocation from their local federation (Kutzik 1967, 1001).

Supporting Jewish hospitals partly as a means to assist Jewish physicians was more than ethnic philanthropy; it was exemplary *tzedakah*. According to Maimonides (who was also a physician), the highest form of *tzedakah* enables a person to become economically self-sufficient. This can be achieved by helping the person find gainful employment and ensuring his livelihood through patronage (Taub 2001, 39–40). Helping Jews find careers in medicine met this criterion. As an Indianapolis rabbi has observed: "We can't expect all Jews to be tailors."[22]

JEWS HAD LESS NEED FOR JEWISH HOSPITALS AND VICE VERSA

Changes in American society after World War II eliminated many of the problems that Jewish hospitals were founded to address. They became increasingly irrelevant to the Jewish community and vice versa.

With the decline of anti-Semitism in the United States, it became easier for Jews to train and practice at non-Jewish hospitals and to join the faculties of medical schools. The desire of these institutions "for the best candidates was stronger than the institutionalized anti-Semitism." Jewish hospitals, in turn, had more difficulty attracting the most talented Jewish physicians for their residencies and staffs (Aufses and Niss 2002, 13).

As non-Jewish hospitals became more welcoming to Jews, demand among Jews for Jewish hospitals fell. In 1962, a Catholic hospital in Reading, Pennsylvania, installed a kosher kitchen—the first non-Jewish hospital to do so (Solomon 1967, 147). As Jews joined the middle class, many moved to the suburbs. It became less convenient and more dangerous to visit Jewish hospitals because most were located in depressed inner cities where Jews once lived.

American Jews also found they had bigger problems than residual anti-Semitism in medicine. Although, as Alan Dershowitz observes, "American Jews—as *individuals*—have never been more secure, more accepted, more affluent,[23] and less victimized by discrimination or anti-Semitism," American Jews *as a community* "have never been in greater danger of disappearing through assimilation, intermarriage, and low birthrates."[24] Many Jewish leaders share Dershowitz's view that the community "is at imminent risk, unless we do something dramatic *now* to confront the quickly changing dangers" (1997, 2). Jewish federations dramatically reduced their allocations to hospitals and health care (from 25 percent of federation allocations in 1961 to 2.3 percent in 1981) and increased their support for Jewish education (from 9.9% of domestic allocations in 1961 to 25.7% in 1981) (Bernstein 1983, 337–38). As for anti-Jewish prejudice, American Jews are more eager and able to combat it head-on, and not merely indirectly through philanthropy. This is reflected in the activities of groups such as the American Jewish Committee and the Anti-Defamation League, founded in 1906 and 1913, respectively.

As Jews had less need for Jewish hospitals, these institutions became less demonstrably Jewish. According to a 1957 survey, Jews comprised only 38.4 percent of the patients in Jewish general hospitals. As their revenue from fees and government grants grew, Jewish hospitals became less dependent on Jewish philanthropy: in 1959, private philanthropy covered less than 15 percent of their operating costs (Lurie 1961, 448, 318). Philanthropy became even less important in the 1960s with the advent of Medicare and Medicaid, which reduced the need for hospitals to provide uncompensated care. Boards of Jewish hospitals paid less heed to demands to maintain kosher kitchens, exclude pork products from cafeterias, and bar Christmas decorations (Kraut and Kraut 2007; Gee 1992).

JEWISH HOSPITALS BECAME LESS COMMERCIALLY VIABLE

Since the early 1980s, changes in the hospital industry have squeezed out most freestanding community-based hospitals, a category that included all Jewish hospitals. Until 1983, the federal government paid most hospitals to treat Medicare patients on a "cost-plus" basis, which enabled them to recover their full costs and earn some profits. In 1983, Congress introduced the Prospective Payment System (PPS), which set fixed Medicare payment levels for various medical conditions. Because Medicare patients constituted around 40 percent of the average hospital's inpatients, the new system gave hospitals strong incentives to contain their costs and provide services more efficiently. "Hospitals that could provide care [to Medicare patients] within the price limit could pocket the savings," while "those that could not had to absorb the losses" (Shortell, Morrison, and Friedman 1990, 4).

After 1983, more large for-profit systems entered the hospital industry, making it more competitive. A substantial number of community hospitals closed.[25] Others joined multi-hospital systems, seeking economies of scale and more bargaining power to negotiate with private insurance companies. A significant number sold their facilities, mostly to for-profit systems, and used the sale proceeds to endow grant-making foundations. Between 1983 and 1999, 107 nonprofit hospitals took this route, which resulted in the creation of "conversion foundations" with a combined total of $13.2 billion in assets (Champion 2000). In 2006, there were at least 185 foundations with assets generated by hospital conversions, with $21.5 billion in assets.[26]

The differences between nonprofit and for-profit hospitals have become less discernible. As noted above, Medicare and Medicaid reduced the need for hospitals to provide uncompensated care. Changes in the hospital industry have impaired the ability of hospitals to supply such care. Absent philanthropic support and government subsidies, a hospital must finance charity care through cross-subsidization, that is, with surpluses earned from self-paying and insured patients. This became more difficult as competition reduced profit margins and as private insurance companies imposed their own prospective payment systems and scrutinized hospital utilization more strictly (Shortell, Morrison, and Friedman 1990, 6).

THE END OF JEWISH HOSPITALS: WAS IT GOOD (FOR THE JEWS)?

In the past quarter-century, changes in the hospital industry forced directors of Jewish hospitals to make some difficult decisions. Could their institution stay both competitive and institutionally Jewish? Should it join a nonprofit system to become more competitive, even if this meant forfeiting control by members of the local Jewish community? Should they sell the institution and use the proceeds to support other charitable causes and organizations? If so, which causes and organizations should they support?

For two reasons, these boards had wide discretion to redefine their institution's mission and redeploy its assets. First, almost all Jewish hospitals were organized as non-membership nonprofit corporations, instead of charitable trusts, and derived most of their wealth from income for services and goods rendered.[27] (The present value of the Jewish community's past financial contributions is relatively small.) They thus lacked a single major donor whose instructions they were obliged to follow, absent extraordinary circumstances. Second, Jewish hospitals were organized as freestanding institutions. This set them apart from some church-sponsored hospitals, whose articles of incorporation guarantee the sponsoring church or affiliated entity a formal role in their governance. These articles may grant that church or entity a say in key matters such as merger or sale. They may also provide that, upon the hospital's dissolution, its assets will go to that church or entity.

In 1983, there were twenty-four Jewish general hospitals outside New York.[28] Of these, seven still operate as Jewish hospitals, six have merged with non-Jewish systems, and three went bankrupt after struggling to stay open.[29] The remaining eight were sold to other systems and the proceeds used for grant making.

The Jewish hospitals that survived found a niche and formed their own systems.[30] Mount Sinai in Miami represents one type of Jewish hospital: it serves a substantial number of observant Jews and meets their religious needs and cultural sensibilities. Mount Sinai in Chicago is another: it serves mostly poor African American and Hispanic individuals from the surrounding neighborhood, Lawndale, which once housed Jewish immigrants from Eastern Europe. The hospital remains connected to Chicago's Jewish community through Jewish directors, donors, physicians, and volunteers as well as its affiliation with Chicago's Jewish federation, which provides grants and loan guarantees, and lobbies on its behalf for more public support.

A third type of Jewish hospital strives to honor its Jewish origins through excellence in teaching and research.[31] This institutional striving to be "the best" has been attributed to the "Jewish love affair with education,"[32] the "well-documented need for achievement among Jews," and "ethnocentric pride" (Feldman 1976, 230). Other explanations are possible. Jewish hospitals did not become excellent because they were Jewish; they had to meet high standards in order to provide residencies and internships to Jewish medical school graduates. (Beware the regress: why were all those Jewish graduates striving to be excellent physicians?) When that need waned, some Jewish hospitals came to see the pursuit of excellence as the better part of their mission.

Ironically, these same stereotypically Jewish characteristics—the love of education and the pursuit of excellence—pushed some Jewish hospitals to merge with non-Jewish systems. Their directors saw merger as a means to maintain first-rate training and research programs. In the end, they decided it was more important for their institution to be excellent than to be Jewish.

By the 1980s and 1990s, many people in the Jewish community were questioning "whether, with the passing of time, the Jewish hospital remains a necessary concept" (Wagner 1991). Advocates for these institutions pointed to their role in generating good will and countering anti-Semitic attitudes. Jewish hospitals were also needed, they argued, as insurance in the event of a resurgence of anti-Semitism in the medical establishment.[33] The latter claim is implausible and smacks of fear-mongering. In any event, there are far more direct and efficient ways to combat anti-Semitism in medicine, including watchdog groups and anti-discrimination laws.

The plurality of Jewish hospitals have sold their facilities to other systems and become grant-making foundations.[34] Their total assets exceed $1 billion, which represents almost 5 percent of the combined assets of all hospital conversion foundations. All eight of the foundations that were formed from the sale of Jewish hospitals make at least some grants to expressly Jewish organizations and causes, some more than others. Most concentrate their Jewish grant making on the health and human services needs of elderly Jews, recent immigrants from the former Soviet Union, people with disabilities and special needs, Holocaust survivors, and other vulnerable and underserved Jewish populations.[35] They connect their focus on health care to the mission and values of the Jewish institution they succeeded and whose sale created their endowment.

The largest of these, Rose Community Foundation, focuses its Jewish grant making on the health of Jewish life rather than on the health of Jewish individuals. It supports "efforts to create and sustain a vibrant Jewish community," especially through "outreach to unconnected Jews, experiences that promote Jewish growth, leadership development, and organizational development." This entails, among other things, grants to Jewish studies programs and student organizations at universities, Jewish youth groups, festivals and conferences that celebrate Jewish learning and culture, Judaism 101 classes, a "Shalom Baby" program for families with newborns, and special programs for intermarried couples and children of interfaith marriages.

For many Jews, donating to the Jewish federation's annual campaign is a way to affirm their membership in, and concern for, the Jewish community. Jewish federations reinforce this perception, declaring that a donation "is a noble expression of devotion to the entire Jewish people," "demonstrates a love of community," and makes "a proud statement of commitment to our individual communities and to every individual Jew." There's a risk that large-scale grant making by Jewish foundations might reduce or "crowd out" more modest giving by individual Jews. To counter this effect, Rose Community Foundation helps Denver-area Jewish organizations expand and improve their fundraising activities.

Getting people to write a modest check to the federation is not the only way to connect them to the community. Another way is to get them more involved in directing the community's philanthropy. Rose Community Foundation has developed creative ways to engage young Jews in its grant making. In one program, a group of Jewish teens collectively decide how to give away $50,000 in grants to Jewish and non-Jewish organizations in the area. In the process, the teens become more involved in the Jewish community and "learn about and practice the Jewish traditions of *tikkun olam* and *tzedakah*, and . . . about responsible grant making." In another program, young adults give away $94,000 "in a primarily Jewish way," as part of a larger initiative "to deepen the connection of Jews in their 20s and 30s with Jewish life." Through their participation, these young people invest far more of themselves than they might by simply writing a check.

Almost all of the eight new foundations make substantial grants to non-Jewish organizations and causes. In addition to helping their direct beneficiaries, these grants may indirectly generate good will for the Jewish community. All but one of the foundations publicize their origins in the Jewish community, including the Jewish Healthcare Foundation of Pittsburgh, the Jewish Heritage Foundation of Greater Kansas City, the Jewish Fund of Detroit, and the Healthcare Foundation of New Jersey ("Founded by the Jewish Community"). These foundations resemble Jewish donors who, as Gary Tobin explains, support non-Jewish causes in part because they "do not want non-Jews to assume that they support only Jewish causes, or that Jews are too insulated or self-concerned. Some feel that if Jews are too isolated and provincial, the hospitable atmosphere of the general society will not respond to Jewish needs" (Tobin 2004, 285). In this vein, a director of one foundation believes that "all the money in our endowment is Jewish money, and it is a powerful example for the wider community that as Jews we care about the health and well-being of all people."

Such considerations differ in crucial ways from *darkhei shalom* ("for the ways of peace"), a concept unfamiliar to most non-Orthodox Jews. In its purely pragmatic formulation, *darkhei shalom* sees the non-Jewish world as a bit like Cossacks at the gate, who must be appeased in order to avert a pogrom. Few American Jews think that way. When non-Orthodox Jews support general organizations and causes, they are more likely to see themselves as engaged in the work of *tikkun olam* ("to repair the world"). (See Judy Failer's excellent discussion in this volume of how some Orthodox Jews understand *tikkun ha-olam*.) Reform Jewish leaders, for example, declare that "*tikkun olam*—repairing the world—is a hallmark of Reform Judaism as we strive to bring peace, freedom, and justice to all people."[36] Many Jews see *tikkun olam* giving as a means to express their Jewish values and commitments. For this reason, they may donate to Jewish charitable intermediaries such as Chicago's Mount Sinai Hospital, the Jewish Fund for Justice (which promotes social and economic justice in the U.S.), the American Jewish World Service (which promotes economic development in the Third World), and Mazon ("food"): A Jewish Response to Hunger. The good relations such gifts may generate is a bonus.

CONCLUSION

Like other nonprofit hospitals, Jewish hospitals conferred significant benefits on the community at large. During the era of anti-Semitism, they were especially important for Jews. For the poor and observant, they expanded access to free and amenable hospital care. For Jews seeking careers in medicine, they expanded opportunities for training, research, and practice. For the Jewish community as a whole, they generated good will and reduced a source of resentment among non-Jews.

In the United States today, people incur few penalties for being of Jewish descent or self-identifying as Jews. It has also never been easier for someone of Jewish descent to exit the community—to *not* be a Jew—even without converting to Christianity. For several decades now, Jewish hospitals have done relatively little to promote Jewish continuity. No Jewish community without a Jewish hospital would consider building one. Had these institutions been owned by federations instead of being independent, more would have been sold, closed, and given away and the resources they held and consumed used to address more pressing matters. This was true of church-affiliated hospitals, which responded to overcapacity in the hospital industry by exiting it more quickly as compared to independent nonprofits. The reason for this, explains Henry Hansmann and colleagues (2002, 8), is that "religiously-affiliated hospitals often have an owner of sorts, if not in the formal legal sense then at least in the functional sense that . . . the church . . . exercises substantial control over them." When a church has a portfolio of agencies and ministries, it has more incentive to shift resources among them in order to maximize the portfolio's value to the church and its flock. Jewish hospitals are more like unaffiliated secular hospitals, whose directors need only take stock of their own organization's activities.

A quarter-century ago, majority-Jewish boards controlled the fate and assets of twenty-four hospitals outside New York. A substantial number merged their institutions with non-Jewish systems, a move that effectively jettisoned their Jewish identity and put their assets beyond the reach of the Jewish community. Some joined with Christian systems and created improbably named entities such as Barnes-Jewish/Christian (BJC) Health-Care in St. Louis (*oy*), Jewish Hospital & St. Mary's HealthCare in Louisville (*vey*), and Beth Israel Deaconess Medical Center in Boston (*iz mir*). Others stayed the course in ways that serve both Jewish and general communities, as with Chicago's Mount Sinai. (It is also true that Mount Sinai generates significant good will for the Jewish community without consuming much of its resources—a bargain!—and likely could not be sold in any event.)

On balance, Jewish philanthropy in the United States would be more robust today if more Jewish hospitals had sold their institutions and become grant makers. Most Jewish communities can find more innovative and urgent ways to perform *tzedakah* and engage in *tikkun olam* than by operating nonprofit hospitals.[37] Additionally, the future of American Jewry would be more secure if foundations financed by hospital sales would devote more resources to Jewish education, religion, culture, and communal life. This grant-making agenda advances what I see as the fondest and most fundamental hope of many founders of Jewish hospitals: to help American Jewry survive and thrive as a distinct community. (A related hope inspired Hadassah, a Zionist organization for American Jewish women, to build nonsectarian hospitals in the land of Israel.)[38] The institutions they founded countered the greatest obstacle to Jewish flourishing in *their* time—anti-Semitism. Foundations such as Rose Community Foundation keep faith with these founders by counteracting the gravest threat to Jewish flourishing in *our* time—the alienation of many Jews from Jewish heritage and communal life.

What would these founders think about hospitals with half-Jewish names and no connection to the Jewish community? They might derive as much joy from them as American Indians do from cities with Indian names but no Indians that they relinquished for a pittance. Had founders anticipated this outcome, they might have taken more steps to prevent it. For example, they might have drafted articles that protected the institution's Jewish mission from tampering by future boards, granted a governance role to the federation or other entity that serves the interests of the Jewish community as a whole, and devolved the hospital's assets to that entity upon sale or closure.

The denouement of Jewish hospitals presented opportunities for fresh and dynamic Jewish philanthropy. Some of these opportunities were pursued, while a few were squandered. Their story offers a valuable lesson for philanthropic Jews and other communities of faith and fate. When founding and funding charities that partly serve to secure their collective survival, they should consider what happens if and when a charity ceases to serve that end. In that event, the community has a right and perhaps a duty to ensure that the entity's resources be recouped and reapplied in ways that both preserve themselves and benefit society.

NOTES

1. I borrow this expression from Peter Berkowitz, who uses it to describe the situation of students of Leo Strauss in the academy ("The Reason of Revelation: The Jewish Thought of Leo Strauss," *The Weekly Standard* [Washington D.C.], May 25, 1998).

2. See *Pirkei Avot* 1:14 (quoting Hillel the Elder, a Jewish sage who lived in the first century CE) ("If I am not for myself, then who will be for me? And if I am only for myself, then what am I? And if not now, when?").

3. Yossi Prager, "Jewish Giving: Keeping the Faith Alive," *Philanthropy Magazine*, May 1, 2005.

4. Kraut and Kraut 2007, 6. See also Lurie 1961, 318: "All cities with Jewish populations of 30,000, with the exception of Washington, D.C., have established a general hospital under Jewish auspices, as have also three cities with less than 15,000 and eight cities with from 14,000 to 40,000 Jewish population."

5. Numbers and Amundsen 1986, 2–3. Some Christian churches valued the hospitals they sponsored in part because of their perceived efficacy in drawing nonbelievers to their faith.

6. The duty to give charity stems from the requirement that we do justice, *tzedakah*, from the root *tzedek*, "righteous" (Wurzburger 1994, 47).

7. "Hebrew Charity," *New York Times*, April 16, 1871.

8. "General Grant and the Jews," *New York Times*, January 18, 1863, 4.

9. "Military Wards of the Jews Hospital," *New York Times*, September 16, 1862.

10. Kutzik 1962, 311, quoting "The Jew as a Citizen," [Philadelphia] *Evening Telegraph*, October 19, 1872.

11. Wurzburger (1994, 49) argues that "there is no conceptual difference between the two formulations [*mipnei darkhei shalom* and *mipnei eivah*], which, for all practical purposes, are equivalent." Robert Novak (2000, 152) sees them as opposite versions of the Golden Rule, with *mipnei darkhei shalom* corresponding to "love your neighbor as yourself," and *mipnei eivah* corresponding to "what is hateful to you, do not do to someone else."

12. B. Gittin 61a, cited by Wurzburger 1994, 48.

13. Feuer 2001, 406, citing *Responsa Avnei Yashpei* [*Yoreh Deah*, 1:193]; emphasis added.

14. Ibid., 83 (citation omitted).

15. Spitzer n.d., quoting R. Moshe Feinstein (1895–1986), whom Spitzer describes as "arguably the most influential modern halakhic authority."

16. Maimonides, Mishneh Torah, Laws of Gifts to the Poor 10:8.

17. Davis 1949, 70 (internal quotations omitted, emphasis added).

18. Shakespeare, *Merchant of Venice*, Act I, Scene 1, 180.

19. Bleier, Donnelly, and Granowitz 1997, 113, quoting Dr. Sidney Kaufman.

20. Ibid.

21. Ginzberg and Rogatz 1961, 19, 39. According to a 1929 survey of Jews in the New York City area, support for Jewish hospitals was motivated in large part by "the desire of Jewish physicians to have institutions in which discrimination against Jewish doctors would not exist" (Lurie 1995, 32).

22. Rabbi N. Schuman, Congregation B'nai Torah, Indianapolis, interview by R. Katz, February 22, 2008.

23. According to Pew's 2008 survey, Jews have the highest income levels among major religious groups in the U.S.—46% make more than $100,000 per year. By contrast, only 19% of Catholics make over $100,000 per year. See Pew Forum on Religion & Public Life, "U.S. Religious Landscape Survey," http://religions.pewforum.org.

24. Dershowitz 1997, 1; emphasis in original. To cite one statistic, the percentage of Jews marrying non-Jews has risen from 9 percent in 1965 to 52 percent. See United Jewish Communities, "A Brief History of the Federation System," www.ujc.org/page.html?ArticleID=1039&page=3.

25. Between 1980 and 1987, 519 of the nation's hospitals closed, according to Shortell, Morrison, and Friedman (1990, 9).

26. Grantmakers in Health, "Connecting to Community and Building Accountability," www.gih.org/usr_doc/October_2007.pdf.

27. Mt. Sinai Hospital in New York (formerly Jews' Hospital) was initially organized as a membership nonprofit corporation whose members, typically small donors, elected the board of directors. The hospital was later reorganized as a non-membership nonprofit corporation, which empowered its directors to select their own successors. I know of only one Jewish hospital founded with a charitable trust—the Nathan and Miriam Barnert Memorial Hospital in Paterson, New Jersey. In 1914, Nathan Barnert deeded land in trust to the Barnert Hospital Association, a nonprofit corporation, for the creation of a hospital, on condition that the hospital "shall be non-sectarian, and the food supplied for use therein shall be provided in accordance with the Hebrew

Dietary and Kosher; and the said hospital shall be devoted as far as practicable to the accommodation of poor people without accommodation" (Baum 1914, 121). The hospital declared bankruptcy in 2007, and its assets may revert to Barnert's heirs.

28. My sample consists of twenty-four hospitals in twenty-three cities outside New York. New York hospitals must be analyzed separately in part because state law does not allow for-profit hospitals. See N.Y. Pub. Health Law § 2801-a(1). These were Sinai Hospital of Baltimore, Beth Israel Hospital (Boston), Michael Reese (Chicago), Mount Sinai Hospital Medical Center (Chicago), Jewish Hospital (Cincinnati), Mount Sinai (Cleveland), Rose Medical Center (Denver), Sinai Hospital (Detroit), Mount Sinai (Hartford), Menorah Medical Center (Kansas City), Cedars-Sinai (Los Angeles), Jewish Hospital (Louisville), Mount Sinai Medical Center (Miami), Mount Sinai Medical Center (Milwaukee), Mount Sinai (Minneapolis), Touro Infirmary (New Orleans), Beth Israel Medical Center (Newark), Passaic Beth Israel Hospital (Passaic, New Jersey), Barnert Memorial Hospital Center (Paterson, New Jersey), Albert Einstein Medical Center (Philadelphia), Montefiore Hospital (Pittsburgh), Miriam Hospital (Providence), Mount Zion Hospital and Medical Center (San Francisco), and Jewish Hospital of St. Louis.

29. The three were Minneapolis, Passaic, and Paterson.

30. The survivors were Baltimore, Chicago (Mount Sinai), Los Angeles, Miami, New Orleans, Philadelphia, and Providence.

31. According to a 1976 study of hospitals in New York City, Jewish hospitals committed a larger share of their resources to education, teaching, and research than comparable Protestant and Catholic facilities (Feldman 1976, 218).

32. Wagner 1991 (quoting Ruth Rothstein, former president of Chicago's Mount Sinai Hospital: the hospital "will continue [our educational program for residents and medical students] in spite of the costs because we have a Jewish love affair with education.")

33. Ibid.

34. Michael Reese Health Trust, formed from the 1991 sale of Chicago's Michael Reese Hospital (2006 Assets: $119.8 million); The Mt. Sinai Health Care Foundation, formed in 1994 from the sale of Cleveland's Mt. Sinai Hospital (2006 assets: $141 million); The Jewish Foundation of Cincinnati, founded in 1996 from the sale of the Jewish Hospital of Cincinnati (2006 assets: $89.1 million); Rose Community Foundation, formed in 1995 from the sale of Denver's Rose Medical Center (2007 assets: $325 million); the Jewish Fund, formed in following the sale of Detroit's Sinai Hospital (2006 assets: $63.4 million); Jewish Heritage Foundation of Greater Kansas City, formed in 1994 from the sale of Kansas City's Menorah Hospital (2005 assets: $47.8 million); The Healthcare Foundation of New Jersey, formed in 1996 from the sale of Newark's Beth Israel Hospital (2006 assets: $172 million); and Jewish Healthcare Foundation, formed in 1990 from the sale of Pittsburgh's Montefiore Hospital (2006 assets: $127.4 million).

35. See, e.g., the Healthcare Foundation of New Jersey; the Jewish Healthcare Foundation (Pittsburgh).

36. Union for Reform Judaism, "What is Reform Judaism?" http://rj.org/whatisrj .shtml.

37. See, e.g., Mary Jo Feldstein, "BJC settles lawsuit for uninsured patients," *St. Louis Post-Dispatch*, March 19, 2008. (BJC HealthCare, the nonprofit entity that owns the former Jewish Hospital of St. Louis, spent 0.84 percent of its operating revenue

on charity care in 2005, less than the state average of .93 percent and less than the area's other major hospital systems).

38. Hadassah Medical Organization, Mission Statement, www.hadassah.org.il/English/Eng_MainNavBar/About/Mission+Statement/.

REFERENCES

Aufses, A., and B. Niss. 2002. *This House of Noble Deeds: The Mount Sinai Hospital, 1852–2002.* New York: New York University Press.

Baum, M. T. 1914. *Biography of Nathan Barnert, His Character and Achievements: Including Histories of Local Institutions.* Paterson, N.J.: News Printing.

Bernstein, P. 1983. *To Dwell in Unity: The Jewish Federation Movement in America Since 1960.* Philadelphia: Jewish Publication Society of America.

Bleier, C. S., L. Donnelly, and S. P. Granowitz. 1997. *A History of Montefiore Hospital of Pittsburgh, Pennsylvania 1898–1990.* Pittsburgh: Montefiore History Fund.

Bogen, B. D. 1917. *Jewish Philanthropy: An Exposition of Principles and Methods of Jewish Social Service in the United States.* New York: Macmillan.

Champion, S. J. 2000. "Foundations and Endowments: Hospital Conversion Foundations." *Senior Consultant* 3, no. 1 (January): 1–3.

Davis, M. 1949. "Jewish Religious Life and Institutions in America." In *The Jews, Their History, Culture, and Religion,* ed. L. Finkelstein. Philadelphia: Jewish Publication Society of America.

Dershowitz, A. M. 1997. *The Vanishing American Jew: In Search of Jewish Identity for the Next Century.* New York: Simon and Schuster.

Dinnerstein, L. 1994. *Antisemitism in America.* New York: Oxford University Press.

Dorff, E. N. 2005. *The Way into Tikkun Olam (Repairing the World).* Woodstock, Vt.: Jewish Lights Publishing.

Feldman, E. 1976. Characteristics of Catholic, Jewish, and Protestant Hospitals in New York City. Ph.D. diss., Columbia University.

Feuer, Avrohom Chaim. 2001. *The Tzedakah Treasury: An Anthology of Torah Teachings on the Mitzvah of Charity—to Instruct and Inspire.* Brooklyn, N.Y.: Mesorah Publications Ltd.

Fiske, J. 1902. *The Dutch and Quaker Colonies in America.* New York: Houghton Mifflin.

Gee, D. A. 1992. *Working Wonders: A History of The Jewish Hospital of St. Louis 1891–1992.* St. Louis: Jewish Hospital at Washington University Medical Center, St. Louis.

Ginzberg, Eli, and Peter Rogatz. 1961. *Planning for Better Hospital Care: Report on the Hospitals and Health Agencies of the Federation of Jewish Philanthropies of New York.* New York: Columbia University Press.

Hansmann, Henry, Daniel P. Kessler, and Mark B. McClellan. 2002. "Ownership Form and Trapped Capital in the Hospital Industry." Yale Law & Economics Research Paper No. 266. http://ssrn.com/abstract=313827.

Hirsh, J., and B. Doherty. 1952. *The First Hundred Years of the Mount Sinai Hospital of New York.* New York: Random House.

Kraut, A. M., and D. A. Kraut. 2007. *Covenant of Care: Newark Beth Israel and the Jewish Hospital in America.* New Brunswick, N.J.: Rutgers University Press.

Kutzik, A. J. 1967. The Social Basis of American Jewish Philanthropy. Ph.D. diss., Brandeis University.

Linenthal, A. J. 1992. *First a Dream: The History of Boston's Jewish Hospitals, 1896–1928.* Boston: Beth Israel Hospital / Francis A. Countway Library of Medicine.

Lurie, H. L. 1961. *A Heritage Affirmed: The Jewish Federation Movement in America.* Philadelphia: Jewish Publication Society of America.

Lyon, F. A. 1995. *Mount Sinai Hospital of Minneapolis, Minnesota: A History.* Minneapolis: Mount Sinai Hospital History Committee, 1995.

Maimonides. *Mishneh Torah*, Laws of Gifts of [*that belong to*] the Poor (translated by Jonathan J. Baker, 2003). Available at www.panix.com/njjbaker/rmbmzdkh.html.

Novak, D. 2000. *Covenantal Rights: A Study in Jewish Political Theory.* Princeton, N.J.: Princeton University Press.

Numbers, R. L., and D. W. Amundsen. 1986. Introduction to *Caring and Curing: Health and Medicine in the Western Religious Traditions.* Baltimore: Johns Hopkins University Press.

Praglin, L. J. 2007. "Ida Cannon, Ethel Cohen, and Early Medical Social Work in Boston: The Foundations of a Model of Culturally Competent Social Service." *Social Service Review*, March.

Rosner, F. 1986. "The Jewish Patient in a Non-Jewish Hospital." *Journal of Religion and Health* 25, no. 4 (Winter): 316–24.

Salomon, G. 1963. "Communal." *American Jewish Year Book* 63: 145–259.

Shortell, S. M., E. M. Morrison, and B. Friedman. 1990. *Strategic Choices for America's Hospitals: Managing Change in Turbulent Times.* San Francisco: Jossey-Bass.

Solomon, D. N. 1961. "Ethnic and Class Differences among Hospitals as Contingencies in Medical Careers." *American Journal of Sociology* 66, no. 5 (March): 463–71.

Spitzer, J. A. n.d. "The Non-Jew in Jewish Law." MyJewishLearning.com. www.myjewishlearning.com/ideas_belief/Jews_NonJews/NJ_Legal_TO/NJ_Legal_Spitzer.htm.

Taub, S. 2001. *The Laws of Tzedakah and Maaser: A Comprehensive Guide.* Brooklyn, N.Y.: Mesorah Publications.

Telushkin, J. 1991. *Jewish Literacy.* New York: William Morrow.

Tobin, G. "Jewish Philanthropy in American Society." 2004. In *Philanthropy in America: A Comprehensive Historical Encyclopedia*, ed. D. F. Burlingame, 2:284–88. Santa Barbara: ABC-CLIO, 2004.

Wagner, M. 1991. "Jewish Hospitals Yesterday and Today." *Modern Healthcare*, February 4.

Wegner, B. S. 2007. *The Jewish Americans: Three Centuries of Jewish Voices in America.* New York: Doubleday.

Wurzburger, W. S. 1994. *Ethics of Responsibility: Pluralistic Approaches to Covenantal Ethics.* Philadelphia: Jewish Publication Society.

One Man's Extrapolations: Conclusions after Two Years of Listening

DAVID H. SMITH

The authors of the preceding essays met three times, listened to each other's ideas, modified their own (to a greater or lesser extent) and produced this collection. For most of that time my role as editor was listening and reading; now, after spending considerable time with these essays and their authors, I offer my observations and conclusions. This latter phase of my role is convenient, since my colleagues will have to offer their rebuttals outside the covers of the book. But my spirit will be irenic; I am constitutionally disposed to want to agree with everyone, a viewpoint that does not lend itself to crisp argumentation.

My observations are organized under three headings: the relationship between God and giving, giving as a form of participation within one's own community of faith, and the question of to whom we should give.

GOD

For Judaism, Christianity, and Islam, God is a central figure in religion, but there is little agreement, either among those traditions or within any one of them, about the nature of God, not to mention God's relationship with humankind. All historically affirm that God is creator and transcendent, but this leaves the door open to a lot of recombination of the details.

Western religions are stuck with what someone once called the monotheistic syndrome: the idea that there is a God and that a person's relationship to God is the most central fact of his or her life. Even if we were all clear and in agreement about who or what God is, this syndrome would complicate our moral lives; ethics is conceptually much easier without God.

But the fact is that few if any of us are fully sure about the nature of God. We have scriptures, traditions, images, beliefs, loyalties, and feelings. We may be able to situate ourselves as more or less traditional, more or less devout, than other people we know. Some feel they can and should articulate key insights into God's nature, and we see that ventured in some essays in this book. Still, something escapes our understanding, and these authors would all be uncomfortable with persons who were overconfident about their knowledge of God.

GOD AND GIVING

For these authors, the argument about religion and giving is theological. With the possible exception of Schervish, they believe that it is not sensible to talk of religion without talking of God. Arguments for giving are complicated and enriched by the existence of God; they are not just arguments about moral responsibility.

Three distinct paradigms for understanding the relationship between God and giving appear in these essays. One is the image of command and obedience. God is seen as a political sovereign or commander; believers are to be loyal citizens of God's commonwealth, honoring the sovereign's commands. Another paradigm is the image of God as redeemer, who rescues persons from guilt and punishment for sin and from the fear of death; believers respond in gratitude by helping others. Finally, God may appear as lover, who identifies with humankind; this establishes solidarity and empowers persons of faith to work with God to accomplish God's purposes. Some of the authors use more than one of these metaphors; all interpret them in distinctive ways; each has something important and original to say about the relationship of God to giving.

GIVING AS A RESPONSE TO COMMAND

All the Western traditions refer to God as judge and commander. God's very being creates obligations for the loyal or faithful. If God commands that God's people give, then they must give.

We see this command theme prominently in essays with roots in Muslim, Jewish, and Protestant traditions. It is much less apparent in the more Catholic style of Vacek and Schervish and the kabbalistic authors that Failer discusses. While all of these authors acknowledge the legitimacy of the command/obligation paradigm as a rationale for religious giving, none is entirely satisfied with that. Wheeler is particularly clear on this point.

Arguing that the language of obligation leaves large dimensions of New Testament ethics out of account, she insists that obligation is not enough; emotional engagement and a desire to help are the essence of a truly Christian gift. Bangert takes things in the other order, beginning with the virtue and the emotional roots of giving, then moving into the idea of gift as something that is commanded.

Similarly, Failer, although reflecting a traditional Jewish concern with *mitzvoth*, or commandments, shows how a mystic cosmology can provide a different rationale for giving of self within a traditional Jewish context. Something of the same duality is found in the Muslim tradition as Siddiqui interprets it: the emotional ties of friends and family, at home or abroad, complement the notion of God's commanded *zakât*.

Before turning to the second way of seeing the relationship between God and giving that is reflected in these essays, I want to call attention to two important insights in the command metaphor. The first occurs in Wheeler's essay as she struggles to reconcile the apparently contradictory ideas of gift and command. She reminds us of John Wesley's life: how he was dragged by his brother and friends into helping the poor and how, in taking on that unsought responsibility, his life was transformed. Wheeler makes the point that Wesley's story may be paradigmatic for many of us. Originally joyless doing turns into joyful giving.

I think this gets it just right. Sometimes the heart and mind don't lead the body; they follow it. In the doing, one may discover something totally unexpected. I would never claim that this always happens. Sometimes doing remains a necessary chore. But with giving—as Scrooge found to his amazement—after we do our bit to help, we often end up caring more.

Similarly, Bangert argues that there is a clear relationship between giving—or at least the motive of giving—and taxation. Giving must be tied to justice, he argues, resisting the entirely unchristian notion that charity is somehow optional for Christians. "Doing justly" requires the use of coercion in the form of taxing power.

Again, I think this hits the nail on the head. Justice is the good that charity or love seeks, and taxation is, among other things, a means to that end. I don't want a maximal state, with no room for private largess and philanthropy. But for seriously religious U.S. citizens to argue that we face a dichotomy—either government programs to assist with health and welfare *or* third-sector philanthropy—is to reveal an ignorance of reality. The fact is that government and philanthropy have been working together for decades, if often indirectly. The goals of charity require active efficient government with the necessary resources to perform its part of the job.

GIVING AS A RESPONSE OF GRATITUDE

Just as the command metaphor cannot be jettisoned, neither can the metaphor of gratitude. Gratitude is a feeling, a response of thankfulness, and an emotion. Characteristically, it is associated with love. It is true that many discussions of love in the twentieth century stressed the idea that love is best understood as a command. The constancy and "eternal" character of love as command was central for Kierkegaard and the neo-orthodox writers that he influenced. This constancy was contrasted with the shifting winds of love as emotion, particularly in the work of Kierkegaard himself, as well as in that of Anders Nygren, Paul Tillich, and Paul Ramsey.

In the last quarter-century or more, however, the relationship between love, identity, and the structure of the self has been stressed by feminist writers and others. Distinctions among forms of love—such as among *agape*, *philia*, and *eros*—have come to be seen as less radical than once was supposed, whether in scripture, tradition, or the human psyche. I have already noted the great importance of this expanded understanding of the role of God in giving in the essays by Bangert and Wheeler. To be what it should be, giving must be rooted in a sense that one has been pardoned, saved, or redeemed by God.

In this volume, Vacek develops the strongest stress on the emotional root of love, despite the fact that he explicitly says he is rejecting the gratitude metaphor. In fact, Vacek goes back to roots in Augustine and Aquinas and stresses the emotional power and gratification of love. Love for God, he argues, is at the core of religious life, and that love requires us to give.

Why? Because we ought to love what God loves. Just as I ought to love my friend's dog because of what it means to my friend, even if it is an obnoxious dog, so I ought to love and give to others because they, as well as I, are friends of God. (Thomas Aquinas defined charity as "the friendship of man with God.") The most important fact in my life is that God loves me; God has established the friendship. I now live my life in that context.

I confess that I don't see the radical difference between this argument and the believer's response of "gratitude" that Vacek explicitly rejects. Both metaphors seem to me to rest on a notion of evocation: a gift evokes gratitude, or love evokes love in return. Neither is a syllogistically tight account of the binding character of obligation; neither is the less important for that. However this nuance is to be resolved, the core point is crucial. Giving must have a root in the human heart; it must be well meant as well as well done. Something important is missing in rote religious observance or perfunctory giving, even if the former is grand and beautiful and the latter is financially generous.

What is clear is that all of these writers reject the sufficiency of what Schervish calls the "admonishment model." Simply insisting to people over and over again that they must give more of themselves or more money is, at best, an insufficient strategy.

GIVING AS A RESPONSE TO GOD'S LOVE

Many of these writers use the word "participation" to describe the faithful person's reason for giving. The lover of God participates in the love of God for God's creatures, or in God's quest for justice, or in the attempt to repair the world. I see this most clearly in Vacek's essay and in the kabbalistic mythology, but it may well be more pervasive, and I think it gets at something profound in its radicalness.

Participation is a radical term for traditions that stress the holiness or transcendence of God. It need not entail a blurring of divine and human identity. I participate in the (mis)fortunes of the Chicago Cubs without starting to think that I am a member of the team. But participation does connote a kind of identification. To some degree my well-being is tied up with the cause I have identified with, otherwise I am not a participant but simply a spectator. In participation, the self's range of concern and vulnerability is extended, but difference is not lost.

THE IMPLICATIONS OF THIS INVOLVEMENT

Participation transforms the attitudes of the self, so that the participant wants to do things he did not want to do before. This can happen in devotion to an athletic team; more powerfully, it happens in love relationships. Marrying a musician leads to personal interest or investment in the music that the musician plays or writes. Becoming a parent leads to caring about a child—and the schools the child will attend, the economy in which she will earn her living, and the health of the world polity and ecosystem beyond one's own lifetime. Just so, participation in the cause of God brings about investment in God's cause in the world, in loving or repairing the world.

Insofar as religious persons see themselves as participants in the life and mission of God, they are forced to take themselves seriously. The effect is the creation of a sense of dignity, of respect for oneself as an adopted child, a member of the family of God. This derivative form of self-regard contrasts with self-esteem that results from a comparison with others. Moreover, participation in the family of God establishes a basic equality among persons in terms of their participation in the life of God. Giving becomes a sharing among siblings rather than the condescension of the superior to the inferior. Giving is a transaction going from the dignity and strength of one to the dignity and strength of another, all within the family of the one loving God.

FACTS AND MYTHS OF PARTICIPATION

Is participation optional for the Peoples of the Book? On the one hand, the answer is clearly No. Being religiously serious means being a participant in the community (family, city, or kingdom) of God. Helping is nonnegotiable. The only question is whether to describe the contribution of time, treasure, and talent as a *duty* or a *gift*. If we think in terms of the command metaphor that is so powerful and pervasive in these traditions and their scriptures, the help is a matter of duty. On the other hand, if metaphors of redemption or participation are used, contribution is something that someone who loves God will *want* to do; wanting to help others is an index of whether someone really is a participant, really is transformed.

In the United States, however, giving to religious institutions or for religious motives is clearly an optional matter, as Patrick Rooney's opening essay makes clear. A higher percentage of those who are religiously active give than is true for the population as a whole, but there are significant differences within traditions. If serious giving is an index of religious vitality, Americans are not a particularly religious people. And as Rooney shows, religious giving has fallen as a share of total income.

STRATEGIES FOR ENCOURAGING GIVING

I believe that the focus on participation has implications for strategies to be used if a religious community wants to encourage giving. Wheeler argues that this is a task of evangelism. I think it is better expressed as making persons feel like active members of the community of God by establishing a vivid sense of participation in the community of God. I want to stress two ways in which this can be accomplished.

One is through vivid and powerful experiences of worship. Rooney notes that religious giving is correlated with attendance. If we want to encourage giving and a healthy attitude toward possessions, we should want people to worship. Worship occurs in many different contexts, but for most more or less traditional religious communities, it occurs at a specific time and place on a weekly basis. Dull and boring worship leaves us unmoved. Powerful worship, in whatever form, affects us as persons. It helps us to look at ourselves and our world in a new way. It broadens our vision and empowers us. Religious communities should not be surprised if souls unstirred by worship are also unprepared to pour out resources of time, treasure, or talent. A rich music program and vital liturgy are invaluable assets to a stewardship campaign, as are powerful sermons.

Secondly, participation implies involvement, and to secure our involvement, we must be asked to help. As we begin to work for the community—ushering, making coffee, washing dishes, arranging flowers—we begin to think of the community as *us* rather than as *them*. In Sondra Wheeler's account, John Wesley truly began his ministry when he was asked to help. Certainly a major change in my attitude toward the church came when an overworked rector asked me if I would regularly lead intercessions on Sunday morning. (I admit that it took more than a decade before this led to a significant pledge, however!) Conversion *follows* practice.

GIVE TO WHOM?

If we work with a participatory model of the relationship of humans and God, and if we think of giving as voluntary but not optional, the question of to whom (or what) should I give must arise. Paul Schervish suggests that the means for answering that question is the process of discernment. We are limited by our ignorance and confused in our priorities. In order to correct our "moral compass" (or, as the kabbalists might say, "see the light"), we need to undertake a disciplined program of self-examination, perhaps with a knowledgeable mentor. The process involves at least as much self-discovery as increased knowledge of the world around us. Generalizations about the causes to which people should give are hard to come by; Schervish is confident that careful reflection on the course of one's life and the needs of the world will produce an appropriate choice.

I have great sympathy for this proposal, particularly when applied not only to people whom Schervish calls "hyper-agents" but to all humankind. He is right that persons who have some skill or luck in making money often find themselves in a fog when questions of allocation or distribution come up. I am, however, somewhat less optimistic than Schervish if he is suggesting that discernment is a *sufficient* strategy for directing one's giving. The reasons are simple: finitude and sin. No matter how hard we work, our perspective will be limited, and human tendencies to be competitive and self-deceived need no documentation. Some giving must be targeted with reference to the common conscience of humankind, not simply my own idiosyncratic choices—no matter how reflectively they were arrived at. There must be public checks or limits on an individual's moral compass.

One particular issue, with respect to the beneficiaries of philanthropy, divides these authors, and it is partly on confessional grounds. It is the question of the relative importance of supporting one's own community as opposed to aiding strangers or working for broad social justice causes. Failer and Katz stress commitment to the Jewish people, but a different picture would emerge if they had space and time to focus their attention on Reform congregations, or even the Conservative movement—to say nothing of non-observant Jews. Siddiqui stresses self-support of the Muslim community, noting the contribution to the public good of that endeavor. But he also observes that Muslims provide support for non-Muslim agencies.

At the other extreme, Vacek questions whether money contributed to one's own congregation should even be called a gift or philanthropy. The implication seems to be that the church exists for the sake of the world and that providing for its own sustenance is a completely different *kind* of thing, rather like an athlete's training or conditioning exercises. It is *preparation for*, not the Christian life itself.

How should these two emphases, institutional security (even survival) and a policy of evangelism, social action, or witness, be weighted in decisions about giving? It is impossible to consider this issue apart from historical and sociological factors. Katz is insightful on this point, showing how the rationale for maintaining Jewish hospitals has evolved from providing necessary services to a stigmatized minority in the nineteenth century, into provision in the twentieth century of a vehicle for the careers of Jewish physicians, and finally into an instrument for providing services to all, both because that was important and to win the good will of the larger community. The American Muslim community, especially after 9/11, faces many of the same problems of nineteenth-century Jews—exclusion, misunderstanding, and stigmatization—which may influence decisions about charity.

Christians, particularly American Christians, are used to operating in a majority culture. Although it has been centuries since churchgoing persons could assume that all citizens shared their ultimate commitments (if they ever could so assume), a common Christian frame of reference has existed, as has a strong missionary impulse. The teachings of Jesus, as preserved in the New Testament, stress the importance of helping the stranger of whatever faith. Indeed, the irrelevance of the religious commitments of potential beneficiaries has been something of an article of faith, at least since the nineteenth century. Everything was supposed to turn on the *needs* of the other.

As the role of Christianity in the world changes, it may well be that this principle has to be re-thought. In a provocative essay, Philip Turner has argued that there are strong arguments for supporting one's fellow Christians, especially if we have some responsibility for their imperiled situation. He notices St. Paul's stress on a collection for the support of the struggling churches in the first century CE. Nurturing the lives of the members of the church *may* only be an instrumental value, but if so, it is a remarkably important one.[1]

TIMELESS GIVING?

Finally, two of these essays raise a different kind of issue in assessing requests for, and the results of, giving—namely, the question of systemic change as a goal of philanthropy.

Paula Dempsey argues that the problem of consumer debt is widespread and acute for many Americans. She suggests that some advertising and banking practices are an assault on the financial health of a family comparable to the medical threat of an epidemic. Virtually all of the mainline churches, however, ignore this problem or simply appeal to the need for self-discipline. Dempsey argues that this is inadequate as a response to the plight of vulnerable persons, especially if their resources are limited. Of course, self-discipline is important, but admonition emphasizing individual responsibility is not enough. As with public health, we do not think individual self-protection is adequate protection from an epidemic. Rather, calls for individual action should be combined with a critique of those institutions and cultural practices that sustain an ethos of indebtedness.

The existence of a culture of debt makes community vitality and participation particularly important. If a church's request for funds is seen as yet another mouth to feed or need to be addressed, it will lose every time in a budget crunch. Failing to make a significant commitment to or for the congregation will not send one into bankruptcy or mortgage default. Everything turns on the role the church community plays in the life of the individual or family. That community must be seen and felt to make a difference and to identify with persons in their financial struggles.

In contrast, Robert Katz raises the question of what should be done with religious institutions that seem to have outlived their usefulness, or at least outlived the specific circumstances that called them into being. Should a religious community reclaim resources designated for health care for other purposes now more pressing in the life of the community? Or should the resources continue to work for the purpose for which they were originally given?

Katz suggests that the best course for many, if not all, Jewish hospitals would have been (or will be) to sell the hospital and use the income for addressing problems that are more central to sustaining the vitality of Jewish life in the United States today: problems of assimilation, intermarriage, and indifference. If we assume that Katz's historical analysis is correct and that the driving purpose behind the Jewish philanthropy of the nineteenth and twentieth centuries was to assist the Jewish community rather than to provide medical care to all comers, then hospital boards have a special obligation to be faithful to that core purpose of the original donors and a responsibility to reinterpret that purpose for the present time. Indeed, that reinterpretation is the core of their moral responsibility.[2]

There may, however, be a complication arising from the fact that the demographic of the Jewish community in the United States has changed considerably in two hundred years and that donations were made both before and after 1950. If it is clear that the donors of the past fifty or sixty years shared the founders' concern for the survival of the Jewish people, Katz's case may be airtight. But if the donors' motives changed over the years—if donors in the 1960s, '70s, and '80s were primarily committed to *health*—then the issue is more complicated, although Katz's conclusion may still be correct.

CONCLUSION

None of us involved in the enjoyable work of writing and talking about these issues thinks we have finally resolved them. I know my colleagues have said enough to get a conversation started, and I hope my reflections have served to provide some focal points as the conversation proceeds.

NOTES

1. Philip Turner, "Philanthropy's Inconstant Friend, Religion," in *Good Intentions*, ed. David H. Smith (Bloomington: Indiana University Press, 2005), 127–45.

2. David H. Smith, *Entrusted: The Moral Responsibilities of Trusteeship* (Bloomington: Indiana University Press, 1995).

CONTRIBUTORS

BYRON C. BANGERT is a research scholar, columnist, and ethics consultant who received his Ph.D. from Indiana University in religious ethics in 2004. After more than twenty-five years of parish ministry in American Baptist and Presbyterian churches, he spent three years as Research Associate at the Poynter Center for the Study of Ethics and American Institutions at IU. His publications include numerous articles, sermons, and newspaper columns, and a book in theological ethics titled *Consenting to God and Nature: Toward a Theocentric, Naturalistic, Theological Ethics.*

PAULA R. DEMPSEY completed her Ph.D. at Loyola University in May 2006. Her chapter is based on her dissertation work researching U.S. denominations' publications on personal money management. She is a librarian at DePaul University in Chicago and teaches as an adjunct in the Department of Sociology and the School of Public Service.

JUDITH LYNN FAILER is Associate Professor of Political Science at Indiana University, where she is also Adjunct Associate Professor of Philosophy and American Studies. She teaches in the areas of political and legal theory, constitutional law, and ethics and public policy. She is author of *Who Qualifies for Rights? Homelessness, Mental Illness and Civil Commitment.*

ROBERT A. KATZ is Professor of Law at Indiana University School of Law–Indianapolis and is also Professor of Philanthropic Studies at the Indiana University Center on Philanthropy and an affiliate faculty of the Indiana University Center for Bioethics. Katz researches and teaches nonprofit and philanthropy law and the law of health care organizations.

PATRICK M. ROONEY is Executive Director of the Center on Philanthropy at Indiana University. A nationally recognized expert and speaker on philanthropy, he is frequently quoted by national news media and has served on advisory committees for the Corporation for National and Community Service, the Association of Fundraising Professionals, and Independent Sector. As the Center's Director of Research, he built it into one of the nation's premier philanthropy research organizations. The Center researches and writes *Giving USA* for the Giving USA Foundation and has conducted research for organizations such as Bank of America, American Express, Google, Aspen Institute, Gates Foundation, and United Way of America.

PAUL G. SCHERVISH is Professor of Sociology and Director of the Center on Wealth and Philanthropy at Boston College. For 1999–2000 he was Distinguished Visiting Professor at the Indiana University Center on Philanthropy, where he also served for many years as National Research Fellow. He has served as Fulbright Professor of Philanthropy at University College, Cork, Ireland. He has been selected five times to the *Non-Profit Times*'s "Power and Influence Top 50." Schervish is author of *Gospels of Wealth: How the Rich Portray Their Lives* and, with Keith Whitaker, *Wealth and the Will of God: Discerning the Use of Riches in the Service of Ultimate Purpose* (Indiana University Press, 2009).

SHARIQ SIDDIQUI is an attorney and serves as Director of Legal Services at the Julian Center and Executive Director of the Muslim Alliance of Indiana. He is pursuing a Ph.D. in Philanthropic Studies at Indiana University. He served as Director of Fundraising, Community Development, and Special Projects at the Islamic Society of North America between 1999 and 2004. Siddiqui has written articles on giving and legislation, Muslim philanthropy in America, and the history of the Islamic Society of North America.

EDWARD VACEK, S.J., is Professor of Moral Theology at the Boston College School of Theology and Ministry. He is author of *Love, Human and Divine* and has contributed more than sixty articles to various popular and scholarly journals and books. Vacek has given numerous talks to popular and professional audiences. He teaches moral theology, with special interests in sexuality, emotions, ethical theory, and biomedical ethics.

SONDRA WHEELER is the Carr Professor of Christian Ethics at Wesley Theological Seminary in Washington, D.C. She works in bioethics, the history of theological ethics, and the virtue tradition as well as in biblical ethics. Her publications include *Wealth as Peril and Obligation: The New Testament on Possessions; Stewards of Life: Bioethics and Pastoral Care;* and *The Love We Were Made For.*

INDEX

Italic page numbers refer to figures and tables.

DAVID H. SMITH

is Director of the Yale Interdisciplinary Center for Bioethics and Er̄
tus Professor of Religious Studies at Indiana University, where he
also Adjunct Professor of both Medicine and Philanthropic Studies a
Director of the Poynter Center for the Study of Ethics and America
Institutions. Smith's publications include *Entrusted: The Moral Responsibil-*
ities of Trusteeship (1995), *Early Warning* (1998), and *Good Intentions* (2005),
all published by Indiana University Press.